Designing
Web
Animation

Nicola Brown   Paul Van Eyk

Peter Chen   William E. Weinman

David Miller

New Riders

New Riders Publishing, Indianapolis, Indiana

Development Editor
Suzanne Snyder

Project Editor
Sarah Kearns

Copy Editors
Lillian Duggan
Nancy Maragioglio
Greg Pearson
Cliff Shubs

Technical Editor
Chris Stone

Associate Marketing Manager
Tamara Apple

Acquisitions Coordinator
Tracy Turgeson

Administrative Coordinator
Karen Opal

Cover Designers
Barbara Kordesh
Karen Ruggles

Cover Illustration
David Uhl

Cover Production
Aren Howell

Book Designer
Sandra Schroeder

Production Manager
Kelly Dobbs

Production Team Supervisor
Laurie Casey

Graphics Image Specialists
Stephen Adams
Debra Bolhuis
Daniel Harris
Clint Lahnen
Laura Robbins

Production Analysts
Jason Hand
Bobbi Satterfield

Production Team
Heather Butler
Angela Calvert
Daniel Caparo
Terrie Deemer
Tricia Flodder
Beth Rago
Megan Wade
Christy Wagner

Indexer
Chris Cleveland

Designing Web Animation

By Nicola Brown, Peter Chen, David Miller, Paul Van Eyk, and William E. Weinman

Published by:

New Riders Publishing

201 West 103rd Street

Indianapolis, IN 46290 USA

Printed in the United States of America 1 2 3 4 5 6 7 8 9 0

Library of Congress Cataloging-in-Publication Data

```
***CIP data available upon request***
```

Warning and Disclaimer

Publisher	*Don Fowley*
Publishing Managers	*Julie Fairweather and Jim LeValley*
Marketing Manager	*Mary Foote*
Managing Editor	*Carla Hall*

This book was produced digitally by Macmillan Computer Publishing and manufactured using 100% computer-to-plate technology (filmless process), by Shepard Poorman Communications Corporation, Indianapolis, Indiana.

About the Authors

Nicola Brown's career thus far has been, by necessity, rather short. She spent four years hard labor completing a Bachelor of Science with Honors in Computer Science at Monash University in Melbourne, Australia before entering the Big Bad World.

Currently, Nicola is employed at Sausage Software as a Java programmer, although she started her term there as technical support, wearing her fingers to the bone answering all the e-mail sales and support inquiries. In writing Egor (believed to be the world's first commercial Java applet), Nicola somehow earned the title "JavaGirl."

Peter Chen received his B.A. in Biochemistry and B.M. in Music Education from Oberlin College in 1995. Currently, he works conjunctively for the Stanford University Libraries and the Department of Biological Sciences as a consultant and developer of technological applications for the academic environment, including Web-based education.

On a Macintosh clone, Peter uses BBEdit for HTML authoring, Photoshop and FreeHand for graphical editing, and Opcode's Studio Vision for all his sound applications. On the receiving end, he uses the Real Audio Plug-In, LiveUpdate's Crescendo MIDI Plug-In, and Netscape Navigator 3.0 with its LiveAudio enhancement features.

A classically trained musician, Peter has been composing and working with computer-based music and MIDI over the past 10 years, and maintains a studio at home using equipment by Alesis, Emu, Korg, Lexicon, Opcode, Roland, Tascam, Yamaha, and Zeta.

David Miller is a Multimedia Application Developer and Instructional Technology Specialist for the School of Education and New Media Center at Stanford University. He is a Web site administrator, designer, and programmer in the San Francisco Bay area and teaches classes in Instructional Technology and Web multimedia. Dave is finishing up his Ph.D. at Stanford.

Paul Van Eyk is 32 years old; he purchased his first computer and laser printer at great cost, back in the days when the phrase "Desktop Publishing" was first coined and traditional typesetters refused to worry about it. Paul started his career as an "underground" cartoonist in Amsterdam, Holland, and 16 years later finds himself working as a full-time "Nethead" in Melbourne, Australia. In between, he's been a graphic designer, copywriter, editor, art director, and publisher.

These days, Paul is the Webmaster at Sausage Software, a very "coooool" software company that makes serious yet fun Web Authoring/Design tools like the HotDog Web Editor and Egor, the world's first commercial Java application. The company's products are developed in consultation with, and for, Web authoring professionals everywhere, and they're marketed and distributed almost exclusively via the Sausage Software Web site.

Thousands of people see Paul's work everyday, but most know him only as Webguru. That's his nickname—and it's also his e-mail address and his job title. Sausage Software is that kind of company, the staff are that kind of people, and the Web is that kind of place. Coooool.

William E. Weinman has earned his living as a technologist-for-hire for about 20 years. He has designed software for many large and small organizations, including IBM, Security Pacific Bank, KDD (the major long-distance company in Japan), and the Bank of New Zealand. Mr. Weinman has also designed and constructed electronic musical instruments for popular recording artists, fiber-optic systems for NASA and Bell

Labs, and a broadcast ticker tape for a television station. He has been involved with online computing since he got his first acoustically coupled modem in 1978.

You can often find Mr. Weinman playing with Jezebel, his Gibson L6-S guitar, in blues bars around Texas; or studying Native-American shamanic medicine in Arizona; but it may be easier to send e-mail to wew@bearnet.com.

Trademark Acknowledgments

All terms mentioned in this book that are known to be trademarks or service marks have been appropriately capitalized. New Riders Publishing cannot attest to the accuracy of this information. Use of a term in this book should not be regarded as affecting the validity of any trademark or service mark.

Dedication

From David Miller:

To Mom and Dad, for their love and support.

Acknowledgments

From Nicola Brown:

I'd like to thank Simone, Lee, and Peter: patient housemates in the face of adversity; all my friends and my family for encouraging me in everything; and lastly my cat, Sooty, for being so wonderfully furry.

From David Miller:

I'd like to acknowledge all the talented, hard-working people at New Riders, including Julie Fairweather, Suzanne Snyder, Tracy Turgeson, and Sarah Kearns. Thanks to Darren and Dana at Terran Interactive, Charles Wiltgen and the helpful folks at Apple Computer for information on beta software, and all the other companies and individuals who provided software for the CD.

I'd also like to thank Lois Brooks and the staff at Academic Technology Support Services at Stanford University, Charles Kerns, New Media Center, Gary Ernst, Alan Garber, Mary Goldstein, Decker Walker, and my loving and supporting family.

From Paul Van Eyk:

I'd like to thank my wife and three children for their support during the writing process, which has added many hours to my already heavy workload. I would also like to thank my associates Tim Marsh and Ray Moon, for their invaluable assistance; any mistakes made are mine, not theirs.

From New Riders:

New Riders wishes to acknowledge, thank, and put on a pedestal funky groovin' guy Rich Evers for his 11th-hour contribution to this project and for always making us laugh when we need it most.

Contents at a Glance

Table of Contents

by David Miller

Author Biography

David Miller is a Multimedia Application Developer and Instructional Technology Specialist for the School of Education and New Media Center at Stanford University. He is a Web site administrator, designer, and programmer in the San Francisco Bay area and teaches classes in Instructional Technology and Web multimedia. Dave is finishing up his Ph.D. at Stanford.

Principles of Animation in a Nutshell

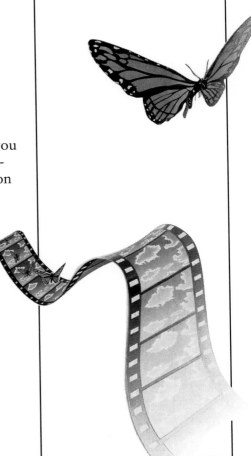

Animated graphics are a recent addition to the rich, multimedia content that is available on the World Wide Web. Creating effective animations within the limitations of Web playback can be a demanding task for the Web designer. If you use television or film as your measure of high-quality animation, the Web has a long way to go to match these production values. Still, the basic principles of animation developed for these other mediums can be applied to Web-based animations. Used judiciously and with awareness of the limited bandwidth of your users, Web animations can add to the enjoyment and information content of your Web site.

Animations are created from a sequence of still images. The images are displayed rapidly in succession so that the eye is fooled into perceiving continuous motion. You perceive the sequence of still images as motion because of a phenomena called persistence of vision. *Persistence of vision* is the tendency of the eye and brain to continue to perceive an image even after it's disappeared.

In the nineteenth century, several popular devices, such as the rotoscope and the zeotrope, capitalized on the phenomena of persistence of vision to produce the illusion of moving pictures. With advances in the fledgling science of photography in the later half of the nineteenth century, John Marey and Eadweard (yes, that's how he spelled it) Muybridge developed devices that took sequences of photographs of moving objects. On a California ranch, which was to become part of Stanford University, Muybridge set up rows of trip wire-activated cameras along a race track and created sequences of photographs of galloping horses (see fig. 1.1). Muybridge made several other photographic studies of moving animals and people. To this day, his published motion studies are used by animators.

Figure 1.1

Animation frames based on the motion studies of Eadweard Muybridge.

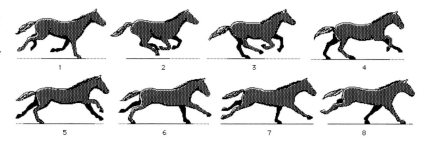

Note

The rotoscope consisted of nested cylinders, with the outermost cylinder having a row of vertical slits along the outside. The innermost cylinder had sequences of moving images printed on the outside. When the cylinders were rotated, the images on the inner cylinder appeared to move when viewed through the slits in the outer cylinder.

The next big technological advance came with Thomas Edison's invention of the kinetograph. The *kinetograph* was a type of camera that was able to take up to 10 photographs per second. Playback was through another device called a *kinetoscope*. Motion picture technology advanced rapidly following Edison's invention. In the early part of the century, J. Stuart Blackton and French artist, Emile Cohl, created short animation films in which each frame was a separate drawing on blackboard or paper. About the same time, Windsor McCay created some of the first cartoon characters, Little Nemo the Clown and Gertie the Dinosaur. Soon, people began drawing on individual frames of motion picture film or celluloid to create animations. J.R. Bray and Earl Hurd are credited with developing the process that today we call "cel animation."

In the 20s, Walt Disney and co-workers developed many of the production techniques, and the graphic idioms and styles, that we take for granted in animation today. In 1928, the Disney studio produced the first full-color cartoon with sound, starring Mickey Mouse. These early animated films were painstakingly hand-drawn by hundreds of artists working in teams. For the next fifty years, cartoons and animated films used these techniques.

Computers entered the picture after World War II, with simple experiments in computer-generated graphics during the 1950s. In the 1960s, computer graphics became a discipline in its own right, spurred on by the work of researchers such as Ivan Sutherland at MIT. John Whitney Sr., who created the special effects for the feature film *2001: A Space Odyssey*, was one of the first artists to integrate computer graphics with film in a series of shorts in the 1970s. The first examples of computer-based animation in feature films and video appeared in the late 70s and early 80s. Special effects in these early movies, such as *Tron* and *The Last Starfighter*, used supercomputers to create their animation effects. Today, you can achieve many of the same effects on desktop computers. Throughout the 80s and 90s, companies such as Industrial Light and Magic, Pacific Data Images, and Pixar brought ever more sophisticated computer-generated imagery to video and film, culminating with the release of *Toy Story* by Pixar in 1995— the first completely computer-generated, animated feature film.

Animation on the Web

The World Wide Web was developed in the early 1990s by Tim Berners-Lee. Initially, it was created as a way to serve hypertext documents on TCP/IP-based, client-server networks, with documents viewed by client software called a *browser*. Soon, other media types, such as GIF graphics and digital audio files, were supported by Web browsers. Animated graphics are one of the latest additions to the media types supported by browsers.

There are several ways to add animated graphics to Web pages. Inline animations are animations that appear directly in the Web page in your browser, much like image files. You can also display animations by launching client-side helper applications that will display animations within separate windows.

Overcoming Obstacles

The biggest factors inhibiting the use of animation on the Web are bandwidth limitations, the asynchronous nature of the Internet, and the differences in platforms and browser support. Typically, Web animations are computer files that must be completely downloaded to the client machine before playback begins. Even small animation files can be quite large and take a long time to download.

Streaming

Some animation programs use proprietary data formats and a technique called streaming as a way around this downloading problem. *Streaming* is the capability of specially formatted time-based media, such as animation, to begin playback before the entire file has been completely downloaded. The rest of the file is downloaded from the server, i.e. streamed, in the background while the animation or other time-based media plays on the client.

Streaming can be tricky to implement, because Internet data is packet-based and wasn't designed for the delivery of continuous, synchronized, time-based data. Interruptions in the continuous data stream can cause stutters and gaps during playback of animation.

Animation Formats

Another problem with Web animation is that once the animation has been delivered to the user, he or she must have the proper helper application or plug-in to display the animation, or their browser must natively support the particular animation format. Several animation formats for the Web exist today, with varying capabilities and uses.

GIF animation uses a special extension to the GIF specification and is supported by most browsers. QuickTime animations use the widely-supported, cross-platform QuickTime movie format. Many Web animation authoring tools can convert between these two formats. Java animations are written in the cross-platform Java programming language, while Shockwave animations are based on the Macromedia Director file format. Other proprietary animation formats include those used by Netscape Plug-Ins from Totally Hip (Sizzler Plug-In) and FutureWave (FutureSplash Plug-In), for example. MBED animations take a different approach and use a newly developed, multimedia description language.

Tip

Compared to video and film, or even CD-ROM, animation on the Web is primitive. Web animations are characterized by small viewing areas and herky-jerky motion. You won't see a Web version of *Toy Story* anytime soon.

So why bother with animation? Animation is good way to draw attention and add interest to an otherwise static Web page. It's also a good way to distract people and prevent them from reading the information you are serving on the Web. So, use animated graphics judiciously. It's probably a good idea NOT to put animations on a Web page that contains a lot of text that you want people to read.

Estimating Download Time

Most users connect to the Web with 28.8 bps modems or less. They will be able to download data at a maximum rate of about 2.5 KB per second. For modem users, it's probably safe to expect about two to three minutes of download time for every 100 KB of animation. These users won't have the patience to sit through long downloads just to see your spinning logo.

Users might put up with longer download times, if they perceive an added benefit. Animations that provide game play, illustrate a dynamic process, enhance the visualization of complex data, clearly and succinctly explain a task, bring increased interactivity, or have a "wow" factor such as navigable 3D environments or an interactive character, might be worth the download time for some users.

Bandwidth Considerations

Corporate and university local area networks or intranets have bandwidth and network speeds that are often an order of magnitude greater than what is available to the average home user. Typical transfer rates are in the range 10–50 KB per second. In this environment, Web animation can be a powerful tool for training, instruction, and sharing of information. The Web enables information providers to serve rich, multimedia, "just-in-time" content that can communicate more effectively than other delivery methods. Figure 1.2 is from a series of Web-based instructional materials that uses animation to illustrate a process—in this case, installing Netscape Plug-Ins.

As bandwidth increases, Web animation will become more practical. In the meantime, it's probably best to be kind to Net bandwidth and be judicious in the use of Web animation.

Figure 1.2

A GIF animation for instructional purposes.

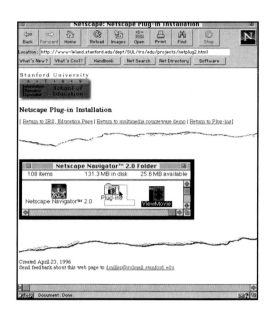

Animation 101

Computer animation software can perform many of the tedious and repetitive animation tasks that have been historically performed by teams of animators working day and night for weeks or months. Plus, computer animation software provides all the benefits of digital editing. Some artists think computer animation has a certain coldness or sterile style compared to hand-drawn animation. This stylistic gap has been reduced as tools and animators evolve.

The following section describes basic animation principles and terminology, including specific aspects of computer animation, as follows:

- Cel animation
- Flip-book animation
- Sprite, path, and vector animation
- Frame rate
- Key frames and tweening
- Character animation
- Timelines, tracks, and animation sequencers
- Key frame transitions

- 2D vs. 3D animation

- Animation special effects

- Processing graphics files

This section also emphasizes tools and techniques that are available on relatively inexpensive desktop computers, as opposed to the expensive hardware and software used by many production houses and film studios.

The final section of this chapter provides an overview of techniques that will help your animations look more professional and life-like.

Cel Animation

A *cel* (only one "l") is a term from traditional animation. Cel comes from *celluloid*, the material that made up early motion picture film, and refers to the transparent piece of film that is used in traditional, hand-drawn animation (this transparent film is usually made from acetate, not celluloid, though).

Animation cels are generally layered, one on top of the other, to produce a single animation frame. There is a separate cel for the background layer and a separate cel for each object that moves independently over the background. *Layering* enables the animator to isolate and redraw only the parts of the image that change between successive frames. A *frame* consists of the background and overlying cels and is like a snapshot of the action at one instant in time. By drawing each frame on transparent layers of acetate, the animator can lay successive frames one on top of the other and see, at a glance, how the animation progresses through time. Many of the processes and terminology of traditional, cel-based animation, such as layering, key frames, and tweening, the latter two of which will be discussed presently, have carried over into computer animation.

Flip-Book Animation

Flip-book animation or *frame-based* animation is the simplest kind of animation to visualize. As a kid, you probably had one of those flip-books that had a series of drawings in the margins of successive pages. When you thumbed through the book rapidly, the drawings appeared to move.

On a computer, flip-book animation means displaying a sequence of graphic files. The simplest and slowest form of this is the slide-show. Slide-shows are typically used to support a presentation and can be an effective and relatively bandwidth-friendly way to provide multimedia information on the Web. Slide-shows can be created with some of the animation software featured in this book.

To produce animation or the illusion of motion, graphic images are displayed in rapid succession. Each image is slightly different from the one before. The graphic images are displayed so fast that the viewer is fooled into perceiving a moving image. In film, this display rate is 24 images or frames per second, but on the Web you will probably have to settle for less. For playback on a computer, the entire graphic file has to be "painted" on the computer screen for each animation frame.

The problem with this form of animation, on bandwidth-sensitive mediums such as the Web, is that it's hard to update each frame fast enough so that the viewer perceives smooth, continuous motion.

Apple Computer's QuickTime, Macromedia's Shockwave, and much of the animation software featured on the CD use various algorithms to compress files, so that instead of having to update the entire screen display for each frame, as you do in flip-book animation, you only update the parts of the screen display that have changed between frames. This compression leads to smaller file sizes and faster playback.

Sprite, Path, and Vector Animation

Sprite-based animation is another kind of animation. Sprite-based animation is sometimes called *cast-based* animation, as in a "cast of characters." It is very common in computer arcade games and computer animation programs. Sprite-based animation is similar to the traditional animation technique where an object is overlaid and animated on top of a static background graphic. A *sprite* is any part of your animation that moves independently, such as a flying bird, a rotating planet, a bouncing ball, or a spinning logo. The sprite animates and moves as an independent object. In sprite-based animation, a single image or series of images can be attached to a sprite. The sprite can animate in one place, for example a rotating planet, or move along a path, like a flying bird.

Sprite-based computer animation is different from flip-book style computer animation in that for each successive frame, you only update the part of the computer screen that contains the sprite. You don't have to update the entire screen display for each frame, as you have to do with flip-book style animation.

File sizes and bandwidth requirements for sprite-based animation are typically less than those for flip-book style animation. Sprite-based animation programs typically use an off-screen buffer to composite frames to provide fast, smooth animation.

Motion Paths

Sometimes sprite animation is called *path-based* animation. In path-based animation, you attach a sprite to a motion path. A *motion path* is a curve drawn through the positions of the sprite in successive frames. The sprite moves along this path during the course of the animation. The sprite can be a single, rigid bitmap that doesn't change or a series of bitmaps that form an animation loop or cycle.

For example, you could create a short, self-contained three- or four-frame animation loop of a bird flapping its wings. Most computer animation software enables you to create animation loops of this sort.

To create an animation of this bird flying across your screen, do the following:

1. Place the loop on the left edge of the screen in the first frame.

2. Move it progressively further to the right in successive frames.

The path of the flying bird is its motion path; when animated, you will see the bird flapping its wings as it flies across the screen.

Spline-Based Animation

When objects move, they usually don't follow a straight line. Motion paths are generally more believable if they are curved. Computer animation programs typically enable you to create spline-based, curved motion paths. *Splines* are mathematical representations of a curve.

> **Note**
>
> Some 2D computer animation packages designed specifically for the Web include TotallyHip WebPainter, FutureWave CelAnimator, DeltaPoint WebAnimator, and GEO Emblaze Creator. Some 2D animation software you can use to create Web animations include Macromedia Director and Action, Vividus Cinemation, Motion ToolWorks ADDmotion and PROmotion, Adobe After Effects and Premiere, Linker System, The Animation Stand, Autodesk Animator Pro, and Animator Studio.
>
> Some 3D computer animation packages include Macromedia Extreme 3D, Specular Infini-D, Strata Studio Pro, Hash Animation Master, Caligari trueSpace, and Autodesk 3D Studio Max.

To define spline-based curves, you first position a series of anchor points. The curve itself passes through the anchor points. The anchor points define the beginning and end points of different parts of the curve. Each anchor point has control handles that enable you to change the shape of the curve between two anchor points. Figure 1.3 shows a spline-based motion path for an animation of a jet fighter—note the anchor point with control handles.

Figure 1.3

A spline-based motion path for a jet fighter.

Motion Path ———

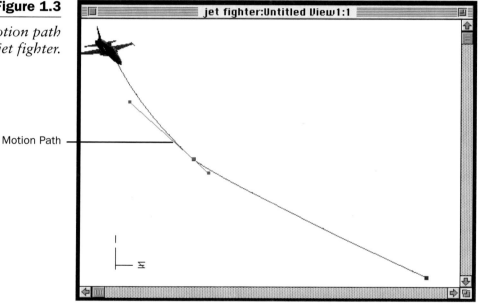

Note

If you use a 2D drawing program like Macromedia FreeHand or Adobe Illustrator, you are already familiar with spline curves. These programs use a type of spline curve called a Bézier curve.

Most animation programs enable you to vary the rate of motion along a path. If a motion path has a sharp bend, for example, an object approaching the bend will slow down as it approaches the bend and then speed up as it comes around the bend. Some programs provide very sophisticated control of the velocity of sprites along paths.

Vector-Based Animation

Vector-based animation is similar to bitmap-based sprite animation, but instead of using bitmaps for sprites, vector-based programs use mathematical formulas to describe sprites. These formulas are similar to the formulas that describe spline curves.

Because objects are mathematical formulas, and not bitmaps, file sizes are much smaller. Another benefit of vector-based animation is that graphics are scalable; i.e., they can be enlarged without becoming jagged or pixellated. Vector-based animation holds promise for Web animation. Several of the plug-ins and authoring tools listed in Appendix A, such as Sizzler and FutureSplash, use vector-based animation.

> **Note**
>
> *Pixellated* means that you can see the individual square pixels that make up a computer-generated image. Pixellation, or the "jaggies," is a common problem in computer-generated images, especially along curved and high-contrast edges.

Frame Rate

Frame rate is expressed as the number of frames per second (fps) of animation. Frame rates for film are 24 frames per second. Video frame rates are 30 (actually 29.97, but who's counting?) frames per second. For Web animations, you will want to minimize the frame rate so as to reduce the total file size as much as possible.

The minimum frame rate before unacceptable jerkiness sets in depends on the particular animation. Frame rates of 10–15 frames per second typically yield acceptable results, although you may be able to get away with 5–8 frames per second. Web playback can be affected by many variables outside the author's control, so consider Web frame rates to be estimates.

Key Frames and Tweening

In traditional animation, lead animators draw the most important frames or *key frames*. These frames establish the main dramatic poses, define the flow of action, and create the animation's graphic style. The hundreds or thousands of intermediate frames that appear between these main key frames are typically drawn by hordes of animators sweating away for days and weeks at light tables. This process of creating intermediate frames between key frames is called *tweening*.

> **Note**
>
> Key frames are typically drawn at the most important or extreme poses that define the action, or at places where the action or viewpoint changes or shifts.

Computers follow this same model. Fortunately, the computer will generate most of the intermediate frames—all you have to worry about is creating the key frames.

On the computer, you place key frames along a timeline. The distance between key frames on the time line determines the amount of time between key frames. The frame rate determines the number of intermediate frames that are generated.

For example, if the frame rate is 10 frames per second and you have a key frame at second 1.5 and second 3.5, the computer will generate 20 intermediate frames.

For complex animations, it's a good idea to rough-out your animation before you commit to rendering key frames. First, sketch the main poses and positions. Then, create a *spacing chart*, which is a sketch map of the action with rough key frames positioned relative to time along a horizontal axis. An example of a spacing chart is shown in figure 1.4. Try to avoid the even spacing of key frames, which tends to make animations look mechanical. Vary the number of in-between frames between key frames. Small numbers of in-between frames will make the action appear faster between key frames, and large numbers of in-between frames will make the action appear slower. Varying the number of in-between frames will make the rate of the action appear to ebb and flow, more like the natural world.

Figure 1.4

A spacing chart.

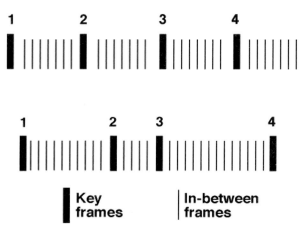

Character Animation

Character animation is a special branch of animation. It is the kind of animation that you typically see when you watch cartoons. It differs from other kinds of animation, such as motion graphics or animated logos, in that character animation involves complex organic shapes with multiple secondary, hierarchical motions.

Although it is fairly easy to animate a single, rigid bitmap over time, animating a believable "living" character is quite an art and takes a lot of work. The techniques that make animated characters believable can also be applied to inanimate objects. Many of these techniques are discussed in a following section on animation techniques.

Timelines, Tracks, and Animation Sequencers

Computer animation software typically mimics the process of traditional cel-based animation. Most programs contain a database of media objects, sprites, or "cast-members." These objects can be placed on a virtual light table or "stage." Computer animation software provides multiple layers that you can use to set up your animation. Each animated object is placed on its own layer, much like layers of animation cels in traditional animation. Figure 1.5 illustrates the layering and database user interface of Macromedia Director. Sprites from the database of media objects or "cast" are placed on the virtual animation stand or "stage." Sprites in this animation occupy layer 3 from frame 1 to frame 10.

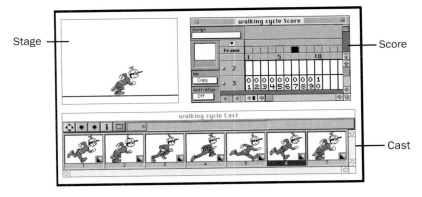

Figure 1.5

Macromedia Director user interface.

Most computer animation software uses a track-based timeline or sequencer to choreograph animation. Track-based timelines and sequencers provide a visual overview of the animation. Each track represents a property that animates over time. The track contains the key frame and animation information for that property. To inspect a property along the track, you typically position a playback head at a particular time or frame along the track. Each individual object can have several animation tracks associated with it. For example, a single object could have a separate track for each of several time-varying parameters, such as position, size, shape, velocity, or surface properties.

Note

Tracks in animation software are similar to tracks in a music recording. Instead of each instrument or vocal having its own track, each object parameter has a track with the animation software acting as the "visual mixer."

You create a key frame by picking a point on the timeline and then choosing a value for a time-varying parameter, such as position or color, at this single point in time. The computer generates or "tweens" intermediate frames between key frames, interpolating the values for the parameters you've specified. Figure 1.6 illustrates an animation sequencer from a 3D animation program—note the track in the lower window. The jet fighter object has a position track with a key frame near frame 5 and an orientation track with a key frame near frame 3. In this case, to set another key frame, you would do the following:

1. Move the playback head to the frame or time where you want to add a new key frame.

2. Select the property track you want to animate.

3. Enter a new value for the property.

Different animation software will handle this differently, but the concept will be similar.

Figure 1.6

An animation sequencer.

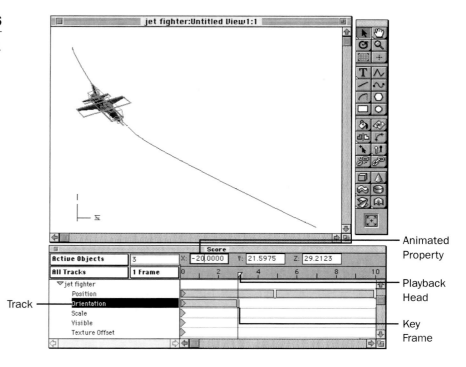

Smoothing Frame Transitions

Because key frames mark transitions between properties in your animation, it is important to make these transitions appear smooth. Many computer animation programs provide ways of smoothing out the rough edges in key frame transitions caused by linear motion paths and lack of correct registration.

Linear Motion Paths

These rough edges are caused because most computers create linear motion paths between position key frames. Linear motion paths contain sharp angle bends at the key frames. Figure 1.7 shows a linear motion path between three positions of a bouncing ball. Many programs will automatically smooth the sharp corners for you. In some programs, motion paths are fully editable curves.

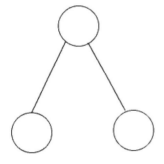

Linear MotionPath   Curved MotionPath

Figure 1.7

Linear vs. curved animation paths.

Registration

To ensure smooth transitions between frames, each frame must be carefully aligned or registered with other frames. Traditional animators typically keep their drawings registered by using a light table with a peg bar and drawing paper or acetate that has punched holes that fit into the peg bar. Another handy tool is a sheet of acetate with a ruled grid that is laid out in the same aspect ratio as the animation frame. The grid can be used to align pieces of the animation consistently from frame to frame.

Note

If you remember back to the flip-book, the drawings on each page were kept aligned and in register because the book was bounded on one side.

A *registration point* is a point on each cel or frame that lines up with the same point on every other cel or frame. Choosing the correct registration point is especially important when you create an animation loop or cycling motion. Usually, the best place to put a registration point in an animation loop is at a point on the object that remains stationary during the loop. Computer graphics programs usually have grid and alignment commands that will help computer-based animators register their drawings, as illustrated in figure 1.8. Figure 1.9 illustrates the registration tool in Director. To set a registration point in Director, do the following:

1. Select the registration tool from the tool palette.

2. Click on a point on the bitmap graphic.

Figure 1.8

A superimposed grid for alignment.

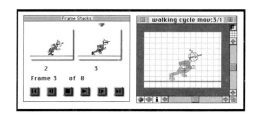

Figure 1.9

Setting a registration point in Director.

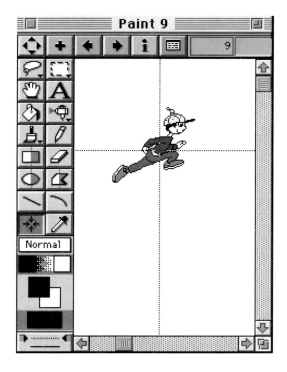

2D versus 3D Animation

Animation software falls into two broad categories, 2D and 3D. 2D animation programs require the artist to add perspective and shading. 3D programs will do a lot of this work for you, but 3D animations typically require a longer time to set up and create. Many 3D programs have integrated drawing, modeling, animating, and rendering tools that enable you to create your animation entirely within one program. Which type of animation software you use depends on the type of project, budget and development time, and the graphic style you are trying to achieve.

Animation Special Effects

Animation special effects go beyond traditional frame-by-frame techniques. Computer-generated special effects produce animations that would be very difficult to reproduce by other techniques. Special effects include some of the flashier elements of animation, such as explosions, fire, and the creation of life-like organic shapes.

- *Color-cycling* or palette animation takes advantage of the way computers display colors. Monitors set to 8-bit color depth can only display 256 colors at any one time. These 256 colors are stored in a palette. Each color in the palette is associated with a unique index number. If your monitor is set to 8-bit color depth, every pixel on your computer screen is referenced to this palette and has unique color reference number between 0 and 255.

  You can change the color of a pixel or group of same-colored pixels by referencing it to a different index number in the color palette. For example, if you have a blue-colored sprite that has been referenced to a palette number, you can change it to another color by referencing it to another palette number. You can cycle through a range of colors to provide smoothly changing color gradient effects. Many computer animation programs enable you to create color cycling animation effects in this way.

- *Morphing* is the process of smoothly interpolating between two different images or 3D models. You pick the first frame and the last frame and the computer generates a series of intermediate frames. When played back as an animation, it appears that the first image gradually and incrementally changes or morphs into the second image. Morphing has become a staple of video and film special effects houses; e.g., in the *Terminator* movie series.

■ *Rotoscoping* is the process of drawing on top of existing video, film, or animation frames. Programs such as Fractal Design Painter, Adobe Premiere, and to some extent Photoshop provide a rich set of drawing and painting tools that you can use to draw directly on top of digital animation frames. Rotoscoping is illustrated in figure 1.10.

Figure 1.10

Rotoscoping in Photoshop.

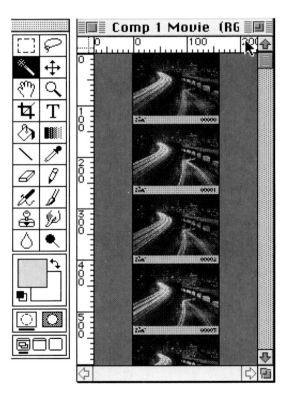

■ *Particle system* animation is a special kind of computer animation that is good for simulating natural phenomena, such as rain, fire, smoke, and explosions. In particle systems, you define behaviors and characteristics of swarms of particles, which can be anything from points to objects. Many of the explosions and special effects in video and film are done with particle systems.

Particle animation systems can be very expensive. One of the few affordable desktop particle animation systems is Final Effects (from MetaTools Software, a plug-in for Adobe After Effects, which runs on Macintosh desktop systems).

- *Inverse kinematics* or IK is a special way of linking separate pieces of a 3D computer model. In computer animation, inverse kinematics is very useful when animating a human, character, or complex organic shape. With IK, when one piece of the model is moved, the rest of the linked pieces follow in a natural, smooth motion. For example, if you move a human model's hand above its head, the motion of the arm and shoulder will follow, mimicking the motion of a real person. Inverse kinematics is different from standard object linking in that the objects have elastic, constrained motions modeled after real humans and animals. Inverse kinematics is hard to program in a computer and is usually only available in high-end animation programs, such as Electric Image and Animation Master.

Processing Graphics Files

Some programs, such as integrated 3D programs and 2D animation programs like Fractal Design Painter and Macromedia Director, enable you to draw your animation frames and create your animation all in one program. Or, you may draw your key frames in one program, export them as separate graphics files, process the files in some way, such as reduce their color depth or dimensions, import them into an animation program, and then use another program to prepare the animation for the Web.

This section provides some general hints on processing graphic files. These hints include using an image processing program, creating frames of larger dimensions than you will later need, reducing your color depth, optimizing your palette, and marking your original dimensions and registration points. Having a macro utility or batch file capability can be tremendously helpful when processing animation files. You'll often generate sequences of separate graphic files that you will need to resize, crop, or otherwise change globally in some way.

Using an Image Processing Program

Equilibrium Technology Debabelizer is an image processing program that contains many useful commands for post-processing animation files. These commands include palette optimization, file conversion, and sprite optimization. All these processes can be automated and run in batch mode. Debabelizer runs on a Macintosh and, unfortunately, there is no equivalent Windows program, although a Windows version of Debabelizer is purportedly in the works.

Think Big

Often, it's a good idea to create your animation frames with larger horizontal and vertical dimensions than the final dimensions you will use for final playback on the Web. Web animations will have dimensions typical of multimedia animation, such as 320×240 or smaller. You may want to repurpose your animations for film or video, however, or use frames in collateral print material. You may also end up changing the size of your animation to fit into a different Web page layout.

It's better to shrink a large graphic rather than increase the size of a small graphic, so it's usually a good idea to create your graphics at a larger size than you need. Once you've created your animation frames, resize them for the Web using a batch processing program or macro. If you create larger graphics, be sure to create them with the same aspect ratio as the Web version. For example, if your Web animation will have dimensions of 160×120, create larger size graphics at sizes such as 320×240, 640×480, and so forth.

Color Depth Reduction

If your graphics are 24-bit, you will have to reduce their color depth if you want to use them in an 8-bit Web animation. Of course, you can create the image at a color depth of 8-bits, but many 3D animation programs have high-quality, 24-bit renderers. You'll often be better off rendering at this higher-quality and then reducing the bit depth in another program for the Web. The quality of a color depth reduction depends on the particular palette and the colors used in the graphic.

Note

Equilibrium Technology has made available free, batch processing scripts designed specifically for Web graphics at the following:

`http://www.equil.comSoftware Scripts.html`

A common problem with reducing color depth is that a smooth gradient, such as a smooth, shadowed surface, will show discrete color bands rather than a smoothly varying color change when it's reduced from 24-bit to 8-bit. Before you reduce the color depth, use Photoshop or other image processing software to add a small amount of noise to smooth gradients and see if this helps reduce banding.

Large areas of flat, solid color in animations can have annoying pixel drift when dithered to 8-bit color. Avoid dithering solid-color areas when you reduce color depth. It's a good idea to output a test color depth reduction to see how the 24-bit animation looks at 8-bit. Consider creating an 8-bit super palette in Equilibrium Technology's Debabelizer. A *super palette* is an optimal palette that is based on the colors found in a range of different images, such as frames in an animation.

Palette Optimization

Web playback places special demands on palette optimization. Different systems have different system palettes. Different browsers assert their own palettes while they are running as the foreground application.

There are 216 "safe" colors that are shared by browsers on different platforms. These colors won't dither on different systems and therefore are good to use for flat areas of color. Lynda Weinman's recent book from New Riders, *Designing Web Graphics*, discusses Web palette issues in detail.

Preserve Dimensions and Registration Points

As you post-process separate animation frames, you may want to preserve the original dimensions of each frame in order to preserve registration points. Outline each frame with a solid line or paint small, solid-color squares in the upper-left and lower-right corners of the image. When you import these graphics into an animation program, the original size and registration points are preserved. If you want to crop your frames to reduce file size and save disk space, consider doing this as the last step, after the animation has been set up, so that you don't lose your registration points.

Note

Dithering is the process by which an image processing program approximates the original high-bit depth color with a more limited range of colors. It usually involves replacing the original high-bit depth color with a pattern of other colors, which our eyes merge and tend to perceive as continuous color.

Pixel drift occurs in animations because the dithering pattern is not consistent between frames. Colored pixels within a dithered pattern will appear to shimmy or move back and forth.

Warning

Some animation programs, such as Shockwave, enable you to assert a custom palette at the price of changing all the colors in the rest of the computer display.

Note

You can download the cross-platform browser-safe palette from Lynda Weinman's Web site at the following:

```
http://home.earthlink.net/
~lyndaw/
```

Animation Techniques

This section discusses the following basic techniques, which make your animations more professional, life-like, and believable:

- Onion-skinning
- Cut-outs
- Ease-in/ease-out and velocity curves
- Squash and stretch
- Cycling
- Secondary action and overlapping action
- Hierarchical motion
- Anticipation, action, reaction
- Line of action
- Exaggeration

These techniques include ways of drawing animations and ways to choreograph and stage your animations. Timing is everything in choreographing animations. Watch your favorite cartoon animations to see some of these techniques in action.

There are no hard and fast rules. What technique works best for you depends on your particular animation and design goals. Experiment with a few techniques using rough sketches to see which one works the best.

Onion-Skinning

Onion-skinning is a drawing technique borrowed from traditional cel animation that helps the animator create the illusion of smooth motion. In traditional cel animation, each frame is drawn on layers of transparent acetate or cels. Rather than working on each frame in isolation, animators lay these transparent cels one on top of the other. This enables them to see previous and following frames while they are drawing the current frame.

Onion-skinning is an easy way to see a complete sequence of frames at a glance and to see how each frame flows into the frames before and after. Many 2D animation programs, such as Macromedia Director, Fractal Design Painter (see fig. 1.11), and FutureWave's CelAnimator, support onion-skinning. You can even use the layering and transparency features in image processing programs such as Photoshop to simulate onion-skinning.

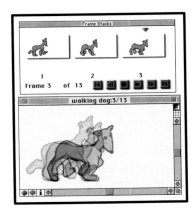

Figure 1.11

An example of onion-skinning.

Cut-Outs

Animation *cut-outs* are another technique borrowed from traditional cel animation. When the motion of a character is limited, for example, to a wave of the hand, it is easier to just redraw the hand and arm rather than redraw the entire character for each frame. The character can be drawn once and used as a background. The separate hand graphics or cut-outs are composited on the background figure to simulate movement. An example of cut-outs for different arm and hand positions is shown in figure 1.12. This technique is useful to animate limited motion, such as mouth movements during dialogue.

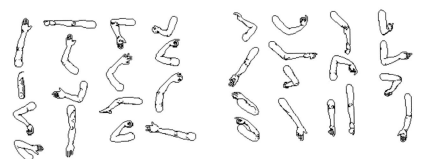

Figure 1.12

An example of cut-outs for different arm and hand positions.

Tip

You can draw an animated figure in separate pieces or as separate closed curves. Draw a separate piece for each part of the figure that will move independently. In a character animation, for example, make a separate piece for torso, head, limbs, and facial parts. Create a library of possible positions for each piece. You can then mix, match, and composite the pieces in different ways. Cut-outs are easy to create in computer graphics programs.

Traditional 2D computer graphics programs—e.g., Macromedia FreeHand—have features such as layering and blending of Bézier curves that make it easy to generate and experiment with cut-outs.

Ease-in/Ease-out and Velocity Curves

In the real world, objects generally don't move at a constant rate—they are affected by gravity. A race car slows down as it banks into a curve and speeds up as it comes out of a curve. An airplane gradually builds up to cruising speed. A transition from one motion state to another, such as starting, stopping, or turning, is typically rendered as a key frame. The gradual slowing down and speeding up as objects approach and leave key frames is called ease-in and ease-out.

You could lay out these velocity changes by hand. Slow movement has small changes between frames. Fast movement has large changes. Transitions between one motion state and another are hard to lay out smoothly. Fortunately, this is one area where computers can help out.

Most computer animation programs enable you to control the deceleration and acceleration of objects (ease-in, ease-out) by a specified amount over a certain range of frames. For example, you can take an object from zero to top speed in 60 frames for a gradual acceleration, or in 5 frames for a fast acceleration. The computer makes sure the animation looks smooth. Some programs have more detailed velocity control and enable you to assign velocity curves to an object. *Velocity curves* are editable spline curves that define the velocity of an object at any given point. Velocity curves are usually depicted in a separate track in animation sequencers with velocity increasing along the Y-axis. Figure 1.13 illustrates a velocity curve track in the program After Effects.

Note

A velocity curve for simple deceleration followed by acceleration (ease-in/ease-out) would be U-shaped.

Squash and Stretch

Squash and stretch means your animated object should have "give"; i.e., should move as if it was made up of something soft and squishy like a sandbag or water balloon. Have your animated object stretch in the direction of movement. Then, when the object stops, changes direction, or hits an immovable object, show the object compressing or squashing in the direction of movement. Squash and stretch is a simple way to give the feeling of weight to an object in motion. It is also a good way to show anticipation, recoil, and follow-through. Figure 1.14 is a composite of a bouncing ball animation illustrating squash and stretch. Note that as the ball flies through the air, it stretches in the direction of movement.

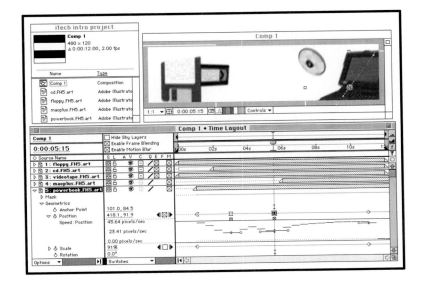

Figure 1.13

An example of a velocity curve in Adobe After Effects.

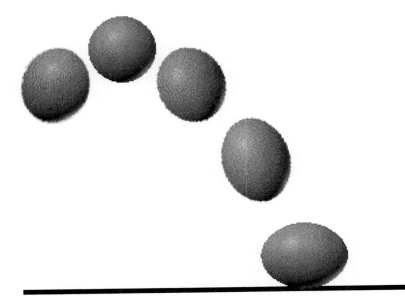

Figure 1.14

Squash and stretch.

Cycling

Many actions are repetitive and can be decomposed into a single cycle or looping action over a few frames. The classic example of animation cycling is a walking, two-legged figure. A complete cycle for a walking, two-legged figure is two steps. You could animate a two-step cycle in 10 frames. Once you create this cycle, you can have your walking figure take an infinite number of steps by just repeating the 10-frame loop.

Figure 1.1 at the beginning of this chapter is an illustration of a cycle for a galloping horse. It's important to pick the best registration point for a loop. Pick a point that remains stationary during the loop. Figure 1.9 illustrates setting a registration point in Director.

Secondary Action and Overlapping Action

It's easy to assign a static bitmap or sprite to a motion path and have it move across the screen—it's also pretty boring. One way to create interesting animations is to add secondary actions to the main action. Secondary actions can be simple. For example, if you are animating a spaceship moving across the screen, you can add simple secondary actions such as a flickering flame emanating from the exhaust pipes, a rotating turret, or a waving alien in the cockpit. If you are animating a flying superhero, show his cape fluttering. These kinds of secondary actions can be added with a simple two- or three-frame animation loop.

Overlapping action and follow-through add a dimension of time to secondary actions. Don't have all of the parts of your character or object arrive in the same place all at the same time. For example, when your flying superhero stops and lands on the ground, show his cape fluttering into position a second or two after he comes to a complete stop.

Loose, flowing parts of an object such as the tails of animals, hair, and clothing are commonly used to show follow-through. Figure 1.15 shows one way to animate a loose, flowing part of an object, such as a cape or tail. When you animate into a key frame or position, bring the object or character and its loose flowing parts, or its dangling limbs, slightly past the position. Then, bring them back into the key frame position.

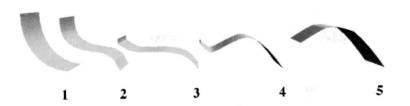

Figure 1.15

Animating secondary action.

1   2   3   4   5

Hierarchical Motion

Hierarchical motion is created by attaching or linking an object or animation loop to another object or loop, so that the first loop moves with the second. The flying bird animation discussed previously is an example of hierarchical motion. First, create a short three- or four-frame loop of a bird flapping its wings. Then, attach this loop to a second object—in this case, a motion path—so that the flapping bird flies across the screen.

The Solar System is another example of a hierarchical motion system (see fig. 1.16). Moons revolve around their planets. Planet-moon systems revolve around the sun. The sun revolves around the galactic core. Each sub-system, such as a planet-moon system, is linked to the next system higher up in the hierarchy, in this case the sun. The sub-system follows around the higher system wherever it goes.

Figure 1.16

An example of a hierarchical motion system—the Solar System.

Many computer programs enable you to set up hierarchical links between objects and animated sub-systems. In the Solar System example, here is the procedure you would follow:

1. Create the rotating planet and rotating moon as separate animation loops.

2. Attach the rotating moon to an elliptical path around the planet, creating a second-level loop.

3. Link the combined planet/moon loop to an elliptical path around the sun for a third-level loop.

If, subsequently, you moved the sun to a different position, the planets and moons would all move with the sun to the new location.

Anticipation, Action, Reaction

Watch your favorite cartoon characters. You'll see that they are masters of the "set up." The mouse holds the flowerpot over the open door, waiting for his nemesis, the cat, to come charging through. You know what is going to happen, and it adds to your enjoyment. The main comedic premise of many cartoons is this kind of anticipated action/reaction between two characters. Anticipation extends to inanimate objects, too. The fuse on the bomb gets shorter and shorter; a couch stretches and bends just before it breaks into a thousand pieces. You can add to the anticipation and help set up the viewer by showing some small movement prior to the primary motion, like a baseball pitcher getting ready to throw. Get set, wind-up, it's the pitch!

For every action there is an equal and opposite reaction. (Did you know Isaac Newton was an animator?) This is sometimes called *reaction-recovery*. Watch your favorite cartoon and you'll see an ebb and flow of action, reaction, recovery—like a pendulum—between characters. Often, you really won't see the action taking place. What you see is the anticipation, the set-up, the start of the action, and then the reaction. This is called a "fake."

To illustrate a "fake" in the preceding flowerpot example, you might animate a stretched, motion-blurred flowerpot falling toward the cat's head. The next frame might be the cat's head squashing under the weight and pieces of the flowerpot falling off its forehead. The actual contact between the two objects is never drawn.

This sort of faking can be used in other situations. Your character leans back, preparing to dash off. In the next frame, he takes his first step into the run. The next frame is a motion blur effect. The motion blur effect is animated from point A to point B. The character then is shown wobbling to a stop.

Line of Action

The *line of action* is an imaginary line that extends through the main action of your animation. For effective Web-based animations, make the line of action simple and direct.

The line of action is commonly arc-shaped or curved rather than straight. In figure animations, it typically follows the main characters spine and goes through the character's head, arm, or leg. In some cartoons, the line of action is S-shaped or made up of opposing arcs that change in a rhythmic, wave-like motion.

Look at newspaper cartoons or comic books and try to sketch in one or two lines that follow the main action. When you create your own animations, sketch in the line of action first and draw the rest of your animation around it. Figure 1.17 shows a line of action through a running figure.

> **Note**
>
> A good way to see how animators achieve their effects is to rent a video of your favorite animated feature film or videotape your favorite cartoon show and step through it frame by frame on a VCR.

Figure 1.17

Line of action.

Exaggeration

Exaggeration is another way to add impact to your animations. This is especially true of Web animations, which are generally small in size because of bandwidth considerations. They will play in tiny little rectangles in your Web page, maybe 32 pixels on a side. They may be competing with other page elements or other windows on a computer screen.

If you want your animation to be noticed, exaggerate the colors and motion. Zoom a graphic element from zero to full size in a second or two. Exaggerate the secondary motions so that they're noticed. If you are animating an old jalopy, have it bounce up and down on its worn-out shocks. Or if you are animating a spaceship, bend back the tail fins as the spaceship accelerates to warp speed.

Exaggerated *foreshortening*, where the parts of an object closest to a viewer loom large, can be especially effective in producing the illusion of depth. Figure 1.18 shows a foreshortened jet fighter.

Figure 1.18

Foreshortening.

Conclusion

Used with consideration of your users and with awareness of the limited bandwidth available, Web animations can add to the enjoyment and information content of your Web site. When placed in appropriate places on your Web site, animations can be the hook that bring people back for a second visit. If used improperly, animations can be annoying and get in the way of users viewing the content of your site.

Currently, there is a multitude of ways to add animations to your site. The most popular techniques are described in this book. Which technique works for you depends on your server, your network connectivity, the design goals and purposes of your Web site, the availability of tools, your user profile, and the availability of viewers.

Also, be aware that this will all be changing in the next year. Faster Internet access will make multimedia content more practical. Probably the most talked about Web innovation has been the cross-platform Java programming language. Java multimedia extensions from Sun, Macromedia, and Silicon Graphics, Apple Computer's QuickTime Media Layer and QuickTime extensions to Java, and Adobe System's Bravo imaging engine for Java, had just been announced at the time of this writing.

These extensions to Java promise the capability to embed "mini-viewers" with downloadable multimedia objects, removing the need for plug-ins or explicit browser support to view your content. Similar features will be present in Microsoft's OLE/ActiveX controls. How all this will play out remains to be seen. In the meantime, this book will provide you with a rich tool kit that you can use to add animations to your Web sites today.

by Paul Van Eyk

Author Biography

Paul Van Eyk is 32 years old; he purchased his first computer and laser printer at great cost, back in the days when the phrase "Desktop Publishing" was first coined and traditional typesetters refused to worry about it. Paul started his career as an "underground" cartoonist in Amsterdam, Holland, and 16 years later finds himself working as a full-time "Nethead" in Melbourne, Australia. In between, he's been a graphic designer, copy writer, editor, art director, and publisher.

These days, Paul is the Webmaster at Sausage Software, a very "coooool" software company that makes serious yet fun Web Authoring/Design tools like the HotDog Web Editor and Egor, the world's first commercial Java application. The company's products are developed in consultation with, and for, Web authoring professionals everywhere, and they're marketed and distributed almost exclusively via the Sausage Software Web site.

Thousands of people see Paul's work every day, but most know him only as Webguru. That's his nickname—and it's also his e-mail address and his job title. Sausage Software is that kind of company, the staff are that kind of people, and the Web is that kind of place. Coooool.

Animation: Getting It All Together

This chapter will offer tips and perspective on how to best prepare a Web site for graphics and animation. It will discuss the fundamentals of design, as well as the general rules to follow when applying these fundamentals. After reading this chapter, readers will have a solid understanding of how to integrate the various design elements to achieve an exciting, dynamic Web site.

Basic Design Rules and File Formats

In many ways, designing for the Web is significantly different from designing for print media such as magazines. But many "Golden Rules" exist that apply to both media. Some of these rules are discussed in the subsequent sections.

White Space

The first rule of thumb is to not create cluttered, "busy" pages if you can help it. Leave enough white space on a page, so that the eye can easily identify the main components of a page (text blocks, pictures, and so on).

Although it can be tricky to achieve good visual balance on a Web page, it can be done. For example, clever use of tables allows accurate placement of text blocks and graphics balanced with white space. Java animations can also be placed inside tables.

Signal-to-Noise Ratio

Although it can be tempting to plaster Java animations all over a Web page simply because you can, the end result will assault the senses in the same way as a pinball machine's many flashing lights. On the Web, "Content Is King." Web users are generally sophisticated enough to appreciate quality information without a great deal of visual effects—particularly if those effects do not significantly add to the information or in fact detract from it.

Most Web sites provide specific information (a "signal"), which is why people visit them in the first place! If your Java animation does not enhance the "signal," it's just plain noise.

Small is Beautiful

One important Web design rule that is irrelevant to print media is "keep it small"—this refers to file sizes. As anyone who has spent any time surfing the Web knows, there are few things more frustrating than waiting (if even just a few minutes) for a graphics-rich page to download over a slow modem connection.

A number of techniques exist today for reducing image file sizes and improving display speed. Minimizing file sizes happens at the image editing/saving stage. Two techniques are worth mentioning, both of which occur at the HTML editing stage:

- The height and width technique
- The cutting threads technique

Height and Width Technique

The first technique is the use of the HEIGHT and WIDTH attributes in the <IMG> tag. Using these attributes enables you to tell compatible browsers exactly how large an image is

> **Tip**
>
> It's better to break content into several "bite-size" pages than it is to cram all the information onto one long page. People usually prefer to view several pages in succession than to scroll down one very long page.

before it is even downloaded. This enables the browser to allocate space for the image in the right size and shape, and start flowing text around it while the image is still downloading. This gives the user a "finished" page faster than if the attributes aren't used; if the browser cannot understand the attributes, no harm is done.

While a typical Web page might contain only 10 KB of HTML code and thus download quickly, a small graphic the size of a passport photo can easily be 20 KB or more. Given that Java animations use a number of images to create an effect, it is vital to keep the file sizes of those images to a bare minimum. This is not simply a matter of courtesy to users—it is common sense. If you have a message important enough to tell people about, you don't want them to get tired of waiting for your page to download. The fact is that people simply won't wait—they'll hit the Stop button in frustration and surf somewhere else. They'll also never get your message, which defeats the whole purpose of the exercise.

Cutting Threads

In addition to using the height and width technique for reducing image file sizes and improving display speeds, a second technique also bears discussion—the cutting threads technique.

Sometimes graphics are essential to the information content or acceptable presentation of a page. For example, a corporate Web site may contain a "staff directory" page showing thumbnail photographs of all employees, as shown in figure 2.1. The Sausage Software Web site contains such a page (http://www.sausage.com/newwho.htm). The function of this page presents an interesting design challenge—it has to show 60 or 70 staff members, each person requiring an individual photograph of acceptable viewing size, and each photograph needs to be hyperlinked to the subject's individual home page or "crew card."

The easiest solution is simply to build a table holding individual images in each cell, and attaching a hyperlink to each image. However, this means that the server must send 60 or 70 small files in quick succession. Each file represents a "thread" that requires the server to look up a file and send it down the line before moving on to the next one.

Figure 2.1

Presenting many or large graphics with acceptable download speeds forces design compromises.

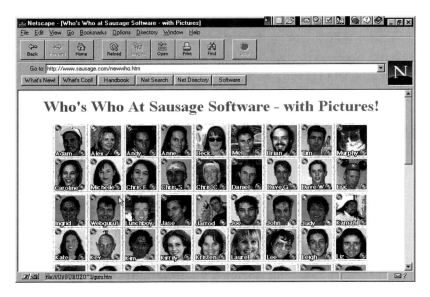

Tip

A useful technique for minimizing the file size of a large transparent GIF is to break it down into component parts and reassemble it inside a table, thereby cutting out the transparent areas. For example, to display a very large letter "H" on a Web page, you can create a table with nine cells (see fig. 2.2). Adjoining cells can be made to fit flush together, and of the nine cells, two can be empty. This reduces the composite image file size in this particular case by a whopping 42 percent!

The alternative is to create one very large clickable image map incorporating all individual pictures. Although this image's file size would be the same as the 60 or 70 individual files combined, it would require only one "thread" and therefore load quicker than the individual files would. Unfortunately, it would still take so long to load that users would get bored waiting for something to look at.

The final design is a workable compromise. Individual images are grouped together in "medium-sized" chunks of client-side clickable image maps, which unlike server-side image maps, have the advantage of not requiring CGI scripting.

Figure 2.2

Tables can be used to greatly reduce image file sizes.

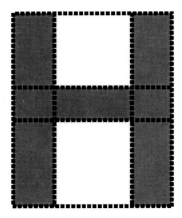

GIF and JPEG Graphics File Formats

The two most commonly used graphics file formats on the World Wide Web are GIF and JPEG.

GIF stands for *Graphics Interchange Format*; this format was adopted by CompuServe as a standard for compressing 8-bit images, which could then be transferred more quickly by electronic means. It has since become a de facto standard for Web browsers.

GIF images can contain a maximum of 256 colors or shades of gray. This makes them well-suited to images such as line drawings and logos or icons with high contrast and a limited palette of colors.

JPEG stands for *Joint Photographic Experts Group*—the people who invented it. It is the most efficient compression format currently available, and it is particularly well-suited to continuous-tone images (such as color or grayscale photographs) with subtle color transitions.

Compressing GIF and JPEG Images

GIF images are compressed using the LZW (Lempel-Ziv-Welch) compression scheme; LZW works by analyzing the binary code representing the image and replacing strings that occur often with shorter equivalent strings. Because it doesn't actually alter any part of the image, LZW is completely "lossless."

Because of the way LZW compression works, it is very good at compressing repetitive data. This means that large areas of "flat" color will compress better in GIF format than JPEG. For example, if you had an image of a landscape with a dramatic sunset, the image would lend itself better to JPEG compression. However, the exact same scene showing a lot of cloudless blue sky would probably compress better (and smaller) in GIF format.

Unfortunately, JPEG is lossy, unlike the GIF format, which indicates that the image will lose a little quality or detail in compression. When saving an image to the JPEG format, you

> **Note**
>
> A *lossless* compression scheme such as GIF is one in which image information or detail is not lost in the process. A *lossy* compression scheme such as JPEG or TIF is one in which some "non-essential" image information or detail is destroyed in the compression process, resulting in a much smaller file size at the expense of a little image quality.

Tip

As a rule, it's probably best to select JPEG's medium compression rate. JPEG is so efficient that the file will still be much smaller than any other format, such as GIF, while retaining acceptable image integrity.

can typically select varying degrees of compression: the highest degree of compression will result in the most loss of detail and, of course, the smallest file size—and vice versa. It's a compromise.

An important point to keep in mind when editing or creating images is that unlike GIF, JPEG is a cumulative compression scheme, which means that your image editor (for example, Photoshop) will recompress the image all over again each time you save it. It can't hurt to save a JPEG repeatedly during a given editing session as it will always reference the "live" version on-screen. Because JPEG is lossy, however, if you were to reopen a previously saved JPEG file and save it again, the image would lose a little more quality.

Ideally, you should save your image to JPEG format only after you have finished all editing. A sensible approach is to save your image in your image editor's "native" format (when working in Photoshop, for example) and save another copy in JPEG format, so that you can come back to the original image and change it at any stage, and keep things like masks and layers for future use.

Palettes and Color Indexing

GIF images are *indexed color* images—that is, they use a specific color palette to translate, for example, a continuous-tone image with millions of colors into a GIF image. This image will (hopefully!) look just as good as the original one, but uses only 256 colors or less.

When using an editor such as Photoshop to create GIF images from scratch or save existing images from a different format into GIF, you can control how the colors are indexed by using different palettes.

Types of Palettes

You have a choice of using a variety of palettes, including adaptive, custom, or system. An adaptive palette will analyze the image and create a unique palette of up to 256 colors taken from the image itself.

Unfortunately, an adaptive palette can look decidedly "off" on an 8-bit video display, which is basically the "lowest common denominator" found on average PCs.

Using a system or custom palette forces the image to use only colors from that palette. Some people argue that an adaptive palette gives the best results. However, browsers such as Netscape Navigator use their own unique palette when displaying images. The Netscape palette is a subset of the Microsoft Windows palette, and colors falling outside that range will be dithered (approximated using similar colors).

An excellent Web site discussing the peculiarities of Netscape's palette behavior can be found at "Victor Engel's No Dither Netscape Palette":

`http://www.onr.com/user/lights/netexp.html`

Choosing the Right Format

You must decide whether to use JPEG or GIF as an image format depending on the characteristics of the pictures you use in your animation, so as to achieve minimum file size and maximum picture quality.

An excellent Web resource on this topic is maintained by the Bandwidth Conservation Society, as follows:

`http://www.infohiway.com/way/faster/`

Besides discussing bandwidth issues, this site presents examples, practical tips and tricks, and an online forum—all features that make the BCS home page well worth a visit for any serious Webmaster (see fig. 2.3).

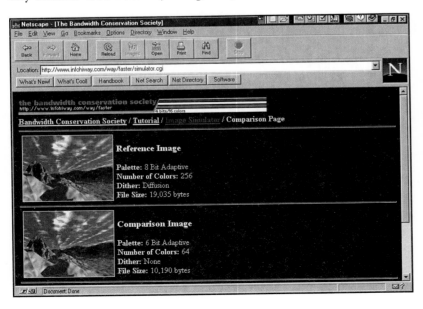

Author Note

In my personal experience, I have found that the majority of people browsing my Web site are Windows users (mainly because my Web site provides downloadable software for Windows users!). However, I prefer to create my graphics on a Macintosh. After experimenting, I decided that the best solution was to index my GIF images with the standard Windows System palettes. This does not discriminate against Macintosh computers, as they tend to display colors much better than most PCs. So everybody's happy…

Much to my chagrin, I was unable to find existing 16-color or 256-color Windows System palettes for Photoshop for the Mac; as a result, I created my own. These are now freely downloadable for all from the Sausage Software Web site at http://www.sausage.com/palettes.htm, and they are also supplied on this book's companion CD-ROM.

Figure 2.3

The Bandwidth Conservation Society is an excellent resource for all Web designers.

Note

In the early days of the Web, many browsers did not support JPEG files as inline images, but that is no longer a concern.

Transparent GIFs

Tip

Typically, you would use transparent GIFs in cartoon-style animations, where you want figures to move around a page and appear to be an integral part of the page, rather than something that happens inside a "box." A series of JPEGs would usually be better for a "movie" made up of continuous-tone images.

Author Note

Transparent GIFs are really quite easy to make, and there are numerous image editing tools available on the Web that can save or export finished images as transparent GIFs.

The best Web resource on transparent GIFs that I have come across is "Transparent/Interlaced GIF Resources" (http://www.cis.columbia.edu/homepages/gonzalu/transparent-gifs/transparent.html). It has details on useful techniques and image editing/GIF transparency tools for Macintosh, DOS/Windows, and Unix platforms. There are even links to online Web resources that will convert images to transparent GIF format for you online!

Personally, I prefer to create and edit images using Photoshop 3.05 on a Power Macintosh. Photoshop is an extremely popular and powerful image editor with excellent support for GIF and JPEG formats.

One significant advantage of the GIF format over JPEG is that GIF images can be "transparent"—that is, parts of the image can be rendered "invisible," allowing a background texture or color to show through. This is not possible with JPEG images, and if you want a transparent image, you have no choice but to use the GIF file format.

Transparent GIF images enable Web designers to escape the rectangular constraints of image file formats. The designer can either leave parts of an image transparent (say, when using Photoshop) or define a certain color as transparent (Magenta, for example) so that when displayed on a Web page, those parts of the GIF image that are Magenta will be invisible and would show instead the page's background color or background image.

Another clever use for transparent GIFs is to use them to position other objects. You may want to indent an image exactly 100 pixels from the left page margin, for example. One way to do this is to insert a transparent GIF (which is entirely transparent and therefore "invisible") first, followed immediately by the image you want to indent.

A better way to do this is to use the HEIGHT and WIDTH attributes of the <IMG> tag to "lie" about an image's size. For example, most experienced Webmasters will build a tiny transparent GIF (say, one pixel in size!), which they use as an all-purpose spacer. When they need the spacer to be 100-pixels wide, they simply add WIDTH=100 to the <IMG> tag and the browser will stretch the image to fit—and because the image is still really only one pixel in size, it downloads very quickly!

Creating Transparent GIFs in Photoshop

This section provides an introductory lesson on how to create transparent GIFs in Photoshop. It is by all means not intended as a general Photoshop tutorial and will only discuss the essential points involved in building a (transparent) GIF optimized for the World Wide Web. Creating JPEG format files will not be addressed at this time because the process requires little special attention beyond deciding whether to use more or less compression when saving an image as a JPEG.

1. When creating a transparent GIF "from scratch" in Photoshop, it is best to start by opening a new RGB image with Contents set to transparent.

2. Next, load the custom Windows System palettes (both 16-color and 256-color) in the swatches palette (see fig. 2.4). This then enables you to select a tool (for example, the Text tool).

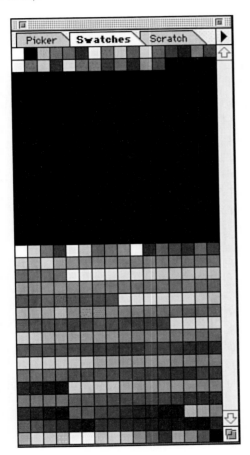

Figure 2.4

Photoshop's swatches palette.

3. Now you're ready to start working. By working in RGB mode, you get to use multiple layers and transparent backgrounds that would be unavailable in indexed color

mode. And by using swatches that contain only those exact colors that you want in the finished GIF, your colors won't be dithered when the image is changed from RGB mode to indexed color mode, or when it is exported as a GIF (essentially the same thing, really!).

4. When you have finished editing your image, save it in the native Photoshop file format before exporting it as a GIF. That way, you'll always be able to go back and edit the file using layers, for example, which you would lose irretrievably if you only kept the GIF.

Avoid Anti-Aliasing

Anti-aliasing is what Photoshop does in RGB mode to avoid "jaggies." For example, a big black letter "A" on a white background will appear smooth when anti-aliased because Photoshop will automatically use shades of gray in pixels along the edges (see fig. 2.5). This fools the human eye into perceiving the ascender as a straight line when in reality it looks more like a staircase. Figure 2.6 displays the "A" when not anti-aliased.

Figure 2.5

Anti-aliasing in action.

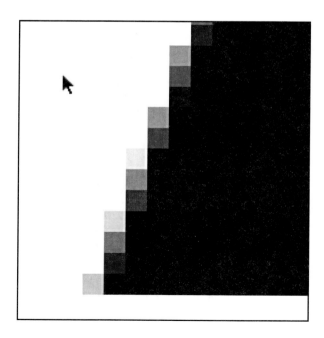

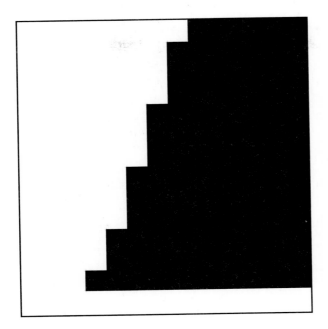

Figure 2.6

Not anti-aliased—note the "jaggies!"

Although anti-aliasing is usually a good thing, it is not when working with indexed colors because Photoshop will anti-alias using colors that do not appear in the palette used for indexing. This will usually have a very poor appearance.

Make sure to avoid anti-aliasing when using tools like Text, Paint Bucket, and so on—many tools have an option for anti-aliasing, which is on by default. Turn it off whenever you see it—it will appear in the Options palette.

Converting an Existing Image to a Transparent GIF

You can take an existing image in any format and convert it to a transparent GIF. If the image already has transparent areas, just export it as a GIF89a (see fig. 2.7).

When you do so, you will see a dialog box with several options that you can select from. These options are reviewed in the following sections.

Figure 2.7

A sample RGB image with transparent areas.

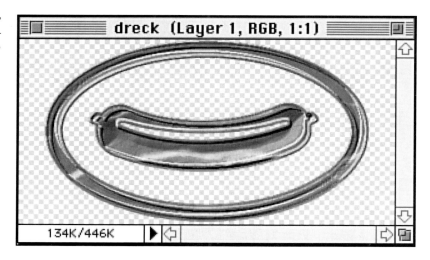

Interlacing

One option that you are presented with in the GIF89a dialog box is *Interlaced*, which is selected by default. GIF images can be interlaced or non-interlaced. To understand interlacing, you can think of the difference between a computer monitor and a television set.

A television picture is broken up into horizontal lines, and constantly redrawn from top to bottom—the "even" lines will stay on-screen while the "odd" lines are redrawn, and then the "odd" lines stay on-screen while the "even" lines are redrawn. A computer monitor, on the other hand, just draws each line in order, from top to bottom, and then starts all over again.

Non-interlaced GIF images take longer to appear on the browser screen; interlaced images will appear quickly, and then flesh out details afterward.

Default Palette

There is another option to consider in the GIF89a dialog box that pertains to the default palette. The default palette is *Adaptive*; you can use that, of course, and will most likely end up with reasonable results on a finished Web page (see fig. 2.8). The author, however, prefers to use a custom Windows System palette, which is accomplished by clicking on Load and selecting the custom palette from the Color Palettes folder inside the Photoshop Goodies folder.

Tip

As a rule, it is a good idea to interlace GIFs—it certainly can't hurt. If a browser cannot take advantage of interlacing, the image will still display anyway.

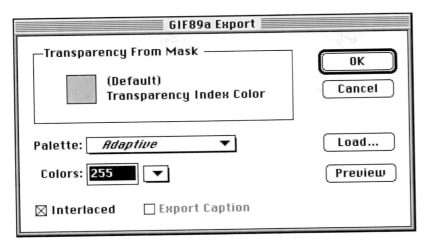

Figure 2.8

Exporting a transparent image to the GIF89a format in Photoshop.

Next, you can click Preview to see which parts of the image will be transparent (they'll show as gray). Click OK, and save the new GIF (see fig. 2.9).

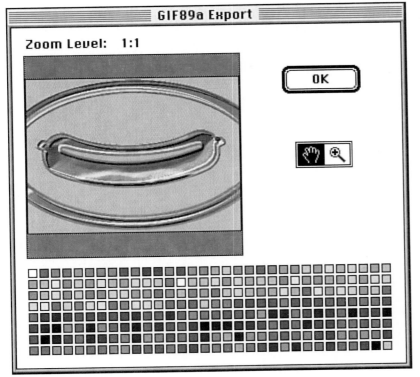

Figure 2.9

The Photoshop GIF89a Export Preview screen.

If the image does not already have transparent areas, you can create them in two ways. One way is to erase or cut unwanted areas to transparent. Another is to fill unwanted areas with a color not used elsewhere in the image. Next, select Mode from the menu and change the image to Indexed Color mode.

You may find that when you try to cut or erase parts of an image, those areas do not become transparent but instead fill with the background color active on the toolbar (white by default). All you have to do is double-click on the Background layer in the Layers palette and rename it (the default will be Layer 0). Now you can cut or erase to transparency.

When you export an image that has already been color-indexed to the GIF89a format, you will see a dialog box that is slightly different from the normal one (see fig. 2.10).

Figure 2.10

Exporting an indexed color image as a GIF89a in Photoshop.

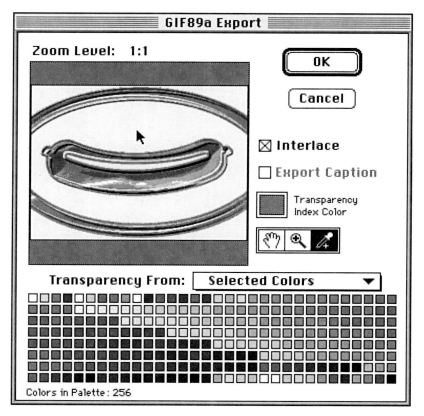

Using the eyedropper, select the color you want to be transparent from the palette displayed or from the image itself and click OK. This is essentially all that is required when converting an existing image to a transparent GIF.

Conclusion

Various rules of thumb should be considered when creating a Web site with various levels of animation and integrated design elements. These rules include understanding how much white space to make part of your site, the signal-to-noise ratio, and the fact that smaller file size images are better than large ones that take a long time to download. Techniques do exist for compressing file sizes that were discussed in this chapter. GIF and JPEG are the two most commonly used graphics file formats on the World Wide Web, and they play a significant role in designing and animating Web pages.

by Nicola Brown

Author Biography

Nicola Brown's career thus far has been, by necessity, rather short. She spent four years hard labor completing a Bachelor of Science with Honors in Computer Science at Monash University in Melbourne, Australia before entering the Big Bad World.

Currently, Nicola is employed at Sausage Software as a Java programmer, although she started her term there as technical support, wearing her fingers to the bone answering all the e-mail sales and support inquiries. In writing Egor (believed to be the world's first commercial Java applet), Nicola somehow earned the title "JavaGirl."

3

Java Animation: Technology Overview

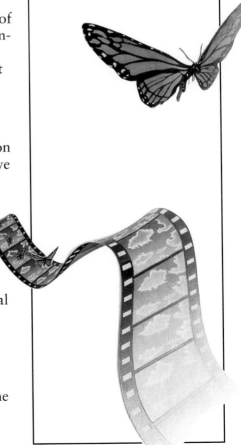

The programming language Java has come into the spotlight of the computing industry in the last six months to a year, spawning heated discussions between passionate advocates and die-hard skeptics, as all new technology tends to do. With respect to the way programs can now be used, Java brings a set of exciting new concepts to users' interaction with the World Wide Web.

In the past, programs were something you bought, installed on your computer (where they took up large chunks of hard drive space), and then ran from your computer. To get the latest version of an application usually involved an upgrade fee and much time spent installing the new version. With Java comes the prospect of programs on demand; that is, to have an applet (as Java programs are known) sitting on a Web page somewhere and fetched over the Net when you need it—an applet that is always the latest version, requires no time to be installed, and takes up no local drive space! Such programs would be paid for by rate of rental—for example, a few cents for each minute spent using the applet. Although the concept of a rental system is commonplace, it has not been implemented anywhere yet.

With the advent of Java, Web pages can now interact with the user. Games ranging from tic-tac-toe to chess now can be played, and constantly updated share prices and the latest

news headlines also are easily available, as are the funkiest animations, full of sound and motion. What a radical concept!

This chapter will not attempt to teach you to program Java. It instead aims to describe the following:

- Some of the history and background of the language—where it came from, who created it, for what purpose it was created, and just why it is worthy of all the fuss that has surrounded it.

- Features of the language, with a description of how the whole Java environment works, from source code to running the applet.

- The differences between an applet and a fully functional application.

- The concern about the language's security aspects, or possible lack of them, and the implications of this.

- How to troubleshoot Java applets, so that they successfully reach the widest audience possible.

- The future of Java, and the possibilities for Java that stretch out ahead.

Because Java is a fully fledged programming language, and this is a book on Web animation, it would be senseless to attempt to teach you how to program in Java in the few chapters assigned to the language and its capabilities. Entire texts exist that are devoted to the study of object-oriented languages, not to mention the abundance of texts recently released aimed at all levels of programmers for Java.

These chapters on Java animation are, instead, composed with the designer in mind. Their purpose is to demonstrate where Java came from, its potential, and where it might be headed in the future, as well as give a taste of how to use it and some of the tools already released in Java that are of use for Web designers and Web authors.

What Is Java?

Once upon a time, all computing was done from terminals connected to a mainframe. The large machine had all the computing power, which was carefully doled out to the programs people ran on it. Into this world came the personal computer, which moved more computing power onto the desktop, but still there remained massive machines that were the mainstay of networks.

Today the network is becoming the computer. Each desktop PC is part of the global network of the Internet, with as much computing power as any other element of the network. To take advantage of these decentralized machines, there needs to be programs that can run on any kind of platform connected to the network, that can be transmitted over the same network, and that are secure enough that everybody feels safe running them.

Java, a full-fledged programming language oriented toward the Internet and the Web, is an example of such a program. This section discusses the following topics related to Java:

- The history of Java's development

- Features of Java

- Java's advantages

- Companies and products that support Java

- Java's future applicability and use in hardware

History of Java's Development

In 1990, Sun Microsystems started a new project called Project Green to investigate the possibility of selling software to the consumer electronics market. Any program written for this market would need to be platform-independent, as it could be running on a variety of devices. Originally, C++ was considered, but the requirements on the language soon made this impractical, and it became apparent that it would be simpler to create a new language with all the features required.

In 1993, Project Green transformed into a company called First Person, Inc., which created the language then known as Oak. Oak was originally aimed to program a variety of networked devices, such as the *set-top box*, a small box that would sit on top of your television to monitor and provide video on-demand.

The technology and the commercial world were not ready for such a product, so in early 1994, First Person, Inc. was dissolved. With the prospect of precious research time being wasted, Sun found a new application for the language in the form of network-savvy programs. In September of 1994, the Java compiler was rewritten in Java—one of the major tests of a language's flexibility due to the complex nature of the task. Java was formally announced in May 1995 at Sunworld 95, and proceeded to take the Web community by storm by showing a taste of the marvels it could perform over the Web with a Java-enabled browser called HotJava.

Features and Design Goals of Java

Java, or Oak as it was known in its earlier days, had specific design goals. These goals required a language that would be able to survive long periods of time with no maintenance and be as sturdy as possible. It needed to be the following:

- **Simple**—programmers new to Java could start programming with only a small learning curve.

- **Object-oriented**—a technique that focuses design on the data (or objects) and the connections between them, rather than a linear progression. As it produces programs that are more modular, components can be re-used or easily modified without affecting the rest of the program.

- **Robust**—reliable even under unusual conditions, especially since the programs are running on a variety of computers.

- **Secure**—programs running in a distributed environment need to be virus-free and tamper-proof to prevent the spread of malicious programs, which can occur all too easily over a network.

- **Distributed**—able to run on a variety of machines connected together (such as over the Internet).

- **Multithreaded**—the ability to have many tasks that are not necessarily related all running at the same time within the one program, with each task attached to a thread of execution.

- **Dynamic**—designed to cope with a changing environment by leaving the binding of a library to the program using that library to the last stage.

- **Architecture-neutral**—Java applications need to run on a variety of systems, composed of different CPUs and operating systems.

- **Portable**—in-built graphical libraries and fundamental data types that do not depend on the system the program is running on.

Java is simple and familiar enough to C++ programmers that getting started programming the language is not a difficult task. These factors make productivity high from the day they start writing code. It is robust so that the software produced is reliable and copes with unusual situations with a minimum of fuss. Java is designed to operate in a distributed environment, such as the Net, which means that it needs to be secure because the programs are exposed to the vast amount of people connected to the network, leaving them open to attacks from hackers. It is architecture-neutral so that the software can run on many kinds of hardware, and it is portable so that the program does not need any kind of rewriting to transfer it from one kind of hardware to another.

> **Note**
>
> Java is based on the C++, Eiffel, SmallTalk, Objective C, and Cedar/Mesa languages.

Java as an Interpreted Language

Two methods are used to translate human-readable source code into machine-readable programs (or *executables* or *binaries* as they are sometimes called). These methods are the following:

- Compilation
- Interpretation

Programs that are *compiled* convert the source to an executable via a compiler, and it is this executable that is run. *Interpreted* programs, on the other hand, have an interpreter convert the source code to instructions and executes the instructions on the fly (as it goes) to machine code (such as Perl or Tcl). Java is essentially an *interpreted* language (although it does have a compiler to convert the source to architecture-neutral instructions, which are then interpreted and run by the interpreter)—to make a compiled language architecture-neutral requires recompilation for every architecture, making the whole process cumbersome.

Because interpreted programs must be converted as they are being run, they are slower in their performance than compiled programs, where all the compilation overhead occurs before the program is actually executed. Java avoids the slowness inherent in true interpreted languages by making the stage between source and instructions compiled. There are also just-in-time compilers (discussed later) that compile the instructions into an executable and then run it, in less time than it would have taken to interpret the instructions.

Kim Polese, the Senior Project Manager for Sun Microsystems when Java was released, described Java in one word: "ubiquitous." Indeed, Java is everywhere. The specification for the language and the compiler is freely available, meaning that interpreters and compilers can be written for any machine platform by anyone who has the time and the inclination. To ensure compatibility, Sun requires that any Java interpreter pass a suite of test programs; this, however, is the only obligation placed on someone porting Java to other hardware.

Why Is Java So Cool?

Java has a variety of advantages over conventional languages available today. It has been designed with a networked environment in mind, which means it is just perfect for the Internet! Not only does it have the support for creating Net- and Web-related software easily through its base library classes, but it also is forged to deal with the problems that arise from being network-oriented.

From a programmer's point of view, an advantage of Java is that it prevents some of the all too common errors relating to memory handling, which is unfortunately one of the main causes of crashes in programs written in languages like C and C++. Java prevents such errors because the language handles all the allocation and de-allocation of memory as the program runs, rather than relying on the programmer. Writing code in Java also is cost-effective because it saves in porting time; the program needs to be written only once, and it is immediately able to run on any platform that has a Java interpreter, with no additional programming time involved. This facet of Java is one to make managers happy, as it results in minimal maintenance costs.

From a user's point of view, Java has amazing potential for programs—applications that run over the Web, but are stored on someone else's machine. Imagine having very little software on your computer other than a Java interpreter and an Internet link. You can simply download the programs you need at the time, instead of having them clutter your local hard drive.

People desiring to publish information on the Web find Java a fascinating concept because Web pages previously were essentially static—displaying information in a plain, unmoving form. With the advent of Java, you can now display information in a more dynamic and interesting form, from animations to colored, constantly updating charts, or ticker tapes.

In a similar vein, if the applets are running from a location on the Web, the moment the software author upgrades the software, all the users of the software have the latest version. This means that support for new data types and protocols can be added as they're needed, and all users of the program can take advantage of this new support immediately, with minimal distribution costs.

Java Support

Even now, in the early stages of Java's lifespan, many companies have signed agreements with Sun to support the language. Among those businesses are Netscape, Spyglass Mosaic, Oracle, Sybase, Symantec, Borland, and Macromedia. Products emerging from these companies are varied in nature. Several of the companies are writing or already have browsers that support Java. Netscape's Navigator is the obvious one; however, Spyglass is releasing Mosaic with Java support soon. The topic of Java-supported browsers is discussed at greater length later in this chapter in the Troubleshooting Guide.

There are environments to help programmers write code in Java, such as Symantec's Café (http://cafe.symantec.com) and Borland's C++ Development Suite 5.0 (http://www.borland.com). Oracle and Sybase are involved in hooking up databases to Java front-ends over a network. Microsoft's Internet Explorer 3.0 will have Java support, and IBM is currently porting the Java environment to Windows 3.1. This is only a few of the projects companies all over the world are undertaking.

Also on the near horizon is a swathe of cross-compilers, which will take source code written in other languages and convert them to Java. Languages similar to Java will be the first to have cross-compilers written for them: SmallTalk, Ada, and Scheme are high on this list. Such compilers will have a variety of benefits, such as converting existing programs into Java and, as a result, opening up possibilities for making the programs network-oriented. By having the power to convert one language to another, the cross-compiler indirectly exposes more programmers to Java.

Because the specification for the Java interpreter and compiler is freely available, ports of the environment can be expected to appear for platforms other than the Windows 95, Windows NT, Unix, and Macintosh architectures that are currently available. IBM is in the process of porting Java over to AIX, Windows 3.1, and OS/2. Sun also has announced that they intend to create a Java operating system called Kona, slated to appear at the end of 1996, and several other companies have announced their intentions to include Java in their operating systems. These organizations include Apple Computers, Hewlett-Packard, Hitachi, IBM, Microsoft, Novell, and Silicon Graphics Incorporated.

Java's Future Applicability

At this stage, the base classes (or libraries) available to Java programmers cover many Internet- and World Wide Web-related functions, as well as the usual foundation classes. As more companies become interested in Java, however, more classes will become available. On the list of future classes are libraries to handle 3D, VRML, database interfaces, encryption, and authentication. All of these will increase the functionality of Java applets significantly by making them part of the standard distribution of classes.

The advantages of having 3D and VRML classes available are immediately obvious considering the amount of current interest in virtual reality. Having libraries of operations for 3D and VRML as part of the Java system means that applets can perform the complex handling of data that these graphical functions require without having to provide the functionality themselves (which would require transferring all those extra procedures across the Net, increasing download time dramatically).

Future Hardware

On the hardware end, Sun still is aiming toward devices containing Java as it was originally designed to be used—as a means of controlling appliances. Several chips that are solely Java interpreters are slated for release. Coming in three varieties, each chip is intended for a different market. Although picoJava, to be used in cellular phones, was slated for release in mid 1996, no sign has been seen of it yet; for the first quarter of 1997 is microJava, for use in low-end games; and in late 1997 is ultraJava, designed for high-end 3D manipulation and graphics. Because these chips have the Java interpreter encoded directly in the hardware, running any Java programs will be a lot faster because the chip executes the instructions directly, rather than having the operating system process the program first.

Many Internet visionaries see more and more devices becoming part of the Net, such as faxes, pagers, televisions, and anything else that has a CPU of some kind in it. As these appliances become part of the Net, they will need software to drive them and monitor their connection. Java was originally designed with such a purpose, and is ideally suited to fill this niche.

Heralded as the next major home tool, for instance, is the Internet Device—nothing more than a screen and some kind of pointing device (such as a mouse, a light pen, or perhaps even a touch-screen) hooked into the Internet and the World Wide Web. This device would provide a very cheap means of having an Internet connection and browsing the Web without paying money for functionality in a PC you might never use.

It has been suggested that this device be just a Java interpreter or a browser that supports Java applets. Once again, the background of Java comes into play as a powerful language designed to be robust and network-oriented. Such a device would be cheap to make and distribute, with little maintenance cost. The usual figure mentioned for the user to buy the device is $500. Instead of replacing the personal computer, the Internet Device is seen to be a preliminary step toward a PC or an addition to one. From the device, you could begin delving into the world of computers and the Net, but would still need a PC to actually create anything (such as a Web page).

Aspects of Java

This section aims to explain a few of the aspects of Java that may be confusing to someone who isn't a programmer, and frequently baffles programmers who are new to Java. The following topics are covered:

- The difference between Java applets and Java applications
- The concept of Java classes
- An example of basic Java code
- A quick overview of how Java code works
- How to view Java applets
- A comparison of Java applets to CGI programs and helper applications

Applets and Applications—What's the Difference?

Java programs comes in two flavors: applets and applications. A Java *application* is much the same as a program written in any normal language—it runs as a stand-alone program with the same restrictions as a normal program. Uses for applications range from monitoring systems for machines in a factory to ftp clients to database management systems.

A Java *applet*, on the other hand, is a program that can be run only through a Web browser. By its very nature, the functionality of a Java applet is severely restricted in order to prevent security compromises. This chapter discusses only Java applets, since this book strictly deals with the subject of Web animation (in which applets are primarily used). Many books on Java programming are available on the market, including New Riders Publishing's *Programming with Java*. An example later in this section provides a brief sample of easy Java applet code.

Java Classes

Any class (a kind of library file) residing on the local system is implicitly trusted. This is how the fundamental operations available to Java programmers are allowed—by distribution of the base classes with the Java environment (which contains the compiler to translate source to byte code, an interpreter to run the byte code, a debugger, and a few other useful tools).

These foundation classes contain programming rudiments like text manipulation, mathematical operations, graphical routines, file input and output, as well as functions on URLs and data containers. The breakdown is as follows:

java.applet:	Controls an applet. Required for creating Java applets. Contains start, stop, and initialization functions.
java.awt:	Abstract windowing toolkit. Looks after windows, buttons, and menus, and tracks multiple images as well as sounds. For animation, the class java.awt.MediaTracker is particularly worthy of note.
java.awt.image:	Image processing. A separate library to the java.awt classes. Handles filtering images and pixel manipulation.
java.awt.peer:	Classes used when porting all the GUI elements in java.awt to a new platform. Not used by normal programs.
java.io:	Input and output. Primarily used for file I/O. Mostly unused for applets because they have no file access.
java.lang:	Math and string manipulation and error-handling routines.
java.net:	Structure for networking, such as dealing with URLs and low-level socket handling.
java.util:	A variety of handy data-storage functions.

Note

For more information on the java.awt and java.applet classes, see the *Java API Reference: java.applet and java.awt API Packages* (New Riders, 1996).

Because these base classes reside on the local system, the applet is allowed to access them with no restrictions at all. If the user has installed other classes on the local machine, the applet would be able to access them as well. It is assumed that the user (the only person who could have installed the new classes) is confident in the security of what he or she has stored. Therefore, applets accessing these new classes are not considered threats to the system.

Sample Java Applet Source Code

The classic starting program anyone writes in a new language, whether that person is a novice or a veteran code grinder, is the Hello World program, which displays "Hello World" to the viewer.

The following is the code for the Hello World program for an applet. It should sit in a file called HelloWorld.java.

```
import java.applet.Applet;
import java.awt.*;

public class HelloWorld extends Applet {

        public void init() {
                resize(100,50);
        }

        public void paint(Graphics g) {
                g.drawString("Hello World!", 50,25);
        }

}
```

The first two import statements bring in the necessary support libraries to produce an applet (java.applet.Applet) with graphical elements to it (abstract windowing toolkit: java.awt.*).

Next, a class is defined that can be accessed by anybody (it is declared public)—this is called HelloWorld and has the properties of an applet (as it extends class Applet). This class has two operations attached to it: init, an initialization function, and paint. These both get called automatically as part of the applet code.

The init function asks for a window to be set up, 100 pixels wide and 50 pixels high. The paint function is given a handle to the graphical operations allowed on the area of the screen the applet resides in, in the form of the Graphics context g. At position (50, 25) in (x,y) coordinates the string "Hello World!" is drawn.

Creating a Class File for the Applet

So now you have a source file, HelloWorld.java—this isn't much use to the browser or the appletviewer, however, which requires a class file, HelloWorld.class. This file is generated by running the Java compiler on the HelloWorld.java source file. It is this class file that is referenced by the HTML file within the <APPLET> tag.

Java source code is compiled into an intermediate form known as *byte code*, which is stored in a file with a "class" extension. This file is stored on the Web server where the HTML file resides. When a user calls up that particular Web page, the class file is sent over the Web to the client machine. There the browser interprets the byte code and then executes it according to the platform the browser is running on.

To generate the class file from the source file (HelloWorld.java), you follow these steps:

1. Make sure that the directory containing the Java compiler (javac) is in your path. For example, if the Java compiler is in C:\java\bin, under Windows 95 or Windows NT at the DOS command-line prompt, you would type the following:

   `PATH=C:\java\bin`

   Under Unix, setting your path is dependent on what kind of command shell you are running. To find out which shell you are running, type the following at the command line, then look up the man page on the shell reported:

   `echo $SHELL`

2. Enter the following at the DOS or Unix command-line prompt:

   `javac HelloWorld.java`

This will create a file called HelloWorld.class in the same directory as the HelloWorld.java file.

Writing an HTML File for the Applet

Now you need to write an HTML file that references the applet to make it run when accessed by a browser. Follow these steps:

1. Open up a file in your favorite editor called helloworld.html (the name is irrelevant) in any directory.

2. Enter the following HTML code:

```
<HTML>
<HEAD>
<TITLE>Hello World!</TITLE>
</HEAD>
<BODY>
Say Hi to everyone!

<APPLET Code="HelloWorld" Width=100 Height=50>
You're missing out on a fantastic HelloWorld
Applet! <BR>
Perhaps you should fetch a Java-enabled browser.
</APPLET>
</BODY>
</HTML>
```

Here's what this code does:

The width and height parameters are present for the same reason you would include them for an inline image: to let the browser know how much space to leave for the applet, as it will be fetched from the server last.

The lines of text between the start <APPLET> tag and the closing </APPLET> tag are what people who don't have Java-enabled browsers see. It can include HTML tags as well.

Both the HTML file and the class file need to be placed on the Web server by using an ftp client to send the relevant files to the Web server. The class file must be in the same directory as the Web page, as that is how it is referenced in the <APPLET> tag.

Running Applets

Currently, there are only two ways to view an applet, as follows:

- Via a browser

- Through the appletviewer distributed with the Java Development Kit

A browser is sent the text of the HTML page by the server and then the images, and lastly downloads the applet. The applet then fetches all its required files, such as images and sounds, off the server. As long as the client machine is connected to the Net, the browser can read an applet on any Web page out there.

To view an applet through the appletviewer, you must pass the URL or local path to the HTML page and then to the viewer as a command-line parameter. Although the page is not displayed, the applet within the page is read in and run. If no applet is embedded inside the page, the appletviewer does nothing.

For processing the applets, there is no essential difference between a Java-enabled browser and the appletviewer other than the lack of overhead for the appletviewer, which does not have to handle the HTML code.

When the browser interprets the byte code, it first performs checks on the code to ensure the applet is not violating any security restrictions and the byte codes are all legal. If the byte codes are legal, the applet has not been corrupted in transit from server to client machine. After the browser has verified the code, the applet takes over a portion of the Web page, 100 by 50 pixels, and displays "Hello World" in the center of the area (see fig. 3.1).

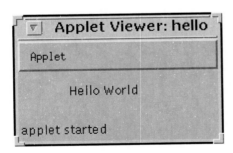

Figure 3.1

HelloWorld applet running within the appletviewer.

An Example Stand-Alone Application

To produce a stand-alone application, you enter the following code into a HelloWorld.java file inside a HelloWorld directory.

```
class HelloWorld {
    public static void main (String args[]) {
        System.out.println("Hello World!");
    }
}
```

This file declares a class called HelloWorld, which has only one operation: main. Function main is called automatically, being passed a list of strings (words) in the *args* parameter, which were arguments to the program when it was invoked. The *public* and *static* keywords tell the compiler how to treat this function.

The operation only performs one action: prints out the text Hello World! on one line to the standard output (usually the screen). The compiler knows to find this functionality in the System library class.

Producing a Class File for the Application

Compiling the code (HelloWorld.java) from the source file to the class file requires the same steps as for an applet, as follows:

1. Make sure that the directory containing the Java compiler (javac) is in your path. For example, if the Java compiler is in C:\java\bin, under Windows 95 or Windows NT at the DOS command-line prompt, you would type the following:

    PATH=C:\java\bin

    Under Unix, setting your path is dependent on what kind of command shell you are running. To find out which shell you are running, type the following at the command line, then look up the man page on the shell reported:

    echo $SHELL

2. Enter the following at the DOS or Unix command-line prompt:

    javac HelloWorld.java

This will create a file called HelloWorld.class in the same directory as the HelloWorld.java file.

3. Enter the following command also at the DOS command-line prompt:

`java HelloWorld`

This application prints out Hello World in the command-line window from which the application was run (see fig. 3.2).

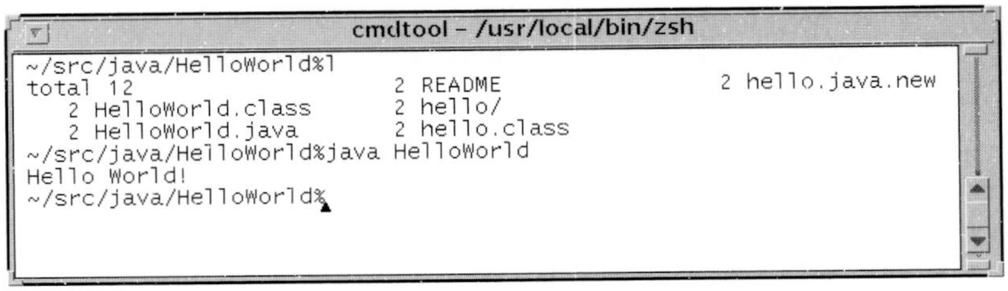

```
                          cmdtool – /usr/local/bin/zsh
~/src/java/HelloWorld%1
total 12                      2 README              2 hello.java.new
   2 HelloWorld.class        2 hello/
   2 HelloWorld.java          2 hello.class
~/src/java/HelloWorld%java HelloWorld
Hello World!
~/src/java/HelloWorld%
```

Figure 3.2

Java application running from Unix command-line prompt.

If the Java interpreter reports an error that it cannot find the HelloWorld class, you may have to set an environment variable called CLASSPATH to point to the directories where the required classes live. Different platforms have different ways of setting up CLASSPATH.

For example, under Unix, use this at the command-line prompt:

`setenv CLASSPATH .:~/classes:/usr/local/java/classes`

Under Windows 95 and NT, use this at the DOS command-line prompt:

`set CLASSPATH=.;C:\java\classes`

The main differences between the applet and the application are the following:

- An applet inherits a lot of its functionality by extending the Applet class.

- Because an applet extends the Applet class, some of the functions called by default are init() and paint(), whereas an application only has main() called by default.

- An applet usually takes up a portion of the appletviewer or browser to display its information by using the resize command, while the application can write information directly out to the screen.

Java Applets versus CGI Programs versus Helper Applications

CGI (Common Gateway Interface) programs need to sit on the server machine in a special directory. They have access to the local file system, as well as the capability to access any machine on the Internet. Service providers usually let no one but themselves have access to the special directory; they do not want to have to check every program their users want to run before putting it online to do any amount of damage to the system.

Applets can run from any directory. Because of the restrictions placed on what applets can control, both the service providers and the users of the client machine are confident they are not endangered by the program being run. Java applets on the same page can talk to one another, providing a mechanism for communication between two users accessing the same page at the same time without the need for the server to be involved in any way. This is something a CGI program cannot do.

A browser uses a table that indicates which application to run for a particular type of file. When the browser encounters a file type it doesn't know how to handle directly, it calls the helper application listed in the table. This means that the application must already be present on the local machine, and that the browser be set up correctly before the page is loaded to ensure that the right helper application is started when the file is encountered.

Java applets circumvent all of this, making life easier for the user as well. Because the latest version of the applet accompanies the data coming down the line, no configuration of the browser is required. The hard drive on the local machine is no longer cluttered with infrequently used applications for strange file types. Instead, the correct handler is loaded with the data from the Web page.

Security Issues

Unfortunately, the nature of applets causes some security issues. How do you know that the program you've just downloaded is not a virus, hasn't been tampered with en-route to your computer, or a myriad of similar concerns? The research team at Sun Microsystems was aware of these issues when they designed Java. Consequently, they built a byte code checker into all interpreters that run Java programs to ensure that the applications have not been tampered with. This section discusses security measures that were built into the Java language, the dependability of the byte code checker, and the possibility of remote security breaches, as well as possible solutions to these problems. It also explores the issue of Java and intellectual property rights.

Built-In Security Measures

Given that people can download programs from across a world-wide network with no guarantee (at least at the moment) of authorship or accountability, Sun wanted to make sure that Java applets would give people running Java on their local machines as much security as possible. The restrictions thus placed on Java initially seem harsh, until you realize why they exist.

Malicious programs, or even just badly written ones, could have the capacity to steal or destroy data on a local hard disk, take over the user's computer (if even only to steal all the CPU cycles), read local files on the computer to figure out how someone could gain access remotely, or a whole host of other spiteful actions.

To prevent these possibilities, the following measures have been set into the Java language:

- There is no access available to the local file system.
- The server machine is the only remote system the applet can access.
- It is not only illegal, but impossible, due to the design of the language, to gain control of arbitrary bits of memory.
- There are checks run on the byte code before execution to prevent illegal instructions.
- Untrusted Java applet warnings are included to prevent the user being fooled into entering sensitive information, such as their password.

Access to the local files on the client machine is not allowed, so that private data cannot be tampered with or even read. Java achieves this by refusing to compile the source code if references to the local file system exist.

In addition, to prevent the introduction of viruses, it is impossible to write new files to the local machine. Java applets can't even check for the existence of files; discovering old programs that have known holes could reveal hidden CGI programs, as well as security weaknesses.

Applets can access only the server machine from which they've been downloaded because otherwise they would be able to perform attacks on any remote machine from the client machine, impersonate a user, or transmit information through an organization's protective firewall.

Java programmers are prevented from gaining access to arbitrary chunks of memory by the inherent restrictions in the language. In C, it is possible to construct a pointer (a handle) into any section of memory; in Java, however, there is no such thing as a pointer. The Java language was designed so that any operation previously performed using pointers can now be achieved in other ways. It is the lack of pointers that prevents programmers from directly accessing your video memory or the system programs that control your hard drive or printer, making it infinitely harder for programs to accomplish evil misdeeds such as reformatting your system or scrambling what is currently on your screen.

Applets are allowed to interact with the screen and keyboard. These functions usually are required for operating and taken for granted. Applets with malicious intent, however, can use this interaction to cause damage. If an applet is so written, it can steal all the processing time of your computer, leaving the computer less able to check for attacks coming from other directions (network ports are a usual means of assault in this circumstance).

Being able to display data on-screen is something you might take for granted, but what if the window looked the same as the one you use to enter your name and password when logging in? You could be easily fooled into entering such sensitive information under the false impression that the Java applet was actually part of the system checks. To prevent the user from being fooled in such a manner, across the bottom of any window not attached to your browser appears a warning in large letters that reads "Untrusted Java Applet," so that you know it's a Java program window.

Security Alerts So Far

CERT, the Computer Emergency Response Team, released several security alerts at the start of 1996. More information on these alerts is available at http://www.cert.org. You also can obtain copies of their advisories and other security-related information from ftp://info.cert.org/pub. CERT has released two advisories regarding Java that have alarmed more than a few people and caused a great deal of consternation among organizations considering the feasibility of using Java commercially.

One caution was in relation to the security manager in the byte code verifier, and the other warned about the capability of applets to reach machines other than the host machine.

In both of these cases, members of Princeton University discovered the security holes while researching the Java environment, and no publicly available applet has been reported to take advantage of the breaches.

Broken Byte Code Verifier

Verification of the byte codes of the applet ensures that no tampering of the program has occurred between the host machine and the client machine. On March 29, 1996, CERT issued an advisory that with the verifier broken, there was no means of ensuring that no modifications have been made to the program in transit.

Additionally, if the byte code verifier is broken, an applet so written can perform any function a legitimate user of the browser can, from reading files, to removing files, to reformatting your hard drive. To achieve this, the applet executes raw machine code on the client machine, which is generally not an easy feat.

This security hole is present in the Java Development Kit versions 1.0 and 1.0.1, but has been fixed in the JDK version 1.0.2. The hole also exists in Netscape Navigator 2.0 and 2.01.

Remote Security Issues

Reported by CERT on March 5, 1996, the security hole was that a malicious applet could reach machines other than its host machine with some clever fooling with the built-in security mechanisms. The applet pretends it is going to its host machine when it actually is reaching out to another location. It can reach only a limited subset of computers in this manner; however, machines behind a firewall are not necessarily safe. This bug is present in the Netscape Navigator version 2.0 and the Java Development Kit versions 1.0, 1.0.1, and 1.0.2. Investigations are continuing, and restrictions are being imposed where necessary.

Although not necessarily a major problem, applets can determine the path from which Netscape Navigator was started. This is mostly a problem for Unix systems, where the path can contain information such as the user name (which can then be used in attacks on the system). An immediate solution is to start the browser from a directory that delivers no information, such as /tmp.

Solutions to These Security Problems

In each of the preceding cases, a CERT advisory has been released notifying people of the problem and any temporary means of preventing the problem. No matter what the problem, the ability to run Java applets can be disabled in the Netscape browser. To disable Java applets, and make your computer safe against any applet, choose Security Preferences from the Options menu, and then select Disable JavaScript.

Software developers generally react quickly in response to CERT advisories. Sun usually releases a bug-fixed version of their developer's kit, which means an updated compiler and interpreter, within a month of the release of such advisories. A new version of Netscape Navigator also follows. Frequently, small patches to the Java Development Kit are delivered by Sun within a few days of the advisories being announced.

Digital Signatures

To ensure that no tampering of programs occurs in transmission from source to end user, verification of the byte code occurs at both ends, as explained previously. It has been suggested that a form of digital signature also is used in the byte code verification. A *digital signature* is a string of text appended to the document being signed; only the owner of the digital signature can produce it. The document, in this case, can be a straight text file, a Web page, or even an executable. Using principles of cryptography, the signature is produced from the document being signed and a digital key (just another string of text). The signature can be checked by the recipient of the document, as well to ensure the document's authenticity.

The digital signatures on the applets provides a means of accountability. Digital signatures will not protect against invasions into your computer, whereby a virus is entered into the source code or the signing program itself is modified to enter a virus during the signing procedure.

Intellectual Property Concerns

Part of the Java environment distributed with the Java Development Kit is a disassembler. The disassembler takes the class file and produces a human-readable version of it that contains a list of all publicly accessible functions, as well as line numbers. You also have the option to print all the instructions passed to the interpreter. These instructions are not as easily readable as the source code (especially since they are not commented!), but are more understandable than mere binary.

Taking this one step further, a couple of the companies that have released programming environments for Java (including Natural Intelligent's Roaster) claim that their debuggers will be able to recreate the source code from a class file. Admittedly this source code will not include comments and will be missing meaningful names for variables, and the code will not be exactly as the original author wrote it. To produce human-readable source code from the machine-readable byte code, however, is an impressive feat.

Unfortunately, this has some disturbing implications regarding intellectual property. When a user can convert a program back into source code, the programmer loses all protection over his

> **Note**
>
> The use of digital signatures has not actually been implemented yet. The process of verifying a digital signature requires that a trusted body (a third-party organization) hold the public version of the private digital key for each person who has a digital key and plans on generating signatures with it. These keys cannot be lost, matched against the wrong owner, or corrupted in any way; otherwise, it will not be possible to verify them.
>
> Who the third-party would be is the subject of much discussion, as is how to implement controls to ensure nothing goes wrong. What kind of methods should be put in place to prevent and detect corruption within the trusted third party? Who watches the watchers?

Author Note

I first heard of the concept of generating source code from a class file at the Netscape Developer's Conference in San Francisco in March 1996, but in all my travels over the Web and in talking to other Java developers, I have not heard it mentioned since. It is possible that the company's claims are true: the generated source code really is impossible to understand (if so, why generate it, though?), or perhaps their claims of producing such a debugger were overstated.

intellectual property in the form of the source code. Ideas, programming styles, and even chunks of code can be stolen and placed into other programs.

The companies' justification for enabling the user to produce source code from class files is that the generated source code is not meaningful without the accompanying comments or useful variable names. Regrettably, any programmer who has had to maintain someone else's code, either for bug fixes or updates, knows that it is possible to work under those constraints and succeed at understanding the source, though it might take a long time and inordinate amounts of frustration.

Disadvantages of Java: An Explanation and Troubleshooting Guide

Java applets don't always work for several reasons, ranging from hardware to software. These problems and the solutions to them are described in the following, so that your impressive Web pages will reach the widest audience possible! This section covers some typical problems Java users experience:

- Lack of browser support
- Slowness of Java applets
- Slow links to host systems
- Timeout

Lack of Browser Support

The primary reason Java animations might not work on Web pages is that not all browsers support Java yet. Netscape Navigator 2.0 was the first browser to support Java, Oracle's PowerBrowser now supports Java, and Microsoft's Internet Explorer 3.0 will have the capability to run Java applets. With the spread of Java across the Net, it shouldn't be too long until all browsers include Java support.

Browsers that support Java are becoming more common, although support on all platforms for a particular browser can be staggered, as evidenced by the information in table 3.1.

Table 3.1

Java-Enabled Browsers

Browser	Platform(s)	Date Due	Notes
Netscape Navigator 2	Mac68K	late Q2 96	
	Windows 3.1	late Q2 96	
	PowerMac		In beta
	Windows 95	released	
	Windows NT	released	
	Unix	released	
Microsoft Internet Explorer 3	Mac68K	mid July 96	
	PowerMac	mid July 96	
	Windows 95	mid July 96	
	Windows NT	mid July 96	
	Windows 3.1		No plans
	Unix		No plans
Spyglass Mosaic	Mac68K	March 96	Delayed; No new release date
	PowerMac	March 96	
	Windows 95	March 96	
	Windows NT	March 96	
	Windows 3.1	March 96	
	Unix	March 96	
SunSoft HotJava	Windows 3.1	unknown	Awaiting IBM's Java Port
	Windows 95	released	
	Windows NT	released	
	Unix	released	
Oracle	Mac68K	late Q2 96	
	PowerMac	late Q2 96	
	Unix	late Q2 96	
	Windows 3.1	released	
	Windows 95	released	
	Windows NT	released	
IBM WebExplorer	Any		No plans

Slowness of Java Applets

Users have complained that Java programs can be slow to run. Although they are slower than conventional programs, there are good reasons for this, and steps are being taken to increase their speed.

Java applets are relatively sluggish to run because they are interpreted, which is considerably slower than executing a compiled program. Compiled programs are quick to run; all the conversion from human-readable source to machine-readable binary has taken place earlier than at execution time. Interpreted programs on the other hand must perform this conversion as the program is running. Many companies are looking at producing Just In Time compilers, which take the byte code and compile it into native code when it arrives on the local machine, then setting the compiled native code to run, which is a lot faster. Symantec and Borland are two companies in the process of writing Just In Time compilers for release in the near future.

Another reason applets are slow to execute is the checks that are made before and while the program is running. The verifier ensures there are no violations of the access restrictions (attempts to access the file system or a machine other than the host machine), that the byte codes are all legal, as are their parameters, that the portion of memory assigned to the applet will not be overflowed when the applet runs, and that the program is not trying to use memory to which it doesn't have access. These tests go a long way toward ensuring robustness and security—the program will not run if any of the tests are failed.

Slow Link to Host System

If the browser has the capacity to run Java applets, but the Java animation fails to display, the link to the server might be too slow. If the applet cannot obtain all the information it needs (images and sound files, in the case of animations) before the link times out, the applet isn't able to run.

To help prevent the browser from deciding that the link to the server has vanished, you can increase the cache size on the local system. This setting is usually found in the Preferences or Options menu of the browser, under the Cache and Network or Advanced heading.

Alternatively, seek out sites that might contain the same applets, but are located closer geographically to you, or have more bandwidth running to them. As a last resort, try going to such sites during off-peak hours.

Conclusion

Java is an exciting new technology that has brought remarkable changes to the way the World Wide Web is viewed. The Web is the prime focus of Java at the moment—the possibilities of what the language can be used for, however, reach far beyond the Web into applications and even hardware devices.

Java brings a thoroughly fresh perspective to the design and use of Web pages in all areas. As it stands, Java can turn a plain and simple Web page into something with life and color that can even interact with the user. Education and entertainment, finance and advertising, even personal Web pages can be thoroughly enhanced by the opportunities Java brings.

If you are interested in learning how to program Java, or are just interested in the language in general, here are a few places that contain the relevant information:

Sun Microsystems: http://java.sun.com

This is where the actual Java Development Kit (the compiler, an interpreter, and basic documentation on how to configure your system to run with the JDK) resides, as well as press information, programming tutorials, and pointers to mailing lists.

Digital Espresso: http://www.io.org/~mentor/jnIndex.html

A service from Mentor Software Solutions (http://www.io.org/~mentor), this is a very good summary of the week's traffic through the comp.lang.java newsgroup. It can save you a lot of time wading through all the articles posted there every week. It also contains announcements of new products and aids.

Gamelan: http://www.gamelan.com

This is an excellent set of pointers to applets around the world, split into categories such as Education, Financial, and Multimedia. A searching facility also exists, which has now become essential due to the sheer number of applets registered there!

JARS: http://www.surinam.net/java/jars/jars.html

Java Applet Rating Service (JARS) judges rate the applets, and winners can then display the JARS-rated logo on their site. Applets included range from a text editor that can pull HTML source from any given URL, to a fully playable Rubik's Cube.

It is hoped that this chapter has provided you with a good insight into Java's background, why it is worthy of so much commotion, and where it can be used today and might be heading in the future. The following chapter continues delving into the aspects of designing for Java applets, with particular emphasis on creating animations.

by Paul Van Eyk

Author Biography

Paul Van Eyk is 32 years old; he purchased his first computer and laser printer at great cost, back in the days when the phrase "Desktop Publishing" was first coined and traditional typesetters refused to worry about it. Paul started his career as an "underground" cartoonist in Amsterdam, Holland, and 16 years later finds himself working as a full-time "Nethead" in Melbourne, Australia. In between, he's been a graphic designer, copy writer, editor, art director, and publisher.

These days, Paul is the Webmaster at Sausage Software, a very "coooool" software company that makes serious yet fun Web Authoring/Design tools like the HotDog Web Editor and Egor, the world's first commercial Java application. The company's products are developed in consultation with, and for, Web authoring professionals everywhere, and they're marketed and distributed almost exclusively via the Sausage Software Web site.

Thousands of people see Paul's work everyday, but most know him only as Webguru. That's his nickname—and it's also his e-mail address and his job title. Sausage Software is that kind of company, the staff are that kind of people, and the Web is that kind of place. Coooool.

Design Aspects of Java Animation for the Web

The World Wide Web has always been pretty exciting, and there are more interesting Web sites out there than any one person could hope to visit in a lifetime. Until Java came into the picture, however, the Web was depressingly static. You could look at a flat page and read the information on it, perhaps even look at photographic stills and graphics—but nothing else really happened. Web pages were as static as pages in a magazine, except of course that you could click on hyperlinks—which would take you to yet another static page.

The cool thing about Java is that it enables Web designers to create Web pages that are truly interactive, interesting, and attractive. Java is a simple, yet effective, way to package sound and animation (which can look like video) without special plug-ins—but animations are just one aspect of Java's exciting capabilities, as follows:

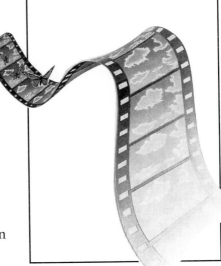

- Java runs on most popular computers, regardless of platform, the only requirement being a compatible browser like Sun's HotJava or Netscape Navigator.

- Because Java applets are fairly small, they download quickly from the server, and because they actually run on

the client (local) computer, they're both fast and very interactive.

- Because Java was developed specifically for the Net and is based on C++, it is particularly stable and powerful.

Technology Overview: Overcoming Java's Limitations

> **Note**
>
> Well-designed Web pages should download quickly. Although there is still a bandwidth problem, with many Web surfers dialing in through slow modems, a good Webmaster constantly strives to deliver the best possible visual and interactive experience at an acceptable speed.

Java is one of the latest weapons in a Web designers arsenal. A few short years ago, however, when the World Wide Web came into being, Web page design was limited to what could be achieved within the original HTML standard. HTML only allowed for text documents, without graphics and certainly without animations.

HTML stands for HyperText Markup Language—the international standard protocol that allows documents to be shared by a variety of platforms. In a nutshell, HTML is an agreed set of tags, such as <H1>, <BOLD>, or <CENTER>, which are interpreted by Web browsers to reproduce a document with various levels of headings and emphasis for different paragraphs of text.

HTML is a dynamic standard; it is constantly evolving. Primarily intended for text-only documents in its original form, HTML was not very useful from a design point of view. There were (and are) limitations to what could be done with graphics and page layout.

HTML Browser Wars: Painful, but Necessary

Since the early days of the Web, when Mosaic was the only browser around, we've seen many new browsers come along that pushed the HTML envelope by introducing non-standard tags. Netscape, for example, has introduced many new tags that at the time were not supported by any other browsers; other companies (like Microsoft) introduced yet more new tags—which were also specific to one browser only.

It can be argued that the various browser companies are deliberately bringing out new tags in a cynical attempt to gain market dominance. If that is true, then Netscape is certainly winning the battle so far. Regardless of the motives of companies like Netscape, by pushing the HTML envelope with "Browser Wars," these competing software companies are gradually giving Web authors better tools to work with.

Perhaps one day HTML will mature and become a relatively static standard, but today it's still difficult for a Webmaster to decide which tags to use. Some purists will argue that a good Web site should look exactly the same on any browser. Those people will use only those standard tags supported by the majority of available browsers, and wait until "rebel" tags are incorporated into the next official HTML standard before using them (currently, we're up to HTML 3).

A more practical point of view is to cater to the majority of people (not browsers!)—and the vast majority of people use Netscape's Navigator browser. A growing minority use Microsoft's Internet Explorer, however, and these two browsers combined probably account for 90–95 percent of Web users.

> **Note**
>
> An HTML tag is part of an HTML file surrounded with greater-than and less-than symbols (an example of which is <EMBED>), and interpreted by a Web browser that controls various attributes of the text, image, or other elements.

Java Browser Support

At this point, only a few browsers support Java. As Sun is the creator of Java, it's hardly surprising that its browser, HotJava, supports Java. Later versions of Netscape Navigator support Java with varying degrees of success; even though they are still prone to crashing (especially on a Macintosh), these versions are becoming increasingly robust.

Although at this stage Internet Explorer does not support Java, Microsoft has announced that future versions will do so (version 3, due out July 1996)—which means that Webmasters can use Java without alienating too many visitors from their Web sites.

Typically, what will happen when someone tries to view a page containing Java with a non-Java browser is that a message will be displayed, advising them to use a Java-compatible browser. Here's an example of a Web page containing a Java animation created with the Egor Animator from Sausage Software, as seen with a non-Java browser (Microsoft's Internet Explorer, fig. 4.1) and a Java-compatible browser (Netscape Navigator, fig. 4.2).

Figure 4.1

A Java animation as displayed (NOT!) by Microsoft Internet Explorer.

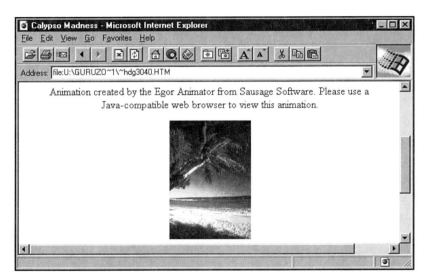

Figure 4.2

The same Java animation as displayed by Netscape Navigator.

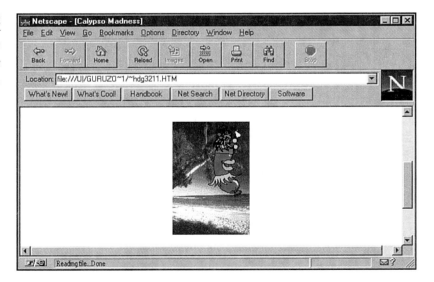

When viewed on a non-Java compatible browser like Microsoft Internet Explorer, the Java applet is ignored, but non-Java elements embedded within the applet are displayed—in this case, a line of text advising the user to switch browsers and a default image (the beach scene).

When viewed on a Java-compatible browser like Netscape Navigator, the Java applet is activated and displayed, but non-Java elements embedded within the applet are ignored—that is, the default background image and the non-Java text warning.

The difference between the two browsers is that Internet Explorer cannot understand Java. When Internet Explorer comes to tags it doesn't know, it ignores them line-by-line until it comes to tags that it does understand and therefore displays.

Here's the source code for the page displayed in figure 4.1 and figure 4.2. As you can see, right near the closing </APPLET> tag is a text warning that will automatically display on non-Java browsers, and an IMG SRC tag for a default background image. The <IMG SRC> tag tells the browser to download and display a certain image (for example, a GIF or JPEG file). The line of text can be used to provide alternative navigational instructions, for example.

The default image can be chosen and positioned carefully so that even if the Java animation itself doesn't display, the default image will still look right in the overall page design.

Tip

It is prudent to offer alternatives for those people with non-Java browsers who might otherwise miss out on vital information or navigational aids.

If your piece of Java is a billboard that advertises sponsors, for instance, you might decide it's not essential information. But if the billboard is a navigation tool where people must choose which page to view next, you should provide other instructions.

```
<CENTER><APPLET Code="anim" WIDTH=120 HEIGHT=180>
<!--This animation was created by Egor, &copy;1996
➥Sausage Software.--> <param name="imagelist"
value="calipso1.gif, calipso2.gif, calipso3.gif,
➥calipso4.gif, calipso5.gif, calipso4.gif,
➥calipso3.gif, calipso2.gif"> <param name="reguser"
➥value="Rob Cumming">
<param name="serialid" value="BAIAH">
<param name="move" value="3,1">
<param name="pause" value="100">
<param name="timeout" value="0">
<param name="bounce" value="true">
<param name="bg" value="#00FFFF">
<param name="background" value="calyback.gif">
<param name="soundtrack" value="callips8.au">
<param name="startup" value="calipso1.gif">
Animation created by the Egor Animator from Sausage
➥Software. Please use a Java-compatible web browser to
➥view this animation.<P>
<IMG SRC="calyback.gif"></APPLET></CENTER>
```

Although Java is not yet supported by all browsers, a Web designer can still ensure that what is displayed on non-Java browsers will still make sense through the judicious use of warning text messages and default background images. Most of Java's other little drawbacks can also be minimized, such as the fact that a Java animation is the last part of a Web page to load and display, discussed next.

Last to Load

Java is the last part of a Web page to actually load. In the case of an animation, for example, the entire page, with text and normal graphics, will appear in the browser window first. The browser will then display a rectangular gray box in the dimensions and placement of the applet window before the Java animation kicks in and fills the window with a color or background image.

Given the relatively slow speed at which most users will download most pages, this means that your Java window may look like a bit of an eyesore until the applet starts to run. The only way to avoid this problem is to design your Web page with a background color that is the same shade of gray as the Java box.

Java Reliability: It's Young, It's Frisky

Another drawback of Java is that it can be a little unreliable. To quote an acquaintance of mine: "Java: it's young, it's frisky, and it's lovable. It's also a bit unruly at times." What that means is that sometimes, a Java applet just won't run. It *should* run, it ran just fine the first time you looked at it, and it might work again next time, but it just doesn't feel like working right now!

As a Webmaster, I have been baffled by reports from some people who are using the right browser (typically Netscape Navigator 2), yet are unable to view my Java animations. So far, the only explanation I've come up with is that when the Java applet starts to run and looks for images, the images don't download fast enough from the server and the applet reports an error—"impatiently" thinking that the images must be missing.

Warning

Java animations run inside a window or box on the Web page. The box can be made to be effectively invisible (for example, by giving the box and the Web page an identical background color), but if the page uses a tiled image as a background wallpaper, the Java window cannot be made to tile seamlessly with the rest of the underlying Web page.

It is usually best to use a background color for the Java animation that is identical to the background color of the underlying Web page; this will allow the Java animation to appear as an integral part of the overall page design.

Luckily, this problem doesn't seem to happen all that often: I've advised people to clear their browser's memory caches, increase their cache size (1 MB for memory cache and 5 MB for disk cache seems to work well), and reload the page, if possible, from a mirror site that is closer or has more bandwidth. This seems to work most of the time. Obviously, Web designers should keep image file sizes to a minimum to avoid this sort of thing; ways to do this are discussed later in this chapter.

Incidentally, a *mirror site* is an "identical twin" of a site that resides on a server in a different geographical location. Mirror sites serve to spread the load around, so that people from different parts of the world are not all forced to view files from just one server, which may be on the far side of the planet and perhaps performing poorly due to the sheer number of people visiting it.

Java's Captive Audience

An amusing characteristic of Java is that it can enable a Web designer to "force" people to view images (say, ones that are embedded in a Java animation), even when they don't want to!

Quite a few people surfing the Web deliberately set their graphics-capable browser to text-only mode. Typically, people do this because they get bored waiting for graphics to download—and who can blame them, when many Webmasters go completely overboard with lots of large unnecessary images on every page.

The browser in text-only mode reads an HTML document and displays it on-screen, but deliberately ignores anything set between <IMG> tags. However, <IMG SRC> tags that are embedded in a Java applet are not blocked out by the browser, because it doesn't know they're there! When the browser comes to a Java applet, it will quickly check for the specified width and height of the applet's window, reserve that much space on the page, and keep reading the HTML code until it gets to the closing </HTML> tag. The browser will then go back to the spot it left free for the applet and start to download the Java code. Once the Java code is downloaded, the applet will start running—and it's the Java applet that then downloads any images required, not the browser itself.

> **Note**
>
> Some Web sites are so popular that they require dozens of identical sites around the world; one such site is TUCOWS. While the central Web site (http://www.tucows.com) resides in Canada, the home page advises users to first select from over 100 locations the mirror site nearest to them.

> **Tip**
>
> To set Netscape Navigator in text-only mode, select Options from the menu and ensure that Auto Load Images is deselected.

This means that if you're sneaky, and want a certain image to be displayed even on Java browsers that have been set to text-only mode, all you have to do is incorporate the image in a Java animation. The animation doesn't even have to be a real animation—just a single frame will do the trick.

The only way for a user to stop the image from downloading and displaying is to switch off Java, as well as Auto Load Images. Most people don't know how.

Procedure: Animating a Web Site with Java

In this section, we will actually go through the steps required to create a miniature Web site that utilizes various forms of Java. The Web pages and the Java effects will be created with a number of specialized Java and Web authoring applications, which are included on the CD-ROM that accompanies this book.

Tools
The HotDog Pro Web Editor (16-bit and 32-bit versions)
Egor
FrameGang
BookWorm
CrossEye
Swami
Flash

The applications in the toolbox were all created by Sausage Software, a world leader in Web authoring tools—and the employer of Paul Van Eyk, this chapter's author.

Sausage Software: Company Profile

Sausage Software is an Australian company that produces world-class Internet tools. This company is renowned for creating the HotDog Web Editor, one of the leading WWW home page design tools available. HotDog is used by some of the largest and most well-known companies, universities, and institutions in the world, including Microsoft, NASA, ABC, and Harvard University.

On Tuesday, February 6, 1996, Sausage Software was the first company in the world to successfully launch a commercial Java applet, simply titled "Egor." Egor enables users to bring a Web page to life with animation and sound.

In April 1996, the company announced its business development strategy for the year. The strategy focuses on the development of a variety of niche application and software tools, to be known as "Snaglets," for Web publishers and Internet users. At peak production, 20 new products will be released each month.

Sausage Snaglets do not require any knowledge of HTML or JAVA programming languages in order to produce impressive and highly individual Web pages from scratch. Snaglets are designed to use either "point and click," "drag and drop," or similarly intuitive command interfaces.

Author Note

"There has been a lot of talk about Java across the world. It was the company commitment of time and resources to develop the language that has enabled us to claim this important world first, proving we are at the cutting edge of Web programming and products," said Steve Outtrim, managing director of Sausage Software.

HotDog

In the course of building our little Web site, I will create Java effects, image maps, and frames using a variety of programs. These programs generate HTML code that I will then paste into the relevant HTML documents, which I will create using HotDog, an HTML editor.

There is no real need to use a dedicated Web editor to create and edit HTML documents; for example, some Web authors prefer to use a very simple text editor such as Windows Notepad. There's nothing wrong with that, provided of course that you don't make any mistakes when typing in HTML code manually.

Many Web designers choose to use a specialized HTML editing tool because the editor will always get the tags right; once you're familiar with the program, you can create lots of HTML code quickly.

My preferred HTML tool is the feature-packed HotDog Web Editor; of course I'm biased, because it was created by the company I work for, but HotDog has been given rave reviews by Web cognoscenti and trade publications world-wide.

HotDog comes in various flavors—a 16-bit version for Windows 3.x users (see fig. 4.3), and a 32-bit version for Windows 95 users (see fig. 4.4). HotDog Pro 32-bit has all the features of the 16-bit version, plus a funky interface and customizable floating toolbars. Fully-functional evaluation copies of each are included on the CD-ROM that comes with this book. The copies will work for 14 days before nagging you to register. Try 'em out—you might like 'em as much as I do!

Figure 4.3

The 16-bit version of HotDog Pro.

Figure 4.4

The 32-bit version of HotDog Pro.

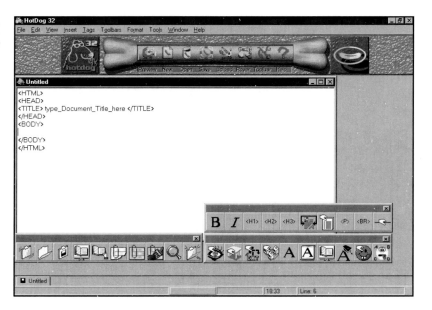

With the in-depth HTML tutorials and reference material, even a total novice can learn everything needed to create world-class Web pages in a very short time (see fig. 4.5).

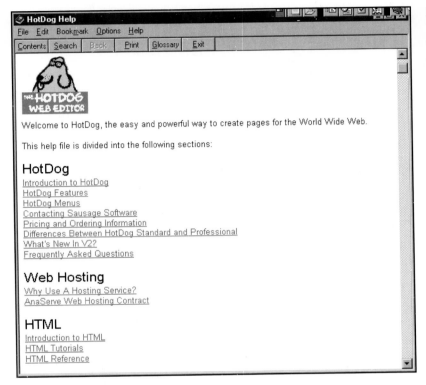

Figure 4.5

HotDog's comprehensive Help files are possibly its best feature.

FrameGang

The Web site I'll be building should allow for easy navigation between a number of pages, and preferably show a Java animation at all times.

This is an appropriate time to use frames, which are a new addition to the HTML code created by Netscape. Although they are great because you can use them to dynamically update portions of your Web page, they can be tricky to create.

Luckily, there's a nifty little utility called FrameGang that will create framed Web pages in moments. I'll start by conceptualizing the screen I want to end up with. I want to center a title graphic at the top of the screen, with some Java effects on either side. Below that, I'd like a frame to hold a vertical toolbar on the left and the main document window to the right.

1. After opening FrameGang, I click on "New" and start by specifying how many rows or columns I'd like to start with (see fig. 4.6).

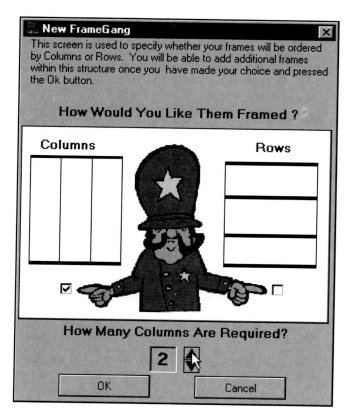

2. Once I've got a basic set of frames, I can add or remove frames by clicking a button on the menu bar (see fig. 4.7). You can have a virtually unlimited number of frames on a Web page; of course, the practical limits are dictated by the screen size and resolution.

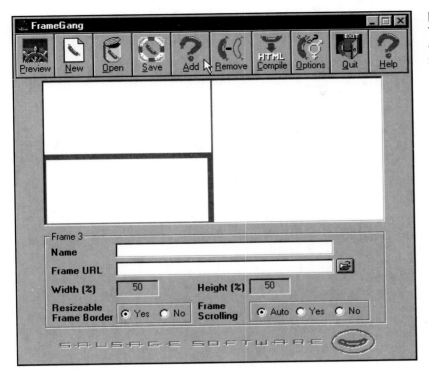

Figure 4.7

Adding or removing frames with a mouse click.

3. Once I've added all the frames I need, I can resize them to suit by simply dragging the dividers or entering absolute values.

4. The final step is to name each frame, and specify an URL (Uniform Resource Locator) for each frame; that is, specify an HTML document to be displayed inside that frame (see fig. 4.8).

   The key to understanding how frames work is to appreciate that all frames do is tell your browser to display more than one Web page at the same time on the same screen. An HTML document with five frames is really just five individual Web pages displayed within the same browser window simultaneously.

5. Once I'm satisfied that my frames are where I want them, in the right size and shape, and I've previewed them to make sure it all looks right, I simply click on the Compile

---

Note

Frames can be a fixed size, expressed in pixels, or they can be flexible. A flexible frame will have its size expressed as a percentage of screen size, enabling the browser to resize it depending on the user's monitor.

These modes of sizing can be used in combination; for example, you may want to specify exact dimensions (using pixel values for height and width) for a frame containing a graphic that you want to be displayed at a particular size. The adjacent frames can simply take whatever space is left over on the monitor.

button (see fig. 4.9). FrameGang then copies the required HTML code to the Windows Clipboard, ready for insertion in your Web document.

Figure 4.8

Naming the frames and specifying characteristics.

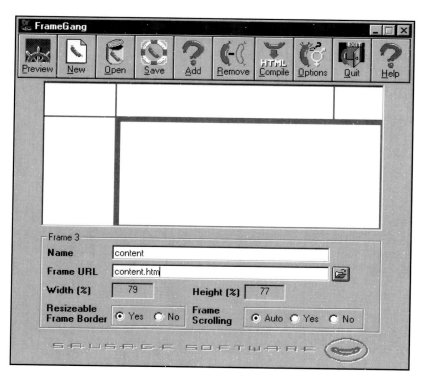

Figure 4.9

Clicking the Compile button copies the relevant HTML code to the Windows Clipboard.

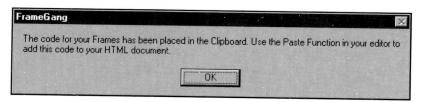

6. I then paste the code into the HotDog Web Editor (see fig. 4.10).

7. Finally, I save this page as index.htm—the default "front door" page for this Web site.

Now I'm ready to create the rest of the site. I will need to create a Web page for each of the frames specified in my frameset. I've just created index.htm, which is effectively a placeholder page that contains no more than the frameset created with FrameGang.

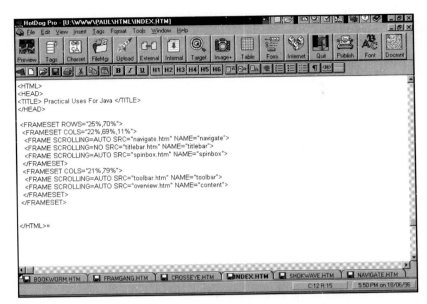

Figure 4.10

Pasting the compiled HTML frameset into the HotDog Web Editor.

8. Using the HotDog Web Editor, I create Web pages as "filler" for individual frames:

- navigate.htm

- titlebar.htm

- spinbox.htm

- toolbar.htm

- content.htm

The content page is different from the others in that it is the only frame that will change content, depending on user actions. The content of the other frames will remain on-screen and visible while the user browses the site. Clicking on the toolbar will switch between pages viewed in content.htm.

Those pages are to contain text and graphics illustrating the individual software programs discussed in this section.

Egor

Having created a set of frames for my Web site, I can now create the content for the individual Web pages that will be displayed in each frame.

I've decided to put a little Java animation in a small frame at the top of the page; rather than learn how to write Java (very difficult for non-programmers like me!), I'll just use a program like Egor, which does all the Java stuff for me (very easy indeed!).

 A copy of Egor can be found on the CD-ROM that accompanies this book. When you start it up, you'll see a screen like the one in figure 4.11.

Figure 4.11

Egor's main screen.

Tip

Egor animations can be simple, consisting of only a few cells, or complex—remember, however, that the more GIF images you include in the animation, the more files the browser will need to download and the longer it will take for the animation to commence.

Egor lets you take graphics in GIF format that you've created with programs like Photoshop and turn them into animation sequences, complete with audio if you want:

1. A click on the Add button on the toolbar brings up a File Manager where you can select which cells to use (see fig. 4.12). Once you've selected a range of graphics files, you can move them around or cut them in Egor's main window.

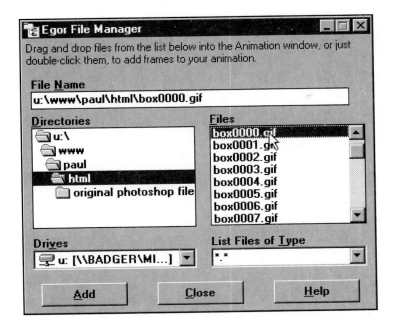

Figure 4.12

Adding images to the animation.

2. Having selected all the files for my animation, I can check it in Egor's preview screen (see fig. 4.13). Once I'm happy that the animation sequence works more-or-less properly, I can add the finishing touches.

3. I'll specify a time-delay between frames; this determines how fast the animation runs. The best way to determine the correct delay between frames is simply by trial and error; preview the animation after every change.

4. I want my animation of a three-dimensional spinning box to loop seamlessly; that is, I want the animation sequence to repeat itself without a break, so that there is no obvious start or end to the sequence. Therefore, I'll leave the "Delay Before Restarting" value blank (see fig. 4.14).

5. If I want to, I can specify the number of times the animation loops, or the length of time I want it to loop for before stopping. Again, because I want an endless loop, I'll leave those fields blank. There are other fields that don't apply to this particular animation because I want it to sit in one spot and not move up or down around the screen. I therefore ignore the Start Position fields (see fig. 4.15).

Author Note

A cute touch is that to delete a cell, you must drag it to the guillotine in the top right corner, which then "chops" it. Gory!

Figure 4.13

Previewing the animation.

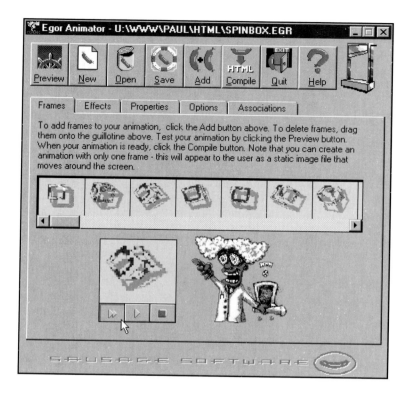

Figure 4.14

Adding the finishing touches to the animation.

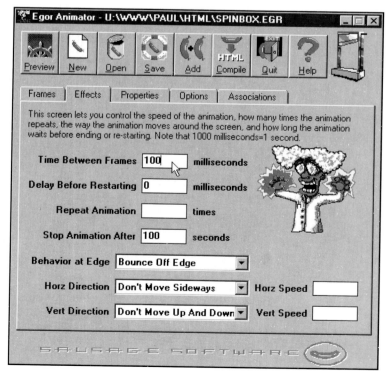

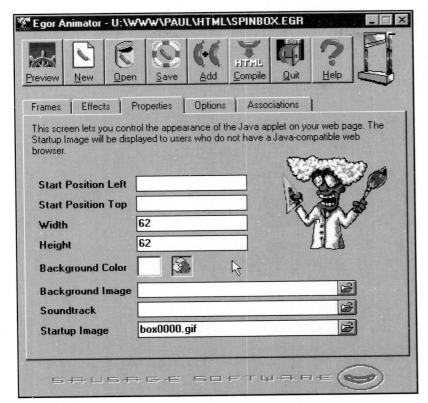

Figure 4.15

The Properties window, where you can specify exactly how the animation displays.

6. I will specify a background color for the Java window—in this case, yellow (see fig. 4.16). I can also choose to display a background image instead of a background color, in much the same way background colors or images can be specified in HTML.

7. I've decided not to use a soundtrack because it would not add significantly to this animation, but would add to the number and size of files to be downloaded before the animation can be displayed. If I were to use a soundtrack, however, I would add it at this point.

8. Finally, I will specify a startup image, which is the first GIF to be displayed in the animation. After previewing my animation one last time, I'm ready to save the file and put the Java applet on my Web page.

9. A click on the Compile button saves HTML code to the Windows Clipboard, from where I paste it into my Web editor. This code will tell the browser used by people viewing my Web page to run my Java animation (see fig. 4.17).

Figure 4.16

Egor's color palette.

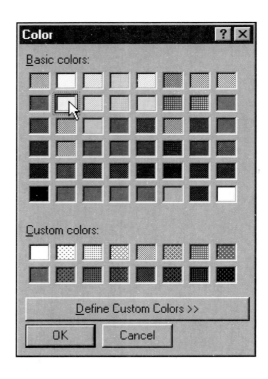

Figure 4.17

Egor copies HTML code to the Windows Clipboard.

That's all it takes to create a simple animation using Egor. You can use Egor to create more complicated animations; for example, you can associate individual sound files and hyperlinks to specific frames. You could also use this to create a billboard advertisement, for instance, which displays different clickable images in succession, and the viewer can be taken to different Web pages by clicking on each image.

IMPORTANT: For any of the Java applets described in this section, it is important to put all associated files where the Java animation can find them. When a Java-aware browser discovers an <APPLET> tag in an HTML document, it looks for a piece of Java code to load—in the case of an Egor animation, a file called "anim.class." This CLASS file is actually the Java program; the code placed inside the HTML document basically just calls up the CLASS file, which then does its thing: loading image files and running an animation, for instance.

> **Note**
>
> Browsers that do not support Java will not display the animation; they will display some text advising viewers to use a Java-compatible browser instead, and they will also display the image I specified in the Startup Image field.

> **Tip**
>
> As a rule of thumb, it is a good idea to place CLASS files and any associated image or sound files in the same directory as the HTML document they are placed on, both on your own computer and on your Web server.

BookWorm

I want to add a list of hyperlinks to my Web page, but I don't want to create a bulleted list that takes up too much space. What I need is a list that can be pulled down by the user, or scrolled to display the full list of links. This can be done with Java, and BookWorm is a neat little application that will enable me to create lists of hyperlinks without knowing how to program in Java (see fig. 4.18). You'll find a copy of BookWorm included on the companion CD-ROM.

1. Using BookWorm is easy. I click on "Add" to bring up a dialog box where I can enter URLs and their descriptions (see fig. 4.19).

   The end users won't see the URL (which is often not descriptive of the nature of the Web page); instead, they'll see your description of that Web site—which is more helpful. I can even specify a "target" on that page; that is, a specific part of the page to jump to, so the user doesn't have to scroll through looking for the part I want them to see first.

2. I don't even have to manually specify all the links—I can actually import my existing lists of bookmarks from Netscape using BookWorm's Import feature, and use those as a BookWorm list!

Figure 4.18

BookWorm's user-friendly interface.

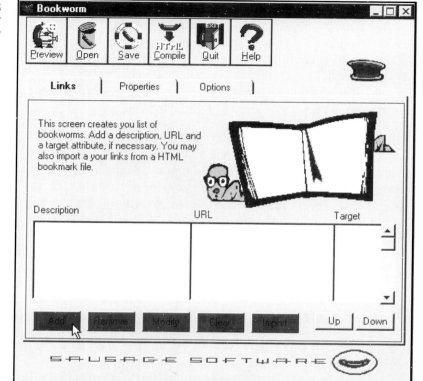

Tip

Importing links is very handy if you are adding a list of your favorite Web sites to your Web page; typically, you would have already bookmarked your favorite pages in your favorite browser, and thanks to BookWorm's Import feature, you don't have to manually enter their URLs.

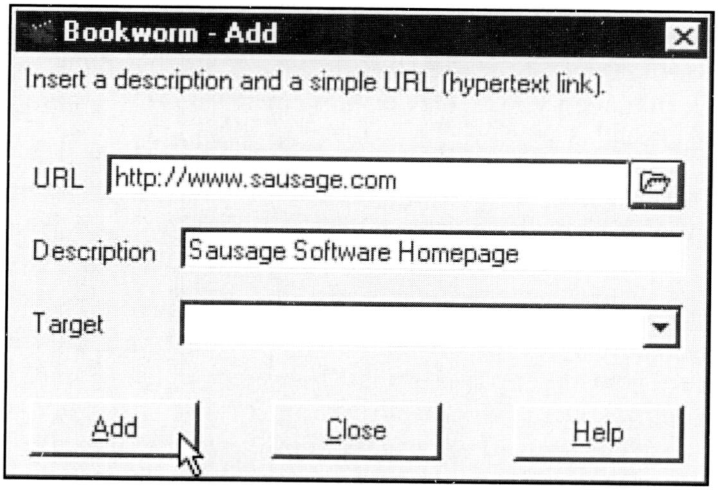

Figure 4.19

Adding hyperlinks to the BookWorm list.

3. Once I've added all the hyperlinks I want, I can define the way the list will display on my Web page. In this instance, I'll choose a scroll list; I could also select a pull-down list or a window list, which places a floating Java window over the browser window.

4. I can specify which font and size I'd like for my text, as well as colors for the text and the list box itself (see fig. 4.20).

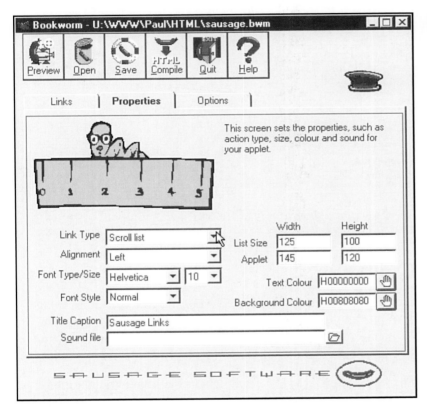

Figure 4.20

BookWorm allows precise control over fonts, sizes, shapes, and colors of lists.

5. I can even specify a sound file—for example, a "Click!" noise—to play whenever the user clicks on the list to activate a hyperlink.

6. Using the Height and Width fields, I can specify exact dimensions (using pixel values) for the list itself and the Java applet window containing it. Of course, if I define the list dimensions as larger than the applet dimensions, only part of the list will be visible.

7. Finally, I click on the Compile button, and paste the code generated by BookWorm into my Web Editor (see fig. 4.21). BookWorm reminds me to ensure that I put copies of the MultiList CLASS file—the actual Java applet itself—in the same directory as the Web page itself.

Figure 4.21

Pasting BookWorm's applet code into the HTML document.

CrossEye

On one side of my framed Web page, I'd like to put an image map as a navigation device; that is, I'd like to have a graphic with different hotspots—each linked to a different Web page (see fig. 4.22).

There are a few ways to create clickable image maps; one of them involves CGI (Common Gateway Interface) scripting, which enables a user to call up external programs (known as gateway scripts) from within an HTML document. These gateway scripts live on a document's Web server and can be used to create interactive forms and image maps.

Image maps involving CGI scripts can be recognized by the fact that when you roll your mouse cursor over the image map, you see the cursor's position in the image map defined on the browser status bar as pixel coordinates relative to the image map. Think of this type of image map as a "server-side image map:" when you click on a particular spot on the graphic, a message goes back to the server and asks the gateway script "take me to whatever link is associated with coordinates X and Y." If there is a hyperlink associated with those coordinates, the server will respond and tell the browser which URL to go to next. The user cannot see an actual URL by rolling over the image map—only a set of coordinates.

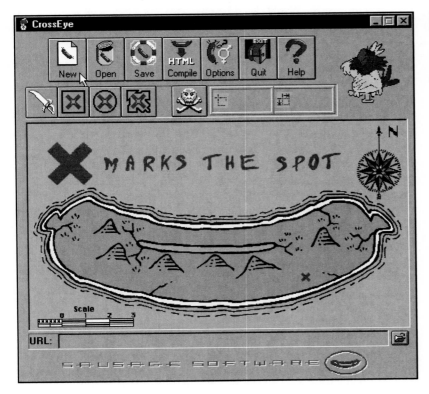

Figure 4.22

The CrossEye interface, complete with treasure map and squawking parrot!

CrossEye works differently. CrossEye creates client-side image maps, which have several advantages over server-side image maps. First off, they're easy to create and require no access to CGI scripts. This is important, because many Internet Service Providers do not allow home page "tenants" to use CGI script for security reasons: used incorrectly, CGI scripts can cause a great deal of trouble on servers and possibly lead to security breaches.

CrossEye has none of those complications. Furthermore, when a user rolls the mouse cursor over a client-side image map, hotspots cause actual URL destinations to appear on the browser status bar. This is more user-friendly than a set of coordinates.

Note

Image maps are typically used as navigation tools, a means of providing a number of hyperlinks within a visual interface. For example, you may want to provide links to your company's headquarters in each U.S. state; a nice way of doing this would be to use a map of the United States as your graphic, with a hotspot within each state's borders.

CrossEye can use either GIF or JPEG format graphics—see Chapter 2, "Animation: Getting It All Together," for information on these file formats and the appropriate use of either type.

I'm going to use a simple graphic showing a vertical list of links in an off-beat typeface, which I have first created in Photoshop:

1. Clicking on the New button brings up a dialog box where I can browse for the correct file (see fig. 4.23).

Figure 4.23

Loading an image file in CrossEye.

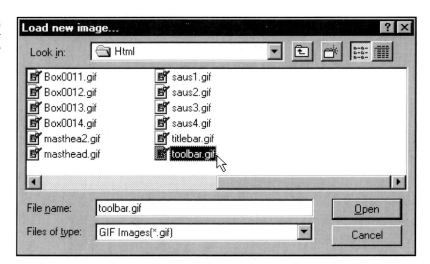

2. Once I've loaded the graphic I want to use for my image map, I define the hotspots by dragging my cursor on certain parts of the image (see fig. 4.24). I can make rectangular, oval, or irregular selections.

3. Each time I make a selection and release the mouse button, a new hotspot is created and CrossEye pops up a window asking for the associated URL (see fig. 4.25).

The URLs can either be absolute or relative references; an *absolute reference* is a reference such as "http://www.sausage.com," which points at a very specific address and would typically be used to link to an external Web page— one that "lives" on a different server from the current page.

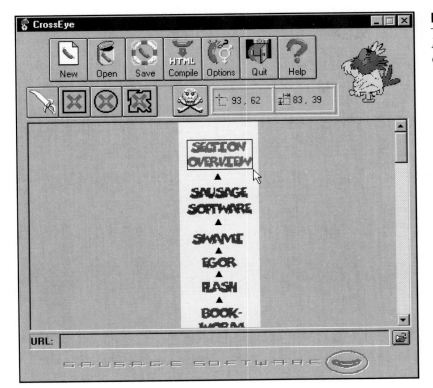

Figure 4.24

Defining hotspots in CrossEye.

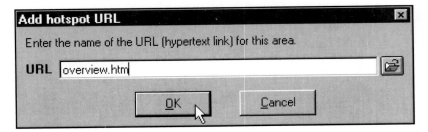

Figure 4.25

Associating an URL with a hotspot.

A *relative reference* is one such as "overview.htm," which points to an HTML document that is called "overview" and is located in the same server directory as the current page. Relative references are most useful when linking to other pages in the same Web site, when that Web site is going to be mirrored at other locations. By using relative references, a Webmaster need not create different pages for every mirror site.

4. The final stage is compiling the code for the image map. I click on Compile, and CrossEye places a copy of the code to be pasted into my HTML document in the Windows Clipboard (see fig. 4.26).

Figure 4.26

The source code for the client-side image map created by CrossEye.

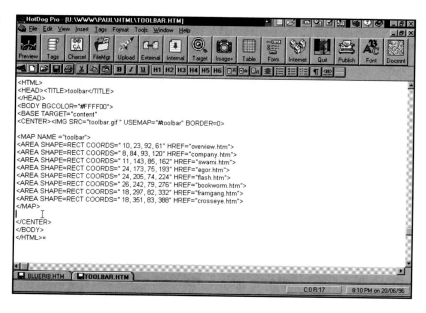

Swami

Java can be used to create *text-only animations*; these are different from graphical animations, such as those created by Egor, because they do not use a series of frames to create an animation. Instead, a text message can be displayed with a variety of effects: scroll, bounce, and so forth. If the message is text-only, without any associated graphics, this use of Java is more efficient than a frame-based animation as there are no image files to download—the "magic" resides in the Java CLASS file.

Swami is very easy to use, with an intuitive interface:

1. I simply select the effect I want and enter the text message I'd like to animate (see fig. 4.27).

2. Next, I specify a background color for the applet (black) and the text color (pale yellow).

3. Swami also gives me full control over the text font, size, and appearance like bold or italic. The effect I've selected—Mexican Wave—causes elements of the text to "float up" from the baseline, so I experiment with the animation controls—start position, horizontal, vertical— and preview various combinations until I'm happy with the results.

Figure 4.27

Swami allows for the easy creation of many animated text effects.

4. Next come the finishing touches: defining the placement and size of the applet window, as shown in figure 4.28—the Java box inside of which the text effect appears on the Web page.

   Although in this particular case I want a simple text effect, centered on my page, I could also incorporate a Swami effect inline, in between normal HTML text. Swami allows sufficient controls to make the effect appear to be an integral (although animated) part of standard text.

5. Having edited and previewed the text effect, I ask Swami to compile the necessary code. I have a choice of compiling applet code or HTML code and copying it to the Windows Clipboard (see fig. 4.29).

Figure 4.28

Swami allows precise controls over the applet window's appearance and placement.

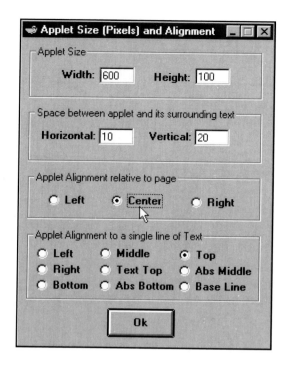

Figure 4.29

Compiling the text effect.

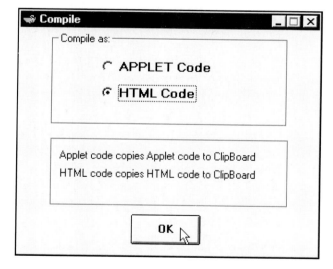

The default mode is applet code—that is, only that code required to describe the Java effect and call the Java applet from within the browser. Because I intend to paste the code into an existing HTML document, applet code is appropriate.

If I select HTML code, Swami will compile all the code necessary to create a new, stand-alone HTML document complete with opening and closing <HTML> tags and everything in between.

6. Finally, I paste the code from the Windows Clipboard into my HTML document.

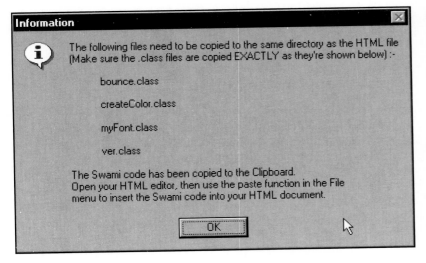

Figure 4.30

Swami thoughtfully reminds you to put all necessary files in the appropriate directory.

Tip

As with all Java applets, it is important to ensure that the CLASS files called on by the <APPLET> section of an HTML document reside in the same server directory (see fig. 4.30). When the user's browser encounters the <APPLET> tag and calls for the Java program to be downloaded from the server, it will look for files mentioned within the <APPLET> tags in the same server directory where the Web page itself resides.

Flash

Java can be used to "take over" the browser's status bar and display text messages. The Netscape Navigator status bar, for example, can be found at the very bottom of the Navigator window, on the left-hand side. This is where Navigator tells the user what it is currently doing; for example, it would show the speed at which it is downloading HTML documents or associated files.

Creating status-bar messages in Flash couldn't be easier, as follows:

1. Simply type in the message and click on Add to enter a line of text; any line can be of virtually unlimited length (see fig. 4.31).

Note

Flash is a convenient Java utility that makes it very simple to display text messages in the browser status bar.

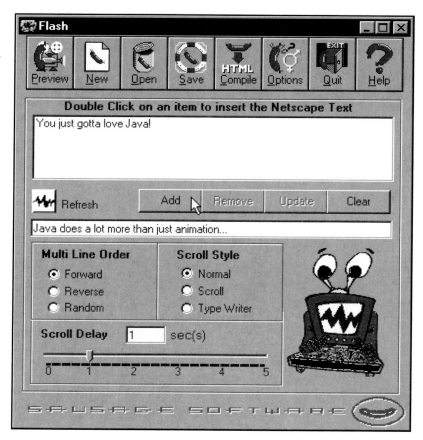

Additional lines can be added in the same way. When multiple lines of text are incorporated in the Java applet, Flash allows them to be displayed randomly or in the order in which they have been entered.

2. Although Java has no control over the size, color, and font of status-bar messages, it can control the speed and style in which the messages are displayed.

The messages can appear as "normal;" that is, a line of text will appear instantly, and display for a predetermined length of time, to be followed by subsequent lines of text if applicable.

They can also appear in the scroll style, which sees the text march across the status bar like ticker tape, or in a typewriter style, where the message appears one letter at a time—similar to watching a telex message appear (remember those?).

3. Once I've defined my message and selected the appearance style, I compile the code ready for pasting into my HTML document. Flash reminds me to place a copy of the appropriate CLASS file in the same server directory as the HTML document (see fig. 4.32).

Figure 4.32

Pasting the compiled Flash code into the HTML document.

The End Result

Now I have all the ingredients for my Web site: an HTML index page that is the frameset placeholder for my other Web pages, and a variety of Java effects to be displayed on various Web pages within the frames. Figure 4.33 displays the end result, a miniature Web site that you can view live at http://www.sausage.com/animate/index.htm.

For simplicity's sake, I have put absolutely everything—HTML documents, Java applets, and graphics files—in the same directory. I can now open up the "front page"—index.htm—in HotDog and click to preview using my favorite browser.

Figure 4.33

The end result.

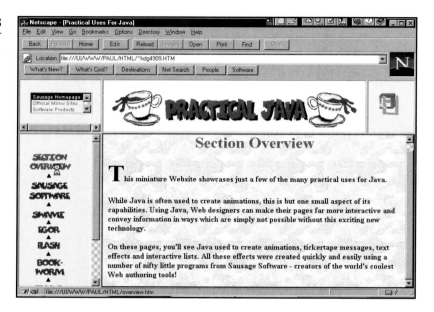

Conclusion

It is almost impossible to tell what we'll be able to do on the World Wide Web in the future. New techniques and major technological breakthroughs appear almost every day. It's probably fair to say that if we can imagine something, we can make it happen on a Web page—if not today, then very soon.

Those of us working on the Web live in exciting times. Regardless of the fantastic tools that may be available to those who follow us in years to come, the tools we have today are enough to allow unprecedented creativity.

Java is truly an empowering technology. You don't need programming skills—even though Java is still in its infancy, you can already easily obtain sophisticated tools that will write Java for you.

Although the scope of this book relates to animation, Java can be applied in many other ways that are of equal interest to Web designers. Some of the useful applications for Java include Interactive Lists, Scrolling Text Effects, Status-Bar Ticker Tape, and Animations.

All you need is a message to share with the whole world—and the imagination to present it effectively.

by William E. Weinman

Author Biography

William E. Weinman has earned his living as a technologist-for-hire for about 20 years. He has designed software for many large and small organizations, including IBM, Security Pacific Bank, KDD (the major long-distance company in Japan), and the Bank of New Zealand. Mr. Weinman has also designed and constructed electronic musical instruments for popular recording artists, fiber-optic systems for NASA and Bell Labs, and a broadcast ticker tape for a television station. He has been involved with online computing since he got his first acoustically coupled modem in 1978.

You can often find Mr. Weinman playing with Jezebel, his Gibson L6-S guitar, in blues bars around Texas; or studying Native-American shamanic medicine in Arizona; but it may be easier to send e-mail to wew@bearnet.com.

Animated GIFs

The Graphics Interchange Format (GIF) was originally designed by CompuServe as a format for users to exchange graphic images. The GIF format has become extremely popular outside of CompuServe, due to its good design, freely available technical specifications, and the ease with which it can be supported by a variety of online applications. The GIF format also has a provision for carrying multiple images in a single file. These multiple image GIF files, also called "multi-block" GIFs, can be used to create animated displays.

Animated GIFs are all the rage right now on the World Wide Web. If you are running a current version of the Netscape Navigator Web browser, it's likely that you have seen many examples of this technique already.

 The current version of the GIF specification is called GIF89a (the full specification is available on the CD-ROM that comes with this book). It can also be found on the author's FTP site at the following location:

```
ftp://ftp.bearnet.com/pub/cgibook/gifspecs.txt
```

Author Note

The CompuServe Information Service (CIS) is the oldest of the major online services. It has been in continuous operation for over twenty years. The author is proud to have been a member of this venerable institution since 1979, although he prefers to receive e-mail at his internet domain, wew@bearnet.com.

Animated, or *multiple-block,* GIFs have been supported by the GIF specification all along, beginning with the first version (GIF87a). The most common application for multi-block GIFs is animation. In fact, CompuServe users have been using the GIF format for small animations all along.

Beginning with version 2.0, the Netscape Navigator supports this part of the GIF format for animation on Web sites. Previously, the only way to create animation on a Web page was to use server-push (see Chapter 8, "Server-Push Animation"), a technique that required a level of access to the server—as well as programming skill—not generally available to most small Web sites. Now that multi-block GIF animation is available to users with Netscape browsers, the World Wide Web is alive with animation wherever you look.

Technology Overview: The GIF File Format

The GIF specification allows a GIF file to have multiple blocks of data, each of which can have different images in them. These images can be set to display, one after the other, or as overlays that partially replace sections of the preceding images. They can also be set to have time delays between them and, with a Netscape extension, to loop as well.

GIF files are formatted as a stream of information so that graphics can be rendered incrementally as they are downloaded from a remote site. This is an advantage for using graphics on the Internet. The format was designed this way to make it more convenient for users of CompuServe's online service. As you will see, it also makes it ideal for streaming animation.

The GIF format is a block-oriented file format—it consists of a stream of blocks, as described in figure 5.1.

Referring to figure 5.1, the required Header Block contains the information necessary for a program to detect that the file is in GIF format. The Logical Screen Descriptor has information that describes the overall dimensions of the file, along with an optional Global Color Table. Optional Extension Blocks are for vendor-specific information, like Netscape's animation looping extension. The Graphic Rendering Block has all the necessary data for rendering each individual image in the stream, and the required Trailer Block is there for a program to easily identify the end of a stream.

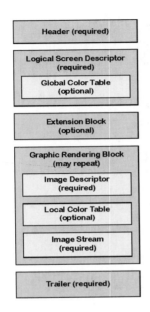

Figure 5.1 ────────────────

The GIF file format.

Tools for Assembling GIF Animations

Multi-block GIF images are easy to put together. Utilities are available on all common platforms for combining individual images into multi-block GIFs. Because I use a PC for my graphics work, the examples in this chapter are explained using the GIF Construction Set from Alchemy Mindworks (available from their Web site) at the following URL:

`http://www.mindworkshop.com/alchemy/alchemy.html`

On the Macintosh platform, you can use GifBuilder (`http://iawww.epfl.ch/Staff/Yves.Piguet/clip2gif-home/GifBuilder.html`); on a Unix machine, you can use GifMerge (`http://www.iis.ee.ethz.ch/~kiwi/GIFMerge/`) by René K. Müller. I have not personally used either of these programs, because I currently do all my graphics work on a PC.

Browser Support

As of the time of this writing, animated GIFs are supported by Netscape Navigator, versions 2.0 and above, and Microsoft's Internet Explorer version 3.0 (now just available in its first beta release). Because of the popularity of animated GIFs on the Web, it is likely that they will be supported by more browsers in the near future.

Procedure: Making the Source GIFs

Animated GIFs are made up of a sequence of individual GIFs. In order to make an animation, first use your favorite graphics program to create each individual frame of the animation. Then combine them into an animation with one of the tools mentioned in the previous section.

As an example for this chapter, I created a series of line drawings to be animated. I drew each of the stick figures on a piece of paper, scanned each one, and then positioned the figures in individual GIF files using PaintShop Pro (a PC-based shareware graphics program that I use and gladly recommend). Figure 5.2 is a screenshot of PaintShop Pro with the series of GIFs to be animated for this example.

Figure 5.2

The source GIFs to be animated.

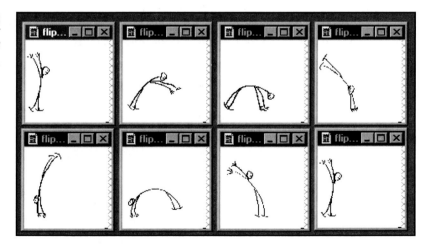

Line art is a good source for animation because it's a flexible medium, and the file sizes can remain small. Each of my source GIFs weighed in at about 300 bytes, and the final animation was about 2.5k. That size file will download in about 2 seconds on a 14.4k baud connection!

Building the Multi-Block GIF

Now that the individual frames have been produced, you can assemble the multi-block GIF. This will produce a GIF file in the proper format for the browser to render the animation.

Tools
GIF Construction Set or other tool (GifBuilder, etc) mentioned earlier
Source frames can be created with your favorite graphics program.

You can start your animation by reading the first GIF of the sequence into your GIF-combining software. In the GIF Construction Set, you can do this easily by opening the first GIF and then saving it with the name you will use for your final animation. Figure 5.3 shows a GIF Construction Set screen with the first frame loaded.

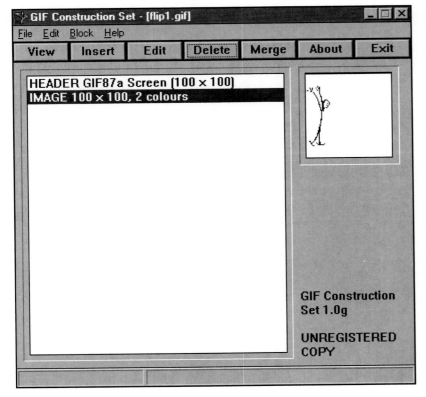

Figure 5.3

The GIF Construction Set with the first frame loaded.

Tip
If you are planning to loop your animation (discussed later in this chapter), you can make it less "busy" by using the first frame for the last frame too; then use a longer delay for the last frame. This will give the effect of a nice pause between loops. Many people find animations that loop continuously to be annoying after a while. This technique can make such animations more pleasant.

Next, import each of the subsequent GIFs. (Don't worry about the control blocks at this stage—you will assemble those next.) In the GIF Construction Set, you need to be careful that you have the last item in the list selected before you insert something new, because it will always insert new items directly after whatever you have selected. Figure 5.4 shows the GIF Construction Set screen after all the images have been loaded.

Figure 5.4

The GIF Construction Set with the example GIFs loaded.

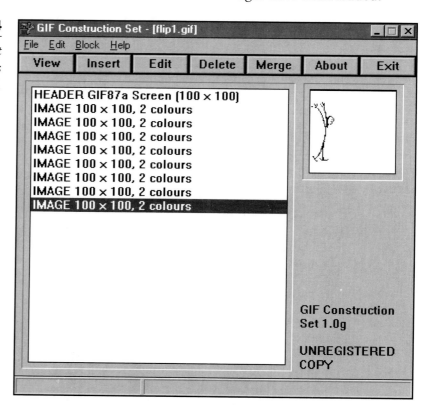

Now go ahead and insert the control blocks. The control block for each image *precedes* that image in the stream. That means that when you insert a control block for a particular image in the animation, it must go before the image that it controls. Figure 5.5 shows the example with the control blocks for the first two images in place.

Once all the control blocks are in place, go back and fill in the necessary information for each one. Four categories of information are contained in each control block—they are explained in table 5.1. These categories may be called by slightly different names in the software that you use; the names used here are from the GIF specification.

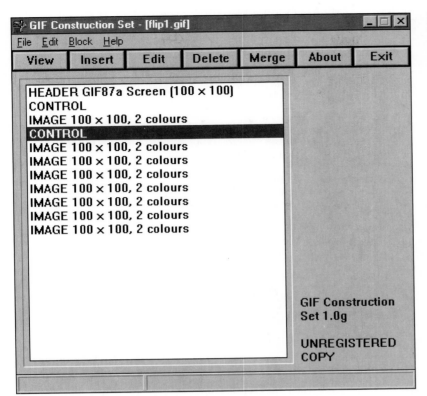

Figure 5.5

Control blocks for the first two images.

Table 5.1

GIF Image Control Block

Field	Description
Transparency information	The transparency information is both a flag and an index. The flag indicates whether or not transparency is used. The index is the position in the color table used for transparency.
The user input flag	This indicates whether or not you want the software to pause for user input before moving to the next frame. This is not supported by any Web software that I know of; it's used for creating "slide shows."
Delay time	This is the amount of time you want the software to pause after this frame is displayed. It is expressed in 100ths of a second (e.g., 50 = 1/2 second).

continues

Table 5.1, continued

GIF Image Control Block

Field	Description
Disposal method	This is what you want to happen after the image is finished displaying and pausing. The choices are as follows: **Nothing:** no action specified **As is:** Leave the graphic in place **Background:** Restore the background **Previous:** Restore the previous image.

Figure 5.6 shows the GIF Construction Set dialog box for editing the image control block.

Figure 5.6

Editing the image control block.

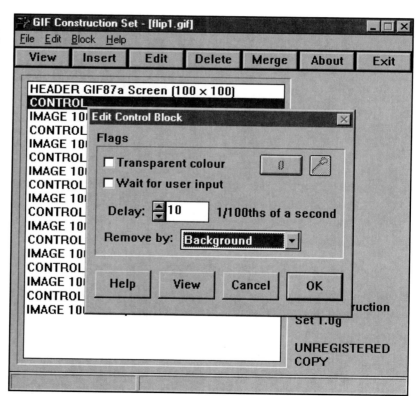

Now your animation is ready to run. You can save it as it is or, if you want it to run more than once, there's still one more step.

Procedure: Netscape's Looping Extension

One final step is to install the Netscape extension block for looping, if you want your animation to loop. This "application extension block" has been defined by Netscape to allow GIF animations to repeat a certain number of times and then stop.

Tools
Netscape Navigator 2.0 or later
GIF Construction Set or other tool
GIF animations

Table 5.2 contains the technical details of this extension block.

Table 5.2

Netscape Looping Extension Block

byte 1	33 (hex 0x21) GIF Extension Code
byte 2	255 (hex 0xFF) Application Extension Label
byte 3	11 (hex (0x0B) Length of Application Block (11 bytes of data to follow)
bytes 4 to 11	"NETSCAPE"
bytes 12 to 14	"2.0"
byte 15	3 (hex 0x03) Length of Data Sub-Block (three bytes of data to follow)
byte 16	1 (hex 0x01)
bytes 17 to 18	0 to 65535, an unsigned integer in lo-hi byte format. This indicate the number of iterations the loop should be executed
byte 19	0 (hex 0x00) A Data Sub-Block Terminator

> **Warning**
>
> Make sure the Netscape looping extension block goes directly before the first image control block!
>
> Depending on the software you are using, you may be able to put the Netscape extension block anywhere in the file. It will not work if you put it in the wrong place in the file.

Figure 5.7 shows the looping dialog box on the GIF Construction Set.

Figure 5.7

*Editing the looping control
extension block.*

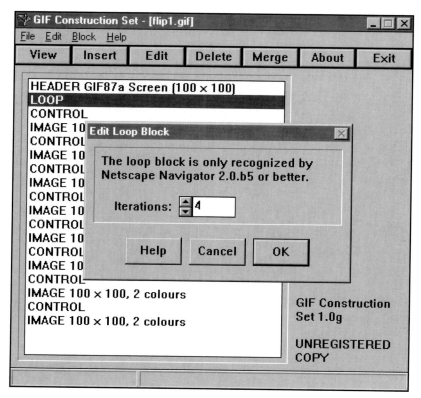

It is important to note that a value of zero for the number of times to loop will cause the animation to loop 1,000 times. If you don't want the animation to loop at all, don't put the loop block in.

Also notice that the looping control block specifies the number of times that the animation will repeat *after it has already run once*. In other words, if you specify the number 4 as the number of times to repeat, your animation will be run 5 times.

Now that you know how to make your animation, there are a few other details you may want to be aware of.

GIF Animation Tips and Tricks

Since Netscape started supporting animated GIFs in their browser products, the Web has become rife with dancing letters and blinking bullets. In some cases, this can be attractive; in other cases, however, it can be more of a nuisance than an asset.

Some of the things to watch out for are animations that take too long to download and animations that distract more than they add to the page.

Keeping Your Files Small

Keeping your files small is important for all the people visiting your site, not just those using 14.4k baud modems. Even if your user is connecting with an ISDN or T1 line, there are many other factors on the Net outside of your control that could slow down the rate of transfer. Your site will be far more popular if it loads quickly.

There are many techniques for keeping images small without losing image readability. A good reference for this subject is Lynda Weinman's[1] *<designing web graphics>* (New Riders, 1996).

In general, it's a good idea to keep your file sizes as small as possible so that your animated displays are accessible to the greatest number of users. As a rule, each 1024 bytes (1k) will take about a second to download at 14.4k baud (your mileage may vary).

On the other hand, because the animated GIFs display as they are downloading, you can have very large files as long as each of the frames are small. Just keep in mind the 1k per second rule, and you should be able to create animated GIFs that are quite long, without users becoming frustrated by the long download times.

In a nutshell, the most valuable thing you can do is keep your palette sizes small. The lower the number of colors in your palette, the lower the overall size of each frame in your animation. You won't always be able to keep them to two colors as I did with the line drawings in this chapter, but you should be able to keep them to 16 or 32 colors. This will reduce the size of your files tremendously as compared to the 256 colors that most graphics programs will default to. Your graphics will download much quicker, and animate much smoother as a result.

---

[1] Yes, she is my sister.

Never Loop for More Than a Few Seconds

When someone is trying to read the text on your page, it can be annoying to have other things vying for their attention in the same space.

While I was writing this chapter, a friend of mine, who is a fine painter, decided to learn how to make animated GIFs. She scanned some of her paintings into her computer and made a beautiful dancing star. Then she made the animation loop, and the first thing she said was, "That's annoying!"

Her solution was elegant, and it is here for your perusal, (`http://www.waterbird.com/links.html`). She put a 60-second delay in the last frame of the animation—if someone sticks around that long on the page, they will see the star dance again. It is much more pleasant, and many animations on the Web could benefit from the same subtle technique.

Conclusion

This chapter has covered all the details you need to create multiple-block GIF animations. This technique has some distinct advantages for the Web designer who wants to spice up a page.

First and foremost, it is much easier to create an animated GIF than any other easily accessible form of animation on the Web. Additionally, the end result uses less resources and less bandwidth than the alternatives. These advantages make it a popular medium for animating small graphics.

As with any powerful technique, there are pitfalls as well. In this chapter, you have learned how to keep your animations lean and bandwidth-friendly, as well as techniques to make them easy to look at without distracting too much attention from the rest of your page's content.

For more details on this and other Web programming techniques, see *The CGI Book* (New Riders, 1996) by the same author as this chapter. I also run a Web site (`http://www.cgibook.com/`) and a mailing list (`webprog-request@cgibook.com`, Subject: `subscribe`) that deal with Web programming issues.

by David Miller

Author Biography

David Miller is a Multimedia Application Developer and Instructional Technology Specialist for the School of Education and New Media Center at Stanford University. He is a Web site administrator, designer, and programmer in the San Francisco Bay area and teaches classes in Instructional Technology and Web multimedia. Dave is finishing up his Ph.D. at Stanford.

6

Creating QuickTime Animations

QuickTime is a multimedia system extension for Macintosh and Windows computers developed by Apple Computer. It is used in numerous multimedia applications, such as CD-ROM and broadcast video production, to deliver cross-platform, time-synchronized digital video, digital audio, 3D "virtual reality" environments, and other multimedia data types.

Why use QuickTime for Web-based multimedia? QuickTime provides standard interface, playback, and compression/decompression features across multiple platforms (see fig. 6.1). Its playback capabilities are included, in fact, as standard equipment with Netscape Navigator 3.0 and Microsoft Internet Explorer 2.0. QuickTime is a mature technology, supported by most multimedia authoring tools, and has become the closest thing available at present to a standard, cross-platform multimedia file format.

Figure 6.1

A QuickTime animation illustrating the standard QuickTime interface.

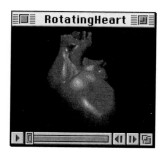

Note

Software-based MPEG playback may also be available by the time you read this.

Although typically used for digital video, QuickTime can be used to play back many different media types, including the following:

- IMA-compressed digital audio
- QuickTime MIDI
- Frame-based and sprite-based animation
- 24-bit graphics
- QuickTime Virtual Reality (QTVR)
- Text
- 3D graphics
- 3D animation

These media types are stored in separate tracks and can be synchronized for consistent cross-platform playback. There are numerous freeware, shareware, and commercial applications you can use to create QuickTime content. Most 2D and 3D animation programs output to QuickTime movies. In addition, there are converters that will convert most other digital video and animation formats to QuickTime format.

Many multimedia firms, video production houses, and CD-ROM publishers have legacy QuickTime content that can be repurposed for the Web. Creating Web-based QuickTime content involves many more variables and limitations, compared to that of CD-ROM publishing, for example. This chapter discusses some of the issues involved in creating

Web-based QuickTime content. New software tools, such as Terran Interactive's Movie Cleaner Pro, are emerging to address the special needs of Web-based multimedia.

One of the most compelling reasons to use QuickTime content on the Web is that QuickTime is now integrated with Netscape Navigator and Microsoft Internet Explorer (see fig. 6.2). Developers can be certain that over 90 percent of end users have QuickTime playback capabilities and can develop content accordingly.

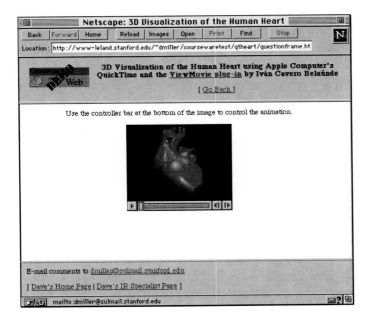

Figure 6.2

A QuickTime animation embedded in a Web page.

Why use QuickTime for animation? Isn't it just for digital video? Both animation and digital video rely on rapid playback of a succession of frames to produce the illusion of moving images. The source for digital video is generally videotape, typically of live action, such as a sporting event or "talking head." Video sources usually contain complex color fields and video "noise." In contrast, animations generally come from computer-generated or hand-drawn sources and are characterized by areas of flat, clean, and consistent colors. For this reason, creating QuickTime animations involves slightly different issues than creating QuickTime video.

Animations created in QuickTime have all the advantages discussed in the preceding. In many cases, however, the file sizes of QuickTime animations are larger—sometimes substantially larger—than sprite-based or vector-based equivalents. New QuickTime compression algorithms developed specifically for the Web may narrow this gap. Another drawback of QuickTime is the limited options for Windows authoring, although it's easy to convert between AVI format (Video for Windows) and QuickTime.

Whether you use QuickTime for your animations or some other format depends on many factors such as budget, time, preexisting content, the format of source material, what authoring tools you have, other media types you want to integrate into your movie, network speed, and the playback capabilities of your users. While this chapter does provide some tips for incorporating digital video in your animations, the main focus is on QuickTime animation. This chapter first gives a brief overview of QuickTime technology. It then discusses the various ways you can provide QuickTime content on the Web, with an emphasis on the new capabilities of Netscape 3.0 and the bundled QuickTime Plug-In. Finally, this chapter provides step-by-step examples of using QuickTime authoring tools and QuickTime Virtual Reality authoring tools to create animations and embed them in your Web page.

QuickTime Technology Overview

QuickTime is a system extension for Macintosh and Windows. It enables applications to display and play back many different kinds of digital media. QuickTime also comes with sophisticated compression-decompression features that are essential for the playback, storage, and editing of digital media.

In a QuickTime file, each media type is stored on a separate track. The tracks are automatically synchronized with each other to provide consistent playback across platforms. QuickTime currently supports many different media types, including digital video, digital audio (including IMA-compressed formats), PICT files, QuickTime MIDI-based music, sprite-based animation, text, 3DMF objects and animation, and QuickTime "virtual reality" environments or QuickTime VR. You can use QuickTime to create movies and animation, create sound-only movies with no pictures, display compressed 24-bit graphics, or enable users to navigate through 3D worlds.

The latest versions of the QuickTime system extension for Macintosh and Windows systems are available free at the following:

```
http://quicktime.apple.com/qt/sw/sw.html
```

To view QuickTime files, you need a QuickTime-enabled viewer. To create content, you need an editing application that supports the QuickTime file format and system extension. A simple viewer and editor is included in the free QuickTime distribution from Apple.

QuickTime Web Browser Plug-Ins

Plug-ins are a new feature of Netscape Navigator 2.0 and later that enable developers to extend the functionality of the Netscape Web browser. Microsoft's Internet Explorer 2.0 for Macintosh also supports Netscape Plug-Ins. At the time of this writing, however, most Netscape Plug-Ins generally don't work in Internet Explorer 2.0 for Windows.

QuickTime Plug-Ins for Macintosh and Windows versions of Netscape Navigator 2.0 include the MovieStar Plug-In from Intelligence at Large and numerous others. Apple Computer's cross-platform QuickTime Plug-In for Netscape 3.0 is automatically installed when you install Netscape Navigator 3.0b4 or later. The QuickTime Plug-In is compatible with Macintosh systems running System 7 or later, and with PCs running Windows 3.1, 95, or NT. The QuickTime Plug-In will play back all existing QuickTime media types directly within an HTML document in Netscape Navigator 3.0 or later and Macintosh versions of Internet Explorer 2.0 or later.

Note

The QuickTime Plug-In from Apple is not compatible with Netscape Navigator version 2.

Besides being part of the standard Netscape 3.0 installation, the latest version of the QuickTime Plug-In for Macintosh and Windows systems is available from the following:

```
http://quicktime.apple.com/qt/sw/sw.html
```

More information on using the QuickTime Plug-In is provided in a following section.

QuickTime Virtual Reality (QTVR)

QuickTime VR (QTVR) is a cross-platform "virtual reality" technology from Apple Computer. QTVR movies are special QuickTime movies that enable users to move through 3D environments, pick up and manipulate 3D objects, and activate hotspots embedded in the 3D scene. The user interacts with the 3D environment with a mouse and keyboard. Users don't need high-end workstations, special headsets, goggles, or other peripherals. QTVR movies are characterized by high-quality, photographic images, fast playback, and small file-size. QTVR is optimized for photographic images, but it also works with computer-generated images.

To view QTVR movies, you need a QuickTime-capable Macintosh or Windows computer. On the Mac, the minimum system requirements are as follows:

- 68030, 25 MHz processor
- 8 MB RAM
- QuickTime 2.0 or later
- System 7.1
- 8-bit video

On Windows, the minimum system requirements are as follows:

- 386SX
- 33 MHz processor
- MB RAM
- QuickTime 2.0 for Windows or later
- Windows 3.1, Windows 95, or Windows NT
- 8-bit video

To add QuickTime VR capabilities to the Netscape QuickTime Plug-In so you can view QTVR scenes embedded in a Web page, you need the QuickTime VR components file. You can download the free QuickTime VR components for Macintosh and Windows computers from Apple's QuickTime Web site, as follows:

```
http://quicktime.apple.com/qt/sw/sw.html
```

A free QTVR player and helper application for Macintosh and Windows systems and sample QTVR movies are also available from Apple Computer's Web site, as follows:

```
http:// qtvr.quicktime.apple.com/
```

More information on using the QTVR features of the QuickTime Plug-In are provided in a following section.

3D Animation in QuickTime

Beginning with QuickTime 2.5, 3D objects are just another media type in QuickTime. You can embed 3D objects saved in the 3DMF file format directly in QuickTime files. The 3DMF or 3D Meta-File format is a file specification from Apple used by QuickDraw 3D and has been adopted as the basis for the file format of VRML 2.0. Users will need to have the QuickDraw 3D system extension installed to interact with 3DMF objects. Animation and geometric data for the 3D object are contained in separate tracks, providing for very compact files. The 3D features in QuickTime were in beta testing at the time of this writing. These new built-in 3D features of QuickTime will provide a powerful new way to deliver 3D animations on the Web.

Codecs

A *codec* is a small piece of software that enables QuickTime to compress and decompress different digital media types—codec stands for COmpression-DECompression. Compression and decompression features are essential when working with digital media because of the nature of storage and playback on computers.

Codecs contain highly optimized software algorithms that will compress a QuickTime movie when you create it, and then decompress it when you play it back. Several different software-based codecs are automatically installed with Quick-Time. Which codec works best for your movie depends on the movie's content. If you compress a movie with a particular codec, the same codec must be installed on the user's machine for the movie to play back. For that reason, it's a good idea to stick with the standard codecs that ship with every version of QuickTime. As of version 2.1, the following video codecs ship with both Macintosh and Windows versions of QuickTime:

- Animation
- Cinepak
- Graphic
- None
- Photo – JPEG
- Video

Lossless Codecs

Lossless codecs preserve all the original movie data when they perform compression. Lossless compression schemes typically use types of run-length encoding, an algorithm that works well with large regions of flat, solid colors. Lossless codecs generally work well with computer-generated animations. In QuickTime, the Animation codec set to the Most quality setting is a lossless compression scheme.

Lossy Codecs

Lossy codecs will discard some of the original movie data when they compress your movie. Once discarded, the data is gone. This is the reason why it's not a good idea to compress QuickTime movies more than once. If you repeatedly use a lossy codec, more data is lost in each compression pass, degrading the movie's image quality. Cinepak is a lossy compression scheme that is commonly used to create movies for CD-ROM.

Compression Forms

Frame differencing is a form of temporal compression—it is a way of compressing your movie based on the changes between frames. Frame differencing works best in movies with little movement between frames; for example, a "talking head" against a static background. In frame differencing, redundant data between frames is compressed or discarded. Thus, the movie doesn't have to store data for the entire frame—it only stores the differences between frames. Temporal compression schemes typically enable you to specify *key frames*, which is a frame against which other frames are compared for differences. Key frames in QuickTime codecs are different from the key frames in animation programs.

Spatial compression reduces the amount of data in a single frame. Run-length encoding, mentioned previously, is a form of spatial compression. In run-length encoding, large areas of flat, solid color can be represented by a simple mathematical formula rather than as a bitmap, thus decreasing file size.

One way to measure the effectiveness of a codec is by the compression ratio. The *compression ratio* is the ratio of the original size of the source material to the size of the compressed material. Another measure of the effectiveness of a codec is the time required for compression and decompression. Some codecs, such as Cinepak, are asymmetric, which means it takes a long time to compress source material, but very little time for decompression during playback.

Codec Availability and Limitations

At the present time, there are no codecs specifically designed for optimal Web playback, although new codecs specifically for Web playback of QuickTime may be available by the time you read this. QuickTime codecs are generally optimized for use with video source and for digital video playback at 16-bit or 24-bit color depths. Digital video is characterized by complex color fields, such as skin tones, and live action motion. In contrast, animation is characterized by areas of flat, solid color or narrow color gradients. Playback at 8-bits is sufficient for many animations. You may get better compression ratios from sprite-based or vector-based animation programs for some of your animations.

Because Web-multimedia is usually downloaded to the client hard disk for playback, file size and download time are the main limiting factors. Once on the client hard disk, playback will be limited by the speed of the user's hard drive and the processing speed of the browser or helper app. Determining which codecs to use for animation and Web playback is discussed in a following section.

Data Rate

Data transfer rate or *data rate* is the amount of information that must be transferred to the user's display for the movie to play smoothly. It is typically measured in kilobytes per second or KB/s. Data rates are usually limited by the user's hardware. Data rates for playback from CD-ROM are typically in the range of 150-200 KB/sec. If a movie's data rate exceeds this amount, the user will experience break-ups and stutters in the video and audio. Fast corporate or university intranets may achieve data rates of 20–100 KB/s. Data rates on the Internet for modem users are around 2.5 KB/sec or less, two orders of magnitude less than CD. And you thought CD was slow! In addition, on the Web, playback can be affected by numerous factors beyond the user's control, such as server load and network traffic.

What this means is that continuously streaming, real-time, high-quality video on the Web is probably not practical today for users on slow connections. QuickTime and other digital video formats on the Web are still a "wait for it to download and then play it" technology. Continuous video compression schemes—for example, "streaming"—and Internet videoconferencing are fairly impractical over all but the fastest modems. This may change in the future, as open, cross-platform compression schemes used in videoconferencing programs, such as QuickTime Conferencing, MBone, and CU-SeeMe, evolve and improve.

What this means for QuickTime on the Web today is that the single most important factor for fast delivery is file size. Reducing data rate, the goal of most CD-ROM productions, takes a back seat to reducing file size in Web-based QuickTime. Low data rates will help reduce file size somewhat at the cost of image quality. Once the QuickTime movie is in the user's disk cache, playback will be limited by hard drive speeds and the processing speed of the browser or helper app.

Other Digital Video Formats

This section discusses some of the other digital video formats that can be used to provide animation on the Web.

MPEG

MPEG stands for *Motion Picture Experts Group*. MPEG is a digital video file format specification and compression standard that was developed by this group. MPEG was one of the first rich media types supported on the Web, and many Web sites have MPEG video and animation.

In the past, MPEG has had limitations, such as the inability to play synchronized video and audio. Essentially, audio and video had to be served as separate files. New versions of the MPEG file format are addressing these specific limitations. Creating MPEG video, however, still usually requires expensive encoding hardware, and additional hardware is typically required to playback MPEG video smoothly.

MPEG is getting a new lease on life with cheaper encoding hardware and support in emerging technologies such as DVD (an acronym in search of a meaning; usually it's taken to mean *Digital Video Disc*). MPEG playback is supported in QuickTime today with additional, relatively inexpensive hardware support. By the time this book is published, MPEG may be installed with QuickTime as just another software-based QuickTime codec. Making MPEG a software-based QuickTime codec will ensure MPEG playback on any QuickTime capable system without additional hardware. Another advantage of the new, soon-to-be-released MPEG features in QuickTime is the capability to easily edit MPEG files. This capability has been very rare in the past because of the way the MPEG file format works and has usually required expensive, hardware-based editing suites.

AVI

AVI stands for *Audio Video Interleave* format. It is the video and animation format for Video for Windows. Most authoring tools on Windows support the AVI format.

The disadvantage of using AVI files for Web playback is that Mac, SGI, and Sun users will have to convert the files to another format for playback. Support for AVI in the Netscape browser is limited to Windows 3.1 and Windows 95 versions.

Also, AVI lacks the sophisticated track-based multiple media support and synchronization capabilities of QuickTime. Codecs for QuickTime for Windows are generally more evolved and efficient than their AVI equivalents. There are numerous Macintosh and Windows programs to convert between AVI and QuickTime. Many are available on this book's CD.

Streaming Video Formats

Streaming is the continuous delivery of time-based media, such as animation, audio, or video, to a user's machine. The user doesn't have to wait for the file to be completely downloaded before viewing the content. The rest of the file is downloaded from the server—i.e., streamed—in the background while the animation or other time-based media plays on the client.

Streaming can be tricky to implement because Internet data is packet-based and wasn't designed for the delivery of continuous, synchronized, time-based data. Interruptions in the continuous data stream can cause stutters and gaps during playback of animation.

Most video streaming technology uses proprietary data formats and buffering systems to implement continuous playback. Web-based streaming video products include Xing Technology's StreamWorks and VDOnet Corp.'s VDOLive. Minimum data rates for streaming video are typically around 60 KB/s, somewhat practical over fast intranets, but barely usable over modem. Even at that rate, video is typically displayed in a small 160×120 window at low frame rates (1–5 fps or less).

MovieStar Maker from Intelligence at Large is an inexpensive, yet powerful, QuickTime authoring tool that is designed to create streaming QuickTime movies. Movies play back with audio and video synchronization and do not require any special server intervention. Users will need the MovieStar Plug-In for Macintosh or Windows systems and QuickTime or QuickTime for Windows installed to take advantage of streaming capabilities; otherwise the movies will behave as normal QuickTime movies.

Tip

If you want to serve QuickTime movies to an internal network, intranet, or high-bandwidth connection, streaming starts to become a viable delivery mechanism; however, you must be willing to accept the low frame rates and minimal image quality that are associated with the streaming option.

Another Apple technology, QuickTime Conferencing, can stream live video and audio. Macintosh versions of Netscape Navigator 2.0 and later are configured to use the free QuickTime Conferencing application as a helper application. QuickTime Conferencing is based on open, cross-platform videoconferencing standards, and a cross-platform version may be integrated with Netscape Navigator version 4. You will need an Internet connection of 112 KB/s or more to view live streaming video with QuickTime Conferencing. You can find out more about QuickTime Conferencing at the following:

```
http://qtc.quicktime.apple.com
```

QuickTime on the Web

There are basically two ways to view QuickTime content on the Web, as follows:

- The first method uses helper applications and is compatible with most browsers. QuickTime movies are downloaded to the client hard disk and then displayed in a separate application such as MoviePlayer, SimpleText, PLAYER.EXE, or PLAY32.EXE. Until early 1996, this was the standard way to view QuickTime content. This is also the way to view QuickTime Conferencing.

- The second way uses Netscape-compatible plug-ins to play back QuickTime content directly in the Web page. To view QuickTime content this way, you will need at least Netscape Navigator 2.0 or Microsoft Internet Explorer 2.0, and one of the supported plug-ins. Beginning with Netscape 3.0b4, a QuickTime Plug-In is bundled with all Netscape browsers and is supported on both Macintosh and Windows platforms.

Helper Applications

A *helper application* is a separate viewer application on the client machine. When your browser encounters a data type it doesn't understand, it can automatically launch the helper application to handle the data type. Your browser knows what helper application to launch, based on the file name extension of the data. For example, if your browser is asked to display a

Note

You can find out more about helper applications at the following:

`http://home.netscape.com/
assist/helper_apps/index.html`

file with the .mov extension, it realizes it is a QuickTime movie, downloads this file to the client's hard disk, and then automatically opens the file with SimpleText, PLAYER.EXE, or PLAY32.EXE.

In your HTML document, you create links to QuickTime movies using the HREF tag. Clicking a link to a QuickTime movie will start the download of the movie file. When the movie file is completely downloaded to the client hard disk, the helper application is opened to play back the movie. Note that your QuickTime movies must have file names ending in the .mov or .qt extensions, and you must configure your Web browser for a QuickTime helper application. Here is an example of some HTML code that creates a link to a QuickTime movie:

```
You can also view a <A HREF="MyQTMovie.mov"> QuickTime
movie </A> if you have your browser set up with the
right helper application.
```

"MyQTMovie.mov" is the path name to the QuickTime movie file on the Web server. In this case, the QuickTime movie file is in the same directory as the HTML document. Note the .mov extension on the file name.

When the user clicks on the link "QuickTime movie," the browser starts downloading the QuickTime movie file called "MyQTMovie.mov." If the user has configured their browser correctly, a helper application is opened to play back the movie after the file has been completely downloaded. If the user has installed a QuickTime Plug-In, clicking on the link will display the movie within a new browser window (see fig. 6.3).

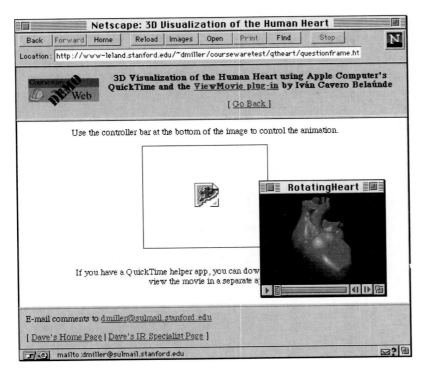

Figure 6.3

A QuickTime animation displayed by a helper application.

Configuring Browsers for QuickTime Helper Applications

To provide QuickTime movies using helper apps requires users to correctly set up their browser. To configure a helper app for QuickTime, you need to tell your browser that files ending in .mov and .qt have the MIME type video/quicktime and should be launched by an appropriate QuickTime player application, such as SimpleText, MoviePlayer, PLAYER.EXE, or PLAY32.EXE.

If you have Netscape Navigator, it should come configured for playing QuickTime content with the MoviePlayer, SimpleText, PLAYER.EXE, or PLAY32.EXE. Different browsers will have different procedures to configure helper apps. The following directions show how to set-up a helper application for QuickTime content in Navigator 2.0. The process is similar in other browsers.

1. From the Netscape Options menu, choose General Preferences/Helpers, as shown in figure 6.4.

2. Click on the Create New Type button.

3. Type in the MIME type "video."

4. Type in the MIME sub-type "quicktime."

5. Type in the file extension "qt,mov."

6. Set the Action to "Launch Application."

7. Click on "Browse," and select the application you want to use to display and play back QuickTime content, such as MoviePlayer or SimpleText on a Macintosh, PLAYER.EXE on Windows 3.1, or PLAY32.EXE on Windows 95/NT.

8. Close the preferences panel of Netscape, and close Netscape. Then, restart Netscape.

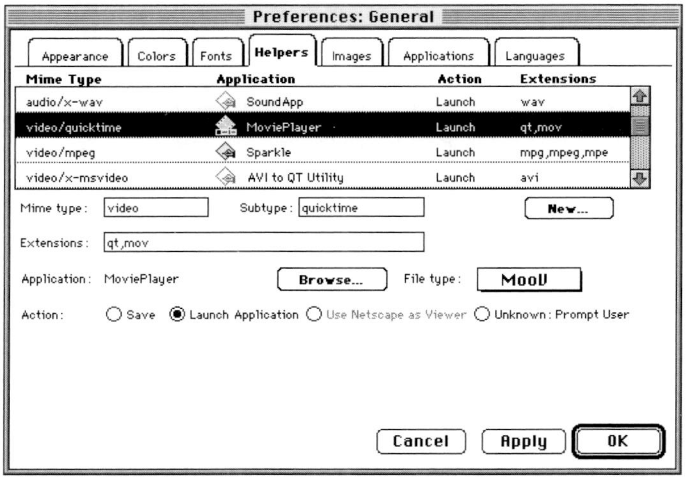

Figure 6.4

The helper app configuration dialog box from Netscape 2.0 for Macintosh.

Obtaining QuickTime Helper Applications

On Macintosh systems, recent versions of the SimpleText application has been shipped with all Macs, and will display QuickTime movies. Also, MoviePlayer, a more full-featured QuickTime viewer and editor, is available free with QuickTime for Macintosh distribution.

You can download the free MoviePlayer application for Macintosh systems or the free PLAYER.EXE or PLAY32.EXE applications for Windows systems from the following:

```
http://quicktime.apple.com/qt/sw/sw.html
```

For both QuickTime and QTVR playback, you can download the free cross-platform QTVR Player from the following:

`http://qtvr.quicktime.apple.com/`

A QTVR extension to the MoviePlayer application may be available by the time you read this.

Internet Explorer 2.0 has a built-in, automatic QuickTime viewer that works much like a helper app. When you click on a link referencing a QuickTime movie, the movie is automatically opened in a separate viewing window. Internet Explorer doesn't require the user to configure anything or have a separate viewing application.

Note

You can also download QuickTime helper apps from Netscape's page at the following:

`http://home.netscape.com/ assist/helper_apps/variety.html`

Plug-Ins

The second way to view QuickTime content on the Web is with plug-ins. Netscape Navigator 2.0 introduced support for external plug-ins. *Plug-ins* are small software programs that extend the capabilities of Navigator 2.0 or later—they can be used to provide viewers for different media types. Media types are viewed directly in the Web page without the need to launch a separate viewer application. Plug-in media are placed in an HTML document using the EMBED tag.

Animation plug-ins are listed in Appendix B, and many are included with this book's CD. Most plug-ins are available free for download over the Internet. Netscape Plug-Ins are also supported by the Macintosh version of Explorer 2.0. The Windows version of Explorer 2.0, however, generally doesn't support Netscape Plug-Ins. This section discusses the QuickTime Plug-Ins that are compatible with version 2 of Netscape Navigator and the Macintosh version of Explorer 2.0.

As of version 3.0b4, a QuickTime Plug-In from Apple Computer is bundled with Netscape Navigator for all Macintosh and Windows systems. This plug-in is not compatible with version 2.0 of Netscape Navigator and is discussed in a following section.

Navigator 2	Navigator 3	Internet	Explorer 2
Windows Plug-Ins	MovieStar	QuickTime Plug-In built-in	Not available
		MovieStar	
Mac Plug-Ins	MovieStar	QuickTime Plug-In built-in	MovieStar
	ViewMovie	MovieStar	QuickTime Plug-In built-in
	MacZilla		

Plug-ins are placed in Netscape's Plug-Ins folder, which is in the same folder as the Navigator application.

QuickTime movies can be placed into an HTML document using the EMBED tag. Following is some sample HTML:

```
<EMBED SRC="MyQT.mov" HEIGHT=144 WIDTH=160 PLUGINSPAGE
➥= "http://quicktime.apple.com/qt/sw/sw.html"
➥AUTOSTART = TRUE AUTOPLAY = TRUE>
```

The value of the SRC parameter shown in the preceding example is the path name to your QuickTime movie on the Web server. Be sure to include the HEIGHT and WIDTH parameters, which are the dimensions of your movie in pixels (add 24 to the HEIGHT for display of the default QuickTime controller).

QuickTime Plug-Ins for Navigator 2.0 include the following:

- ViewMovie from Iván Cavero Belaúnde
- MacZilla from Knowledge Engineering
- MovieStar from Intelligence at Large

ViewMovie Plug-In

ViewMovie by Iván Cavero Belaúnde was one of the first QuickTime Plug-Ins. It is has some nice features, including the capability to use movies as link anchors and image maps. As of this writing, ViewMovie was Macintosh-only, although a Windows 95 version is reportedly in the works.

MacZilla Plug-In

MacZilla by Knowledge Engineering is a Navigator 2.0 Plug-In that plays QuickTime, MPEG, and AVI video; WAV, AU, and AIFF audio; and comes with a built-in game to keep you company during long downloads. MacZilla's unique component architecture enables the plug-in to extend and update itself over the Net with the click of a button. As of this writing, only Macintosh versions were available, although Windows 95 and Windows 3.1 versions had been announced.

MovieStar Plug-In

MovieStar is a QuickTime Plug-In from Intelligence at Large for Mac, Windows 3.1 and Windows 95. The MovieStar Plug-In supports "fast-start" QuickTime, a new feature especially designed for Web playback. Using MovieStar Maker, an inexpensive QuickTime authoring tool, you can perform further Web playback optimization, such as creating streaming movies. Users will need the MovieStar Plug-In to take advantage of these optimizations. If users do not have the MovieStar Plug-In, streaming QuickTime movies will be downloaded to users' hard drives and played back normally.

As of this writing, the MovieStar Plug-In and MovieStar Maker authoring tool were nearing the end of their beta testing. The MovieStar Plug-In supports Netscape Navigator 2.0 for Macintosh and Windows, Netscape Navigator 3.0 for Macintosh and Windows, and Internet Explorer 2.0 for Macintosh. It doesn't support QTVR under Windows. It supports additional HTML tags for compatibility with older QuickTime Plug-Ins, but it does not support some of Apple's HTML tags, including those for QuickTime VR.

QuickTime Plug-In for Netscape 3.0

The QuickTime Plug-In from Apple Computer is automatically installed with Netscape Navigator 3.0b4 or later for Macintosh, Windows 3.1, Windows 95, and Windows NT platforms. The QuickTime Plug-In will play QuickTime content, referenced by the EMBED tag within an HTML document, directly in the browser window. You no longer need a "helper application," although helper applications will still work. The plug-in can play any QuickTime media type, such as digital audio, text, MIDI, and other kinds of media. If you have downloaded and installed the QuickTime VR component, available free from Apple's Web site, you can view QuickTime Virtual Reality movies, too.

The QuickTime Plug-In has features developed specifically for Web playback. The new "Fast-Start" feature displays the first frame of a movie almost instantly and enables the movie to start playing before it has been completely downloaded. This feature reduces the time spent waiting for the movie to download, but is not true streaming video.

Besides being automatically installed with the 3.0 release of Netscape Navigator, the QuickTime Plug-In can also be obtained from Apple's QuickTime site, as follows:

```
http://quicktime.apple.com/sw/sw.html
```

Note

In this release, the QuickTime Plug-In only supports Netscape Navigator 3.0b4 or later. It does not support Navigator 2. Support for other browsers may be added in the future.

In Netscape Navigator 3.0, you can assign different plug-ins to display different types of content, similar to helper apps. To enable the QuickTime Plug-In, you may need to select the QuickTime Plug-In from the \"Options/General Preferences/Helpers" dialog box.

Most of the information presented here regarding the QuickTime Plug-In and Netscape 3.0 is based on beta versions of the software, which were current versions at the time of this writing. Some features will have changed by the time you read this.

System Requirements for the QuickTime Plug-In

The recommended system requirements for the QuickTime Plug-In for Macintosh users are as follows:

- Macintosh or Power Macintosh running System 7 or later
- Navigator 3.0b4 or later
- QuickTime 2.1 or later
- Macintosh Sound Manager version 3.2 or later
- Apple QuickTime Plug-In for Netscape Navigator (automatically installed with Netscape 3.0)
- QuickTime VR (Virtual Reality) components

- Netscape Navigator (Macintosh)
- Sufficient free RAM (9–17 MB)
- For best performance, turn off Virtual Memory

Macintosh RAM requirements depend upon what system and which version of Navigator 3.0b4 or later you use.

The recommended system requirements for the QuickTime Plug-In for Windows users are as follows:

- A 386, 486, or 586/Pentium PC running Windows 95, NT, or 3.1
- 8 MB RAM
- Netscape Navigator 3.0b4 or later
- QuickTime 2.1.1 for Windows
- Apple QuickTime Plug-In for Netscape Navigator (automatically installed with Netscape 3.0)
- Version 1.0.3 or later of the QuickTime VR (Virtual Reality) for Windows software (QTVRW.QTC)

As of this writing, the beta versions of Netscape Navigator 3.0 have steep RAM requirements that may delay its adoption.

Obtaining the QuickTime System Extension

As of this writing, the QuickTime system extension is not automatically installed with Navigator 3.0. To view any QuickTime content, users will need the specific QuickTime system extension for their particular system. The QuickTime system extension for Macintosh, Windows 3.1, Windows 95, and Windows NT is available free from Apple's Web site at the following:

`http://quicktime.apple.com/qt/sw/sw.html`

QuickTime Virtual Reality on the Web

The QTVR extensions enable you to view QTVR scenes embedded in a Web page. To add QuickTime VR capabilities to the Netscape Plug-In, you will need to have the QuickTime

> **Note**
>
> There are two different Windows versions of QuickTime software: 16-bit (for Windows 3.1 users) and 32-bit (for Windows 95 and NT users). In order for the plug-in and QTVR extensions to work on Windows systems, all QuickTime components must be the same type and must match your browser. For example, if you are using 32-bit Netscape, you will need 32-bit QuickTime for Windows, the 32-bit version of the Netscape Plug-In, and the 32-bit version of the QTVR components file. The 32-bit version of QuickTime for Windows runs on Windows 95 and Windows NT only. It will not run on Windows 3.1 under Win32s.

Note

At this time, viewing QuickTime VR files on 16-bit Windows systems such as Windows 3.1 requires running both the 16-bit version of Netscape and the 16-bit version of QuickTime, as well as including the QTVRW.QTC in your WINDOWS or WINDOWS\SYSTEM directory. Viewing QTVR files with 32-bit Netscape and Windows 95 and Windows NT requires running the 32-bit version of QuickTime and including the 32-bit version of QTVRW.QTC in your WINDOWS or WINDOWS\SYSTEM directory.

VR components file. The QuickTime VR components file contains software used by the QuickTime Plug-In to play QuickTime VR Panoramas and Objects. On Macintosh systems, the QuickTime VR components file must be in the same folder as the QuickTime Plug-In. On Windows systems, the file must be in your WINDOWS or WINDOWS\SYSTEM directory.

You can download the free QuickTime VR components for Macintosh and Windows computers from Apple's QuickTime Web site, as follows:

```
http://quicktime.apple.com/qt/sw/sw.html
```

Creating QuickTime Animations for the Web

This section discusses some of the issues involved in creating QuickTime animations for playback on the Web. More specifically, this section discusses the tools you'll need to create Web-based QuickTime and provides general procedures and tips for Web-based QuickTime authoring. Tutorials on using Premiere and the Make QTVR Panorama tool to create QuickTime animations are provided in following sections.

Macintosh QuickTime Tools

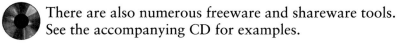

Commercial QuickTime authoring tools for the Macintosh are too numerous to mention. All major 2D and 3D animation programs on the Macintosh support QuickTime output. On the CD that accompanies this book, you will find try-out versions of Adobe Premiere, Adobe After Effects , Macromedia Director 5.0, and Equilibrium Technology Debabelizer.

There are also numerous freeware and shareware tools. See the accompanying CD for examples.

Several programs specifically designed for creating Web-based QuickTime have just been released or announced. The Internet Movie Tool is free from Apple's Web site, MovieStar Maker is an inexpensive QuickTime authoring tool from Intelligence at Large, and the Web Motion Plug-In is an extension to Movie Cleaner Pro from Terran Interactive.

Windows QuickTime Tools

Options for QuickTime-based Windows authoring are limited. Adobe Premiere for Windows will output QuickTime for Windows files. If your Windows authoring tools output to AVI format, you can use one of several conversion tools to convert AVI to QuickTime format. Many of these converters appear on this book's CD. Windows-based QuickTime/AVI converters include the following:

- Intel's SmartVid for Windows and DOS
- TRMOOV.EXE from The San Francisco Canyon Company

Adobe's Premiere for Windows will also enable you to convert between AVI and QuickTime formats.

QuickTime VR Tools

As of this writing, there are two ways to create QTVR movies, both available from Apple Computer:

- The full-featured QTVR Authoring Kit
- The free Make QuickTime VR Object and Make QuickTime VR Panorama Tools

You can obtain the free authoring tools from the following:

`http:// qtvr.quicktime.apple.com/`

At this time, authoring tools are only available for Macintosh systems. A following section discusses how to create a QTVR panorama movie using the free authoring tools.

Guidelines for QuickTime on the Web

At this time, Web-based QuickTime multimedia is a "download and play" technology. Users must download a file to their local hard disk and then play it with the appropriate viewer or plug-in. Thus, total file size is the most important limiting factor. You want to reduce the total file size to as small as possible so users aren't waiting interminably for files to download over slow Internet connections. With that in mind, Web QuickTime should follow these guidelines:

> **Note**
>
> http://www.QuickTimeFAQ.org/ is an excellent source for QuickTime information and software, as well as the home of the unofficial QuickTime FAQ.

■ **Reduce movie size as small as possible.** Stick with one of the standard QuickTime sizes, such as 160×120 or 240×180. If you need to resize an animation, it is probably a good idea to resize your source material, rather than use the built-in scaling features found in most QuickTime authoring programs. Of the QuickTime authoring programs, Adobe After Effects has the best built-in scaling algorithms.

■ **Keep frame rates low.** The lowest acceptable frame rate depends on your content. You may get by with as little as five frames per second. Try not to have frame rates exceeding 15 fps.

■ **Choose an appropriate codec to compress your movie.** If the movie has already been compressed once, compressing it again will degrade the image quality. You may need to experiment with different codecs to determine the quality level acceptable to you. Like everything in multimedia authoring, it's a trade-off. See the section on data rates for a discussion of the tradeoffs involved for Web-based QuickTime. The Web Motion Plug-In for Movie Cleaner Pro promises to provide an expert system tailored for creating Web-based QuickTime. A following section contains suggestions for codec settings appropriate for animations.

Steps for Putting QuickTime Animations on the Web

The procedure for creating a QuickTime animation and putting it on the Web is pretty simple:

Tools
Your favorite animation software (or frames and a QuickTime authoring tool)
QuickTime

1. Make sure your server is set up properly.

2. Use your favorite animation software to create an animation. Output the animation as a QuickTime movie, or output a sequence of frames as separate graphics files and use a QuickTime authoring tool to create the animation.

3. Save movies with the .mov or .qt extension. Follow the 8.3 DOS naming convention if the movie will be transferred to a Windows machine.

4. Save the movie as self-contained and flattened (see fig. 6.5)—you must do this step. It's probably a good idea to save the file with a new name rather than overwrite an existing file.

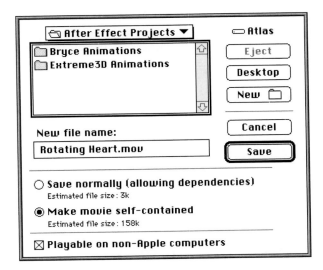

Figure 6.5

The Save dialog box from MoviePlayer.

5. If using an original source, such as uncompressed digital video or a sequence of PICT files, compress your movie with an appropriate codec when you save it (see fig. 6.6). You can typically choose a codec in the Save dialog box of most QuickTime authoring programs. Which codec you use depends on the content. If you are compressing animated computer graphics for display on 8-bit systems, try the Graphics or Animation codecs. If your source is digital video, try using Cinepak. Movie Cleaner Pro provides an expert system that uses answers to English language questions to help you pick the best codec.

Figure 6.6

Standard QuickTime compression dialog box.

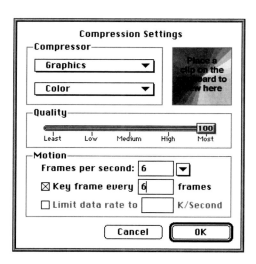

6. You may be able to perform special optimization for Web playback. Many of these optimizations are specific to the authoring tool. Fast-Start playback is a simple optimization performed by many authoring tools and supported by most plug-ins.

7. Embed the QuickTime movie in an HTML document using the EMBED tag.

8. Upload the HTML document to the server. Upload the QuickTime movie file as a raw binary file. Make sure the path to the QuickTime movie specified in the HTML document is correct.

Subsequent sections provide more detail on these steps.

Digital Video Quick Tips

You may want to shoot original video or to digitize from video tape and incorporate the footage into your QuickTime animation. The issues surrounding digital video are worth a book in themselves and there are several good ones.

Here are some tips if you are shooting video for QuickTime:

1. Start with the highest-quality videotape source possible—ideally, you should use Betacam SP. If you can't afford Betacam SP, Hi- 8 or S-VHS are your next best bet. VHS video doesn't digitize very well. It contains video noise

Note

The following is a good book on QuickTime and digital video:

QuickTime: The Official Guide for Macintosh Users
by Judith L. Stern &
Robert A. Lettieri
Hayden Books
ISBN 1-56830-129-4

that digital video codecs will waste time trying to compress and decompress.

2. Avoid fast pans or a lot of rapid motion.

3. Avoid the shakes. Use a tripod at the very least. Shaky video is hard to compress.

4. Use even, low-contrast lighting. Avoid highly reflective objects. High-contrast video will increase the work load on your codecs.

Self-Contained Movies

Saving a movie as "self-contained" ensures that all the data needed to play back the movie is contained within the movie file. Sometimes during the editing of QuickTime files, the QuickTime editing application will insert references to source material on disk, rather than place the actual data into the QuickTime file. Saving as "self-contained" ensures that these references are resolved and that the file will be a stand-alone movie. You must save your movies as self-contained for the Web.

Flat Movies

To prepare movies for playback on the Web, you also must "flatten" them. A *flat* QuickTime movie is a type of movie that can be played on Macintosh, Windows, and some Unix platforms. A flat movie contains all of the data for the movie in what's called the *data fork* of the file. This means that the movie file can be read on platforms other than a Macintosh. Most QuickTime authoring tools provide a "Save As Flattened Movie" option. You can also convert existing movies to the flat format using MoviePlayer, the Internet Movie Tool, FlattenMoov, and some shareware utilities provided on the CD.

Fast-Start Movies

Fast-Start is a new feature of QuickTime movies developed especially for Web playback. Fast-Start movies are the same as regular QuickTime movies, except that some of the movie data that normally is found at the end of the QuickTime movie file is moved up to the beginning of the file. Moving the data to the beginning of the file enables Netscape Plug-Ins such as MovieStar and the QuickTime Plug-In to display the first frame of the movie almost instantly, and to begin playing the movie before the file has been completely downloaded to the client hard disk.

The Fast-Start feature is not the same as true streaming, but does shorten the time that users will have to wait to view a movie over the Web. How much it shortens this time will depend on the particular movie. The Fast-Start feature works best with low data-rate and low frame-rate movies. Large movies will still take a long time to download and a long time to begin playing.

Here is how the Fast-Start feature works.

Fast-Start movies have information, such as the number of seconds in the movie, at the start of the movie file. The QuickTime Plug-In first reads in this information. The plug-in will wait until it thinks the remaining download time is 90 percent of the total movie time before it begins playing the movie. For example, if the plug-in detects it is downloading a 20-second movie, it will start playing the movie when it estimates there are about 18 seconds of download time remaining. Fast-Start is a way to jumpstart playback over networks.

You can create Fast-Start movies with the Internet Movie Tool from Apple, the MovieMaker software from Intelligence at Large, or new versions of Movie Cleaner Pro from Terran Interactive. At this time, there is no way to create Fast-Start movies on a Windows PC. QuickTime developers should be adding a "Save As Fast-Start Movie" feature to their authoring software in the near future.

If you want the movie to start playing as soon as it can, without user intervention, be sure and set the HTML tag AUTOPLAY = TRUE and AUTOSTART = TRUE. Using both AUTOPLAY and AUTOSTART will ensure compatibility with all QuickTime Plug-Ins. See the following section on HTML tags for more information.

A nice feature of Fast-Start movies is that there is no server intervention. Anyone can add a Fast-Start QuickTime movie to their Web page and anyone can play back a Fast-Start movie using the QuickTime Plug-In or MovieStar Plug-In.

The Internet Movie Tool

The Internet Movie Tool is a simple utility from Apple Computer that enables you to quickly convert QuickTime movies for Web playback. The Internet Movie Tool does two things, as follows:

- Flattens the movie for cross-platform compatibility
- Creates a Fast-Start movie for Web playback.

At this time, this utility will only run on Macintosh computers. You can download the Internet Movie Tool for free from the following:

`http://quicktime.apple.com/`

Follow these steps to create a Fast-Start movie:

1. Launch the Internet Movie Tool or drag and drop a movie file on the Internet Movie Tool icon. If you use the drag-and-drop method, the Internet Movie Tool will automatically convert the file and then quit.

2. Select the movie you want to convert in the dialog box and click the Open button.

3. Click Cancel to quit or convert more movies.

Premiere

The latest version of Adobe Premiere (4.2) comes with a special tool for creating CD-ROM movies. You can use this tool to create movies for the Web.

Choose CD-ROM Movie under the Make menu and you will be presented with a dialog box that enables you to set several options, including attaching a special 8-bit palette to your 16-bit or 24-bit movie to ensure high-quality playback on 8-bit systems (see fig. 6.7). At the present time, Premiere will not create Fast-Start movies.

Figure 6.7

The CD-ROM Movie Options dialog box from Premiere.

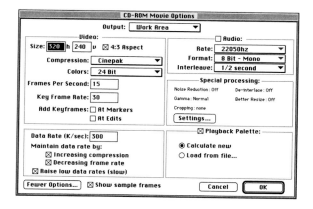

MovieStar Maker

MovieStar Maker is an inexpensive QuickTime authoring tool available from Intelligence at Large (http://www.beingthere.com/). It is designed to work with the MovieStar Plug-In, but you can use it as a general QuickTime authoring tool. It is currently Macintosh-only.

MovieStar Maker supports the creation of Fast-Start QuickTime movies for Web playback. In addition, MovieStar Maker offers other Web optimization features through its "Minimize Video" and "Minimize Audio" options. MovieStar Maker also provides authoring features such as scrolling text and fading.

MovieStar Maker and the MovieStar Plug-In support a proprietary data format that enables a kind of "streaming" playback of QuickTime on the Web. Users need the MovieStar Plug-In for playback. If users don't have the MovieStar Plug-In, a "streaming" movie created by MovieStar Maker will play back as a normal QuickTime movie.

To find out the latest about MovieStar Plug-In and MovieStar Maker, you can visit the following:

http://www.beingthere.com/

Movie Cleaner Pro

Movie Cleaner Pro from Terran Interactive is a dedicated QuickTime compression utility for Macintosh. It contains an easy-to-use expert system that helps you choose the right codec for your movie; in addition, it has sophisticated features such as batch processing, adaptive noise reduction, gamma adjustment, de-interlacing, masking, and automated IMA audio compression (see fig. 6.8). Currently in testing, the Web Motion extension to Movie Cleaner Pro provides features specifically for optimization of Web-based QuickTime.

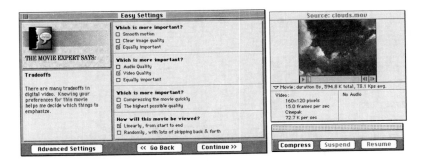

Figure 6.8

Expert system for compressing QuickTime movies from Movie Cleaner Pro.

Codecs for Web Animation

At this time, there are no QuickTime codecs designed specifically for playback of Web animations. You'll want to stick with the standard set of codecs that ships with QuickTime to ensure playback on your user's computers. Most standard QuickTime authoring tools offer access to codecs and their settings in the Save dialog box.

Following are some recommended codec settings to try for your animations. Your particular animation will determine which codec works best for you. Animations typically have large areas of a flat color, which is usually not the case with most digital video. Another fact to remember for Web animation is that once the animation is downloaded to the client's hard disk, the animation will play back from the local hard drive, so that total file size becomes a more important limiting factor than data rate. For codecs that enable you to specify the color depth, such as the Animation codec, be sure to specify a color depth that is the same or less than your source material. For example, don't choose the 24-bit color setting if your source material is 8-bit.

The following offer suggestions for configuration settings:

Video Compression Settings

Compressor: Graphics
Depth: Best
Quality: Most
Frames per Second: 5–10
Key Frame: One key frame per second

Compressor: Animation
Depth: 256 Colors or more (depending on color depth
of source)
Quality: Most
Frames per Second: 5–10
Key Frame: One key frame per second

Audio Compression Settings

Compressor: IMA 4:1
Sample Rate: 6–8 kHz
Sample Size: 16 bit
Use: Mono

Of all the available codecs, the Graphics codec generally creates the smallest file sizes for 8-bit movies. The Graphics codec creates the smallest file sizes in general, with all other settings, such as color depth, frame rate, and data rate, being equal. Of the QuickTime authoring tools tested for this book, Equilibrium Technology's Debabelizer (see fig. 6.9), Apple Computer's ConvertToMovie utility (available on the QuickTime Developer's CD from Apple), and Eduard Schwan's Moover utility (available on the CD) created movies with the Graphics codec that were 10–20 percent smaller than those created in Premiere, all other settings being equal. Your mileage may vary.

Figure 6.9

*Creating QuickTime movies
with Debabelizer.*

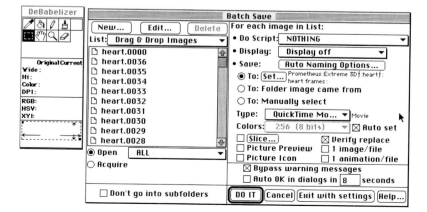

If you have 16-bit or 24-bit source graphics, reduce the bit depth to 8-bit in an image processing program such as Debabelizer before using the Graphics codec. The same advice should be followed when using 16-bit or 24-bit source graphics with the Animation codec set to 256 colors. QuickTime codecs generally do not do a good job of reducing bit-depth of source graphics. If you have 16-bit or 24-bit source graphics and want to create an 8-bit movie, you are better off doing the bit depth reduction of the source graphics in another program, rather than doing it with QuickTime.

Palettes

Digital video generally looks best played back at 16-bit or 24-bit color, but your movie will most likely play back mostly on 8-bit displays. You can save your movie as an 8-bit movie with the Graphics codec, for example, which is optimized for 8-bit color. You can also choose 8-bit or 256 colors as a color setting in some codecs, such as the Animation codec. An 8-bit movie won't look as good on 16-bit and 24-bit displays. All movies, whether 8-bit, 16-bit, or 24-bit, will probably be dithered to whatever is the currently active palette when they are played back on 8-bit displays.

QuickTime enables you to attach a custom 8-bit palette to a movie. QuickTime will use this palette for playback on 8-bit displays. Movie Cleaner Pro, Debabelizer, and Premiere enable you to create and attach custom 8-bit palettes. Custom palettes will not add noticeably to the movie's file size.

The Graphics codec creates the smallest file sizes for 8-bit movies and creates the smallest file sizes in general. For Web playback, you may want to use the Graphics codec for your main audience, and then provide a separate link if you would like users to download a larger, higher-quality 16-bit or 24-bit version.

Cross-Platform Considerations

If your movie will be saved to a Windows 3.1 system, the file name of your movie should follow the DOS 8.3 naming conventions.

PC monitors are generally darker than Macintosh monitors. Some authoring tools have a gamma adjustment that enables you to change the overall darkness of the movie.

Windows computers can only support one video track and one audio track. Many authoring tools, such as Movie Cleaner Pro, will automatically reduce multiple tracks to a single track when you save the movie for cross-platform playback.

QuickTime for Windows plays music tracks using the MPC-compliant MIDI driver. QuickTime MIDI files may not play back on many Windows systems if not configured properly. MACE compressed sound is also not supported under Windows.

On Windows, the standard QuickTime controller is 24 pixels high, while on the Macintosh it is 16 pixels high. If you add 24 to the HEIGHT parameter of the EMBED tag, in order to show the standard QuickTime controller, you will have eight extra pixels at the bottom of your movie on the Macintosh. If the movie is embedded in a frame or you use a background graphic, this extra space will be painted with a solid color.

Procedures for Creating a QuickTime Animation in Premiere

This section describes creating a QuickTime movie for the Web. There are many ways to create QuickTime movies. Most 2D and 3D animation programs will output directly to QuickTime movies. You may want to perform some post-processing on your animation, such as resizing the animation for the Web. In that case, you may want to output your animation as a sequence of PICT files and then batch process the PICT files in another program.

This tutorial assumes you have used an animation program to create a series of PICT files or animation frames. The PICT files should be numbered sequentially, like so:

myPict.01

myPict.02

myPict.03

...and so on

By following this file-naming scheme, you will make it easier for QuickTime authoring programs to create QuickTime movies from a sequence of PICT files.

In addition, make sure all of your sequentially numbered PICT files are in the same folder on your hard disk, as shown in figure 6.10.

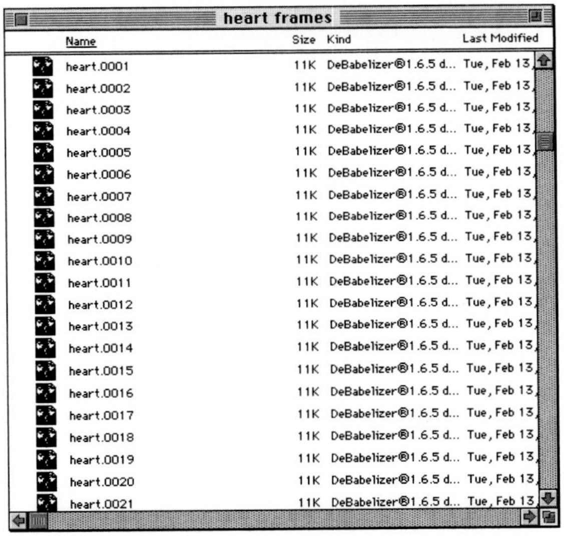

Figure 6.10

Folder of animation frames saved as sequentially numbered PICT files.

This tutorial will describe creating a QuickTime animation with Adobe Premiere. Premiere is a QuickTime authoring tool for Macintosh and Windows. The CD contains a folder containing a sequence of numbered PICT files that you can use to create an animation, or you can you use your own batch of files.

Tools
Pict files or animation frames
Premiere

To create a QuickTime animation in Premiere, follow these steps:

1. Choose New/New Project from the File menu.

2. Choose the appropriate preset for your project or choose Cancel.

 If you're using the PICT files from the CD, choose Presentation 160 x 120.

3. Choose Import/File from under the File menu (see fig. 6.11).

Figure 6.11

The Import/File menu in Premiere.

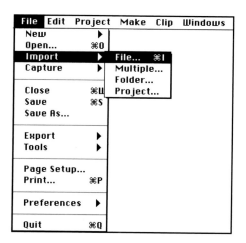

4. Choose the first PICT file in your sequence of numbered PICT files (see fig. 6.12). Premiere will automatically create an animation of the PICT file sequence.

Figure 6.12

The Import dialog box in Premiere.

The animation will play at one frame per second. Double-click on the animation in the Project Window to see a preview of the animation in the Clip Window, as shown in figure 6.13.

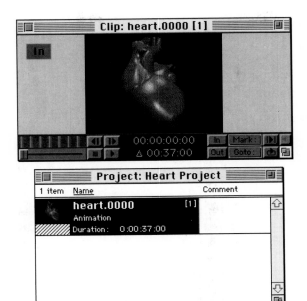

Figure 6.13

Project and Clip Windows in Premiere.

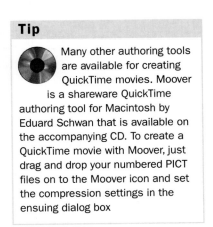

Tip

Many other authoring tools are available for creating QuickTime movies. Moover is a shareware QuickTime authoring tool for Macintosh by Eduard Schwan that is available on the accompanying CD. To create a QuickTime movie with Moover, just drag and drop your numbered PICT files on to the Moover icon and set the compression settings in the ensuing dialog box

5. Drag the animation from the Project Window to Track A in the Construction Window (see fig. 6.14).

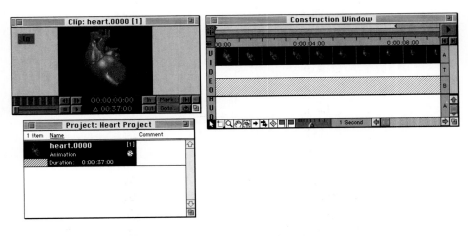

Figure 6.14

Dragging the animation from the Project Window to the Construction Window.

6. Choose Movie under the Make menu.

7. You will be presented with a Save dialog box. Choose Output Options (see fig. 6.15).

Figure 6.15

The save movie dialog box from Premiere.

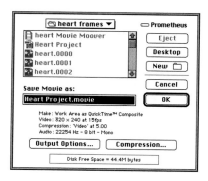

8. Choose the appropriate settings for your movie. Uncheck the audio option if your movie doesn't contain audio. Be sure to select the Flatten option in the lower part of the dialog box—you must select Flatten for Web-based movies. Choose OK when you are done (see fig. 6.16).

Figure 6.16

Output Options for QuickTime movies in Premiere.

9. Select Compression.

10. You will be presented with a standard QuickTime codec dialog box (see fig. 6.17). The Graphics codec works well for 8-bit animations that will play on the Web. Choose OK when you are done.

Figure 6.17

The Compression Settings dialog box.

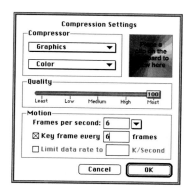

11. Save your movie with a .mov or .qt extension.

Procedures for Creating a QuickTime VR Panorama

This section discusses creating a QTVR Panorama movie for playback on the Web. To create a QTVR panorama, you will need the items described in the Tools box.

Tools
The free Make QTVR Panorama tool from Apple Computer available at the following: `http://qtvr.quicktime.apple.com/newdown.html`
A panoramic PICT file
A Macintosh running System 7 or later, QuickTime 2.0 or later, and enough memory to load the source PICT, plus 2 MB

You can create a panoramic PICT file in a 3D graphics programs such as MetaTools' Bryce or Strata Studio Pro, or you can use a special panoramic camera (see fig. 6.18). You can also create a panoramic PICT file from scratch in Photoshop, Painter, or another graphics program. The right and left edges of the graphic should merge together seamlessly to ensure a true "wrap-around" view. To ensure cross-platform playback, the width of the panoramic PICT file in pixels should be evenly divisible by four and the height should be evenly divisible by 96. The file "gldngate.pic" on the CD is a panoramic PICT file created in MetaTools' Bryce that you can use to create a QTVR panorama movie.

Converting a panoramic PICT to a QuickTime VR panorama involves the following steps:

1. Using an image processing program such as Photoshop, rotate the PICT 90 degrees counter-clockwise (so that the bottom of the image is to the right), as shown in figure 6.19.

Figure 6.18

Panorama rendered in MetaTools' Bryce.

Figure 6.19

Rotated panorama in Photoshop.

2. Start the Make QTVR Panorama tool and open the PICT
   you want to convert, or drag and drop the PICT file onto
   the Make QTVR Panorama icon.

3. The default compression settings work fairly well for
   Web-based QTVR. You will probably want to change the
   dimensions of the movie to something more appropriate
   for Web playback, such as 240×180 (see fig. 6.20).

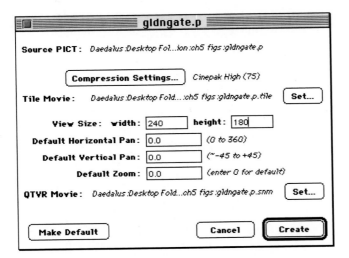

Figure 6.20

The settings dialog box in the Make QTVR Panorama tool.

4. Choose Create.

The PICT is saved as a QuickTime VR panorama.

Adding QuickTime to Your Web Site

The first step in adding QuickTime to your Web site is to make
sure your server is set up to handle QuickTime data. On the
server, the suffix mapping preferences should associate the file
extensions ".mov" and ".qt" with the MIME type "video/
quicktime." Different server packages will handle this differently. If you are unsure how to do this, see your server documentation or contact your server administrator.

Embedding QuickTime in HTML

Add QuickTime movies to your HTML file using the EMBED tag. Here is the minimum HTML code you'll need to embed QuickTime:

```
<EMBED SRC="MyQT.mov" HEIGHT=144 WIDTH=160>
```

The name "MyQT.mov" is the path name to your movie on the Web server (in this case, the movie is in the same directory as the HTML document). The values for HEIGHT and WIDTH are the dimensions of the movie in pixels. Be sure to include the HEIGHT and WIDTH parameters. Add 24 to the height of the movie if you want to display the default QuickTime controller.

Other HTML Parameters

Include the PLUGINSPAGE parameter for users who may not have the QuickTime Plug-In installed. The PLUGINSPAGE parameter directs Web browsers without a QuickTime movie plug-in to a Web page where they can download the appropriate plug-in. The value of the PLUGINSPAGE parameter is a fully qualified URL, in quotes, where the user can download the appropriate plug-in. Here is some sample HTML code:

```
<EMBED SRC="MyQT.mov" HEIGHT=144 WIDTH=160 PLUGINSPAGE
= "http://quicktime.apple.com/qt/sw/sw.html" AUTOSTART
= TRUE AUTOPLAY = TRUE>
```

Setting the AUTOSTART and AUTOPLAY parameters to TRUE will cause the movie to begin playing as quickly as possible without user intervention. The default value is FALSE; i.e., the user must initiate playback. Use this feature with Fast-Start movies to start playback at the earliest possible time. Although you only need one of these parameters, including both provides compatibility with all QuickTime Plug-Ins. The AUTOSTART and AUTOPLAY parameters only work if the movie is visible within the browser window.

Another parameter you may want to use with your movies is the CONTROLLER parameter. The possible values for the CONTROLLER parameter are TRUE and FALSE. The default value is TRUE; i.e., the standard QuickTime movie controller will be displayed with your movie. Add 24 to the height of the movie and give this value to the HEIGHT parameter, if you want to display the default QuickTime controller. If you do not want to show the standard QuickTime movie controller, set the value of the CONTROLLER parameter to FALSE. You may still want to give your users the opportunity to stop playback if they want. See a following section for more details.

There are many more parameters you can use with the QuickTime Plug-In from Apple Computer. For a complete, up-to-date list of the currently accepted parameters, visit the following:

```
http://quicktime.apple.com/qt/dev/devweb.html
```

Hidden Movies

You may want to a hide a sound-only QuickTime movie to provide background music for your Web page, for example. There are two ways to hide a movie on a Web page.

You can use the HIDDEN parameter. The HIDDEN parameter will make your movie invisible. This parameter takes no values.

The AUTOSTART and AUTOPLAY parameters only work if the movie is visible within the browser window. To provide a sound-only QuickTime movie that uses the AUTOSTART and AUTOPLAY parameters, place the movie at the top of your Web page, and specify a WIDTH = 4 and HEIGHT = 4. As of this writing, WIDTH and HEIGHT values less than 4 tend to crash Netscape Navigator.

Transferring QuickTime Files to a Web Server

If you use FTP (File Transfer Protocol) to upload your movie to a Web server, be sure you transfer the file as a raw binary file. The movie file name must have the extension .mov or .qt. Be sure the path name and file name match the names you have indicated in the SRC parameter of the EMBED tag.

QuickTime Unplugged

Even though QuickTime is now standard equipment with all Netscape browsers, many users will not have a QuickTime

Plug-In installed on their machine, or they will be using a browser that is not compatible with Netscape Plug-Ins.

To provide for these users, you can follow these guidelines:

- For browsers that don't support the EMBED tag, use the NOEMBED tag to provide alternate content.

- Always use the PLUGINSPAGE parameter of the EMBED tag to point users to an URL where they can download the appropriate plug-in.

- For users that have helper apps correctly configured, provide a link to your movie with the HREF tag. An added benefit of this approach is that, for users with a QuickTime Plug-In, the movie will open in the middle of a new browser window.

Here is some sample HTML that implements all these suggestions:

```
<EMBED SRC="MyQT.mov" HEIGHT=144 WIDTH=160 PLUGINSPAGE
= "http://quicktime.apple.com/qt/sw/sw.html">
```

```
<NOEMBED>
```

```
<IMG SRC="MyQT.GIF" HEIGHT=120 WIDTH=160>
```

If you don't have the QuickTime Plug-In, but have a QuickTime helper app, click on the following link to view the movie:

```
</NOEMBED>
```

You can also view the <A HREF="MyQT.mov"> QuickTime movie </A> if you have your browser set up with the right helper application.

User Interface and Page Design Considerations

Following are some general considerations for providing QuickTime content on your Web page:

- Animation is the latest whizzy feature of the Web, but it is easy to overdo it. Be kind to network bandwidth and avoid gratuitous animation. Animations tend to be large files that take a while to download. How many times do your users need to see your spinning logo? Animations can be distracting on a page with a lot of text you want users to read.

■ Give users control of playback. Endlessly looping animations can be annoying. At least, provide a way for users to stop playback. This is especially true with animations containing audio. It is very easy to do this with QuickTime by providing the standard QuickTime controller with your animations.

■ Provide an explanation of the features of the standard QuickTime controller, so users know how to start and stop your animation. If you don't provide the standard QuickTime controller, tell your users how to pause playback using the mouse (see fig. 6.21).

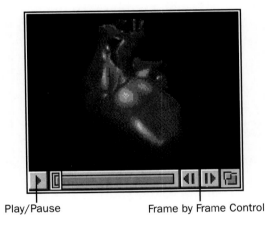

Play/Pause   Frame by Frame Control

Figure 6.21

Features of the standard QuickTime controller.

■ Provide the ability to launch helper apps for users who don't have a QuickTime Plug-In installed. See a preceding section for ways to provide alternate content for users without plug-ins.

■ Be aware that custom palettes can shift colors on the entire display. Sometimes after leaving a page with a custom palette, the original palette will not be restored.

■ Give users short clips or samplers of your full QuickTime movie or display a sample frame as a GIF. Then, give users the choice of downloading the full version after they have seen the sampler.

Fast-Start Movies

If the controller is visible, users may try to click the start button on Fast-Start movies before the movie has finished downloading. You may want to make sure the movie starts with something interesting. Movie Cleaner Pro provides the ability to create a high-quality first frame, for example. If you don't want the user to be able to click the start button, use the CONTROLLER = FALSE parameter and make sure AUTOPLAY = TRUE.

Keyboard Navigation

For navigation of QuickTime and QTVR movies from the keyboard, first select the QuickTime movie or QuickTime VR panorama by clicking on it with the mouse. For keyboard navigation, the movie cannot have an HREF tag associated with it. Once you have selected the movie, use the option and control (shift and control on Windows) to zoom in/zoom out of QTVR movies. Use the arrow keys to step through a QuickTime movie frame by frame on Macintosh. On Windows, the arrow keys do not work.

Saving Movies from the Web

To save an embedded QuickTime movie to your local hard drive, click on the movie and hold the mouse down or use the right-hand mouse button in Windows. A pop-up menu will appear that enables you to save the movie. On the Macintosh, press Command+S to save the movie to disc.

Starting and Stopping Playback

The standard QuickTime controller is a good way to give users control over playback of your movie. If the controller has been hidden using the CONTROLLER = FALSE parameter, you can still give users control over playback using the mouse. The movie must be visible (you can't use the HIDDEN tag) and the movie cannot have an HREF tag associated with it.

On a Macintosh, double-clicking on the movie will start the movie and a single click on the movie will pause it. On a PC, single-clicking on the movie toggles between pause and play.

Mouse control over playback also works for movies with a visible controller (i.e., with the parameter CONTROLLER = TRUE).

Conclusion

QuickTime is now a standard feature in Macintosh and Windows versions of Netscape Navigator. Web developers can be assured that a large majority of users have QuickTime playback capabilities. Users no longer have to download separate plug-ins or helper apps to view QuickTime content on the Web. The Netscape Plug-In architecture has been widely adopted, and other browsers should be supporting plug-ins this year.

Implementation of the QuickTime Media Layer, QuickTime integration with Java, possible QuickTime Conferencing support in Navigator 4, and the sharing of 3DMF file formats between QuickTime's 3D tracks and VRML 2.0 promise many new uses of Web-based QuickTime in the coming year.

by David Miller

Author Biography

David Miller is a Multimedia Application Developer and Instructional Technology Specialist for the School of Education and New Media Center at Stanford University. He is a Web site administrator, designer, and programmer in the San Francisco Bay area and teaches classes in Instructional Technology and Web multimedia. Dave is finishing up his Ph.D. at Stanford.

Animating with Shockwave for Director

Macromedia's Shockwave for Director was one of the first animation plug-ins for Netscape. Shockwave enables Director authors to publish interactive, multimedia content on the Web—you'll need Director to create Shockwave animations. Director is a popular 2D animation and interactive multimedia authoring tool, which is used in CD-ROM publishing, broadcast video and film, interactive ads and marketing materials, kiosks, presentations, games, prototypes, courseware, and just about any application that requires interactivity, animation, or the integration of multiple media, such as text, graphics, digital audio, and digital video.

Note

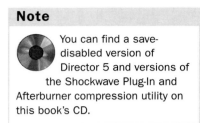

You can find a save-disabled version of Director 5 and versions of the Shockwave Plug-In and Afterburner compression utility on this book's CD.

Shockwave for Director enables the playback of Director files directly in Web pages. Shockwave consists of the following:

- A plug-in for Netscape-compatible Web browsers that plays Director files directly in the Web page
- The Afterburner file compression/post-processing tool
- Special Internet extensions to Lingo, Director's object-oriented scripting language

Figure 7.1 illustrates a Shockwave movie playing on a Web page.

Figure 7.1

A Shockwave "virtual reality" environment playing on a Web page.

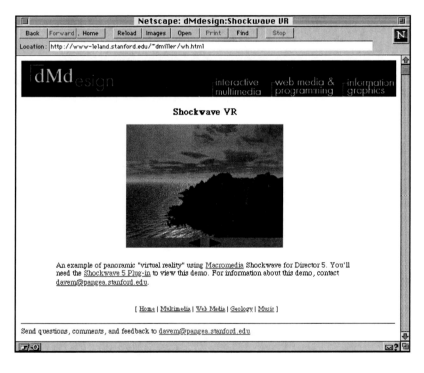

Tip

Users must have the Shockwave Plug-In in the Netscape Plug-Ins folder to play back Director files embedded in Web pages.

Macromedia's Shockwave technology also encompasses two other popular products, as follows:

- FreeHand, a vector-based, postscript drawing package
- Authorware, an interactive multimedia authoring tool popular in computer-based training applications

This chapter focuses on Shockwave for Director. As of this writing, Macromedia had released the beta version of the Shockwave Plug-In for Director 5 for the PowerPC Macintosh and Windows 95. Shockwave for Director 5 has many new features, supports authoring in Director 5, and will also play back Shockwave files created in earlier versions of Director. The final version for PowerPC Macintosh, 68K Macintosh, Windows 95, Windows NT, and Windows 3.1 should be available by the time you read this. The examples in this book use Director 5 and the Shockwave for Director 5 Plug-In.

> **Note**
>
> You can obtain the latest version of the Shockwave Plug-In and Afterburner compression utility from this URL:
>
> `http://www.macromedia.com/shockwave/`

Technological Overview of Director and Shockwave

To create Shockwave animations for the Web, you will need the Director authoring program for either Macintosh or Windows. Shockwave animations created on either the Macintosh or Windows computers play back in any browser that supports the Shockwave Plug-In.

Director is an animation and interactive multimedia tool. Director uses sprite-based animation (discussed presently), but also has limited vector-based tools. Director provides several features helpful to animators, including integrated paint tools, layering, onion-skinning, ease-in and ease-out, and frame-based timelines (see Chapter 1, "Principles of Animation in a Nutshell," for more information on these features). Director also provides several different animation techniques, such as in-betweening, real-time recording, and step recording (also discussed presently).

Director titles can integrate text, graphics, digital video, and digital audio. Interactivity and navigation are provided by Lingo, Director's powerful, object-oriented scripting language. You can also animate sprites programmatically with Lingo. Director does not support motion paths or hierarchical linking, but you can simulate these features with film loops and Lingo.

A Director file is called a *movie*. Director enables you to create license-free, run-time players of your Director movies called *projectors*. A projector contains an embedded playback engine so users can view your Director movie without any additional software.

Tip

 If all you want to do is create short animations and spinning logos for a Web page, Director might be overkill. Competing products, such as WebPainter from TotallyHip, CelAnimator from FutureSplash, WebAnimator from DeltaPoint, Emblaze from the Interactive Media Group, and mBEDLets from mBED Software are cheaper, provide very good animation tools, provide for interactivity (in some cases), and have been developed from the ground up for Web animation. Demo versions of these programs are included on the accompanying CD, but if you already have Director or want to use Director for its many other uses and its cross-platform versatility, then it's relatively easy to put Director content for the Web.

Note

Other Web-based animation tools, such as WebPainter from TotallyHip or CelAnimator from FutureWave, enable the creation of streaming animation. *Streaming* is the capability to start playback of an animation file or other time-based media before the entire file has been downloaded. The rest of the file is downloaded in the background while the animation is playing. The user doesn't have to wait for the whole file to download to see something.

Shockwave for Authorware supports a kind of streaming. As of this writing, Director doesn't support streaming, but probably will support it in the future.

Pros and Cons of Director

One of the best features of Director is that Director files created on one platform can easily be transferred to another platform. A Director movie created on a Macintosh can be easily opened in the Director authoring environment on a Windows computer, and vice versa. Unfortunately, to create a license-free, run-time player for both Macintosh and Windows, you will need a copy of the Director program for Macintosh and a copy for Windows.

You can't create a cross-platform projector on a single platform. A projector created with the Mac-based tool plays only on a Mac, and a projector created with the Windows-based tool plays only on Windows machine. Shockwave provides a way around this limitation, however, because a Shockwave movie created on one platform can be viewed in a Web browser on other platforms.

As with most Web-based multimedia, Shockwave is a wait-for-it-to-download-and-then-play it technology. File size and download time are the biggest limiting factors. Fortunately, to begin with, Director files are inherently compressed. The Afterburner utility compresses Director files even more.

To reduce download time, create Director files that are as small as possible. This chapter provides some tips on how to do that. You can also check out the excellent Shockwave Developer's Guide at this URL:

```
http://www.macromedia.com/shockwave/director5/
contents.html
```

Download time can be affected by many variables outside your control, such as server load and network traffic. Don't expect to put your 20 MB Director projector on the Web. Shockwave movies should be around 100 KB or less. On a 14.4 modem, a 100 KB Shockwave animation can take three or four minutes to download. Small 10 KB movies can download in seconds.

The following table lists some sample download times on different connections. All times are approximate; your mileage may vary.

Connection Size	14.4 KB/s (Home)	56 KB/s (ISDN)	1.5 MB/s (Intranet or LAN)
10 KB	5–10 secs	2 secs	1 sec
100 KB	1–2 mins	15–20 secs	2–4 secs
1000 KB	10–15 mins	2–4 mins	10–15 secs

The following URL has a Shockwave movie that helps you estimate download time based on the file size of your movie.

```
http://www.macromedia.com/shockwave/director5/
moviedocs/download.html
```

System Requirements for Director Authoring

The minimum system requirements for authoring in Director on Windows systems are listed here:

- Windows 3.1, Windows 95, or Windows NT
- 486/66 processor
- 8 MB RAM
- 2X speed CD-ROM drive

In addition, Macromedia provides a list of supported video cards and sound cards. Visit the following site for the latest information:

```
http://www.macromedia.com/
```

The minimum system requirements for authoring in Director on Macintosh systems are as follows:

- Mac OS 7.1 or later
- 68040 or PowerPC processor
- 8 MB RAM
- 2X speed CD-ROM drive

Browser Support

Currently, Shockwave for Director 4 supports Netscape Navigator 2.0 for Macintosh, Windows 3.1, Windows 95,

Windows NT, and partially supports Microsoft Internet Explorer 2.0 for Macintosh. The Shockwave Plug-In is included with Netscape's PowerPack 2.0 add-ons for the Navigator browser and is also available free from Macromedia's Web site:

```
http://www.macromedia.com/Shockwave
```

The Shockwave for Director 5 Plug-In was in beta testing at this writing. It should be available for browsers that support Netscape Plug-Ins on Macintosh, Windows 3.1, Windows 95, and Windows NT by the time you read this.

In addition, Macromedia has announced future Shockwave bundling deals with Microsoft Internet Explorer 3, America Online, CompuServe, and Apple Computer's CyberDog and Internet Connection Kit.

Getting Started in Director

This section gives a brief overview of Director. If you've never used Director or are just starting out, this section provides an introduction to the procedures necessary for creating Shockwave animations in Director—it is not meant to replace reading the manuals. If you've been using Director for awhile, you might want to skip this section.

Director Authoring

Authoring in Director involves several steps, including the following:

1. Creating the content for your Director movie, either in Director or another program, such as Photoshop, After Effects, or Premiere.

2. Importing the content into a Director movie file.

3. Choreographing animations using Director's frame-based timeline.

4. Adding interactivity with Lingo, the object-oriented scripting language of Director.

Exploring the Director Authoring Environment

The Director authoring environment consists of several components, as follows:

- Cast—a multimedia database that tracks where content is stored.

- Score—a frame-based timeline where you set key frames, choreograph animation, and script interactivity.

- Stage—the stage where your cast performs. The stage is what the user sees when they play your Director movie.

- Content editors for different media types.

Figure 7.2 illustrates the Director authoring environment.

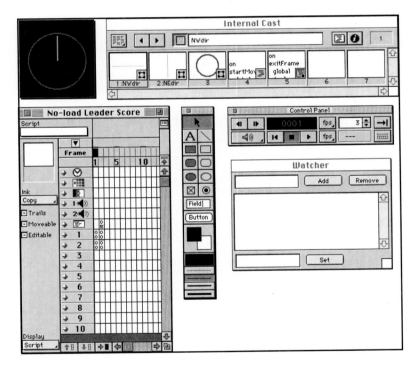

Figure 7.2

Components of Director's authoring environment.

All of the media content—that is, graphics, text, sound, digital video, and the Lingo scripts for your movie—are stored in the *Cast*. Each media element or script is called a *cast member*. Figure 7.3 shows the Director Cast Window for an active project.

Figure 7.3

The Director Cast Window.

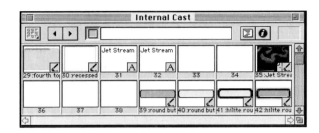

The *Score* is a frame-based timeline that contains 48 layers. In Director, layers are called *channels*. Each channel can contain a sprite. A *sprite* is a copy of a cast member that has been placed on the stage. You can place a cast member on the stage by simply dragging it from the Cast. The cast member is automatically copied into a channel.

The same cast member can be copied into multiple channels; thus, a single cast member can be used to create multiple sprites. Sprites in higher-numbered channels appear above sprites in lower-numbered channels. The Director Score Window is illustrated in figure 7.4.

Figure 7.4

The Director Score Window.

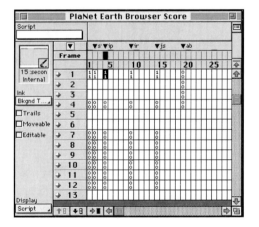

Note

The Director Score resembles a spreadsheet. Channels represent rows and frames represent columns. A single channel at a particular frame is typically called a *cell*—a term that carries over from spreadsheet technology, and one that should not be confused with *cel*.

When the movie plays, it generally follows this sequence:

1. The playback head advances to a frame.

2. The sprites in that frame are displayed.

3. Lingo commands are executed.

4. The playback head advances to the next frame.

You can use the Score and one of Director's animation techniques, such as in-betweening (which will be discussed at greater length presently), to animate your sprites across multiple frames.

The Lingo Scripting Language

Lingo is Director's object-oriented scripting language. You can use Lingo to add interactivity to Director projects. You can also use Lingo to control the behavior and properties of sprites, such as color or position, or to script repetitive authoring tasks.

Although not as feature-rich as a full-blown object-oriented programming language such as SmallTalk or C++, Lingo does support such features as objects, inheritance, and dynamic binding. Lingo also contains useful built-in data types called *lists*, which are similar to container classes and associative arrays.

> **Note**
>
> You don't need to know Lingo to create animations in Director, but Lingo animation sometimes results in smaller file sizes.

Individual scripts in Lingo are called *handlers*. You make a sprite respond to Lingo commands with the Lingo puppetsprite command. For example, the following is a Lingo command that will turn the sprite in channel 12 into a puppet, meaning that the particular sprite is now being controlled by Lingo (that is, is a Lingo "puppet") and is not being controlled by the Director Score.

```
puppetsprite 12, TRUE
```

The Score behavior of that particular sprite is ignored until you turn off the puppeting.

Xtras

Xtras are small software modules, similar to plug-ins in Photoshop, that extend the functionality of Director 5. Xtras replace the functionality of XObjects in previous versions of Director; however, most XObjects still work in Director 5. Xtras can be placed in the Xtras folder in the same folder as the Director application or in the C:\Program Files\Common Files\Macromedia\Xtras folder on Windows 95 and Windows NT, the c:\Windows\Macromed\Xtras directory on Windows 3.1, or the System:Macromedia Xtras folder on the Macintosh.

You can use Xtras in Shockwave movies, but you have to make sure your users have the Xtra and have placed it in the appropriate Shockwave support folder on their hard drive. See the later section on the Shockwave support folder for a discussion on using Xtras in Shockwave.

Afterburner, Macromedia's free file compression utility for Shockwave, is a kind of Xtra called a Tools Xtra. You compress Director movies for playback over the Internet by selecting the Afterburner Xtra in the Xtras menu.

Afterburner is a separate application and drag-and-drop utility for Director 4. In Director 5, however, Afterburner is a Tools Xtra that you place in the Xtras folder in the following ways, depending on the platform you are using:

- Windows 95 and Windows NT—in the same folder as the Director application or in C:\Program Files\Common Files\Macromedia\Xtras folder
- Windows 3.1—in the C:\Windows\Macromed\Xtras directory
- Macintosh—in the System:Macromedia Xtras folder

You can download Afterburner over the Internet from the following:

`http://www.macromedia.com/`

Creating Animations in Director

Director provides several ways to create animations that you can then play with Shockwave. This section describes briefly the many ways—described in the following list—that you can create animations, without scripting, using Director's Score.

- In-betweening
- Cast to Time
- Space to Time
- Step recording
- Real-time recording

You can also create animations with Director's scripting language, Lingo. In some cases, Lingo animation can create smaller Shockwave files.

In-Betweening

In-betweening, or *tweening*, is an animation technique you are probably familiar with if you've used other animation software. *In-betweening* uses the computer to interpolate intermediate frames between key frames. Figure 7.5 shows an example of using in-betweening. (See Chapter 1, "Principles of Animation in a Nutshell," for a fuller discussion of this technique.) To create a key frame in Director, follow these steps:

1. Move the playback head to the frame where you want to create a key frame.

2. Select a channel in the Score.

3. Drag a cast member from the Cast Window and place it on the stage. The cast member is copied into that channel. This copy of the cast member is called a *sprite*.

4. Set the properties, appearance, and position for the sprite by clicking and dragging on the stage, using the sprite properties dialog box or the Tools Palette. You've now set the first key frame.

5. Repeat this procedure for each key frame.

6. Select the range of cells between key frames.

7. Choose In Between from the Modify menu. Director automatically fills in intervening frames. With its In-Between Special command, also accessed from the Modify menu, Director provides ease-in and ease-out (explained in Chapter 1) and additional controls.

Figure 7.5

In-betweening in the Score.

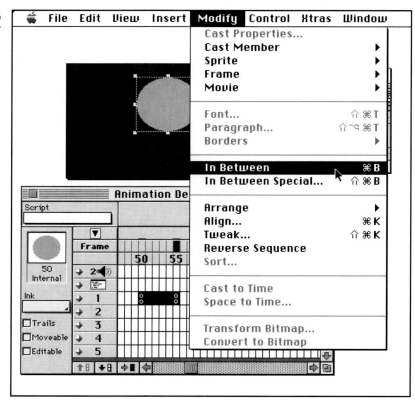

Cast to Time

Cast to Time takes a sequence of cast members in the Cast Window and places them in a single channel in the Director Score. The cast members are placed in the Score, one frame after the other, in the same sequence that they appear in the Cast Window. This animation technique is handy if you've created a series of frames or cels in the Director Paint window or have imported a series of animation frames using the Import/File command. Figure 7.6 shows an example of using Cast to Time. To use the Cast to Time feature, follow these steps:

1. Select a channel in the Score where you want the animation to start.

2. Select the sequence of cast members in the Cast Window.

3. Choose Cast to Time from the Modify menu.

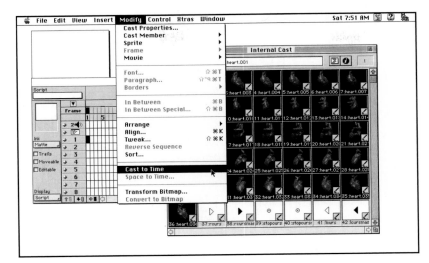

Figure 7.6

Using Cast to Time to create animations.

Space to Time

Space to Time enables you to arrange your entire animation on the stage in a single frame. This technique is similar to overlaying a series of transparent animation cels, one on top of another, and is handy if you want to see the entire animation at a glance.

1. Arrange your sprites in layers so that higher layers represent later frames.

2. After you've arranged the sprites the way you want, select them all.

3. Choose Space to Time from the Modify menu.

Director takes the sequence of layers and turns them into a sequence of frames. Figure 7.7 illustrates using Space to Time.

Figure 7.7

Using Space to Time to create animations.

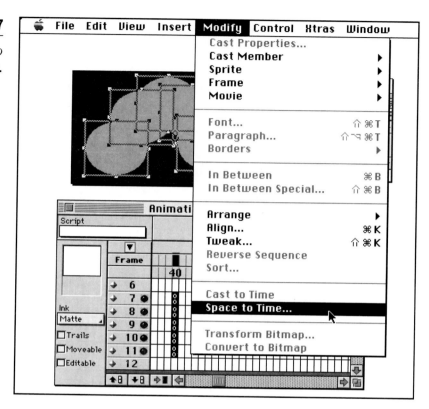

Step Recording

Step recording is a kind of frame-by-frame animation. This type of recording is automatically activated whenever you drag a cast member to the stage. A red indicator light shows up in the currently active channel when step recording is activated for that channel. Figure 7.8 illustrates step recording. To use step recording, follow these steps:

1. Position the sprite in the current frame.

2. Step forward to the next frame using the Control Panel.

3. Position the sprite in that frame.

4. Step forward to the next frame.

5. Position the sprite again, and so forth.

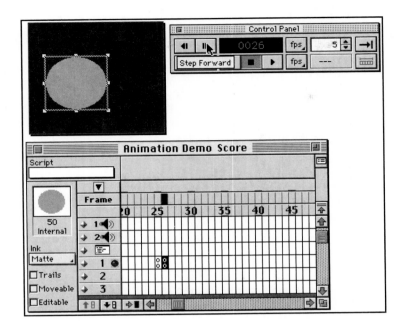

Figure 7.8

Step recording in the Score.

Real-Time Recording

Real-time recording records the movement of the sprite as you drag it across the stage in real-time. Figure 7.9 illustrates real-time recording. To record sprites in real-time, follow these steps:

1. Move the playback head to the place in the Score where you want the animation to begin.

2. Select the cast member you want to animate in the Cast Window.

3. Hold down the Control key and the spacebar. A white indicator light appears in the currently active channel when real-time recording is activated.

4. Drag the mouse across the stage.

5. Release the mouse when you are done recording. Director will create a sequence of sprites in the Score based on your mouse dragging.

Figure 7.9

Real-time recording in the Score.

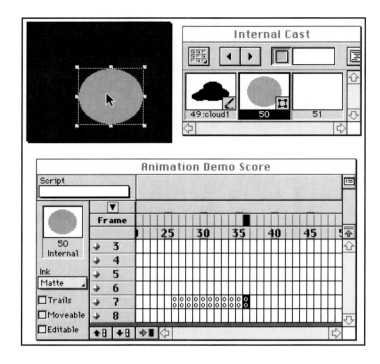

Other Animation Techniques

You can generate in-between bitmap cast members using the Auto Distort command. This command is a kind of poor man's morphing feature.

1. First, select a bitmap in the Director Paint window.

2. Choose one of the distort commands from the Paint window toolbar, such as Skew, Warp, or Perspective.

3. Before you deselect the bitmap, choose Auto Distort from the Xtras menu to create a sequence of intermediate cast members between the distorted and undistorted versions of the bitmap.

PowerApplets

There are two kinds of PowerApplets. The first type consists of utilities for Director for Windows; the second type includes java utilities for Macintosh and Windows. Both types have the same function—to automate the process of creating animations.

Currently, there are three PowerApplets for Director for Windows available, as follows:

- Animator enables users to animate an image or image sequence across the stage using animation paths.

- SlideShow creates Shockwave movies that sequence up to 20 images for presentation on a Web page.

- Icons enable users to create animated bullets and navigation elements.

 You can find PowerApplets on the accompanying CD or by visiting Macromedia's Web site at the following:

```
http://www.macromedia.com/
```

Creating Shockwave Animations for the Web

You create Shockwave animations the same way you create other animations in Director. Most of the things you can do in Director you can also do in Shockwave.

Here are the basic steps you'll follow to create Shockwave animations:

1. Create the Director movie.

2. Convert the movie with the Director Afterburner Xtra by choosing Afterburner in the Xtra menu and save it with the DCR extension.

3. Integrate the movie into an HTML document using HTML's EMBED tag. For example:

   ```
   <EMBED SRC = "myShockingMovie.dcr" WIDTH = 160
   HEIGHT = 120 PLUGINSPAGE = "http://
   www.macromedia.com/shockwave/">
   ```

4. Upload the HTML document and converted movie. Be sure the movie is uploaded as a raw, binary file. The Web server must be configured to associate files with the DCR extension to the MIME type application/x- director.

This section discusses tips and techniques for creating Shockwave animations in Director. Most of these tips and techniques are geared toward helping you create small, compact movies that won't take a long time to download over the Internet.

The following sections include general authoring tips for Shockwave, as well as provide information on animating text, 1-bit and vector-based graphics, ink effects, tiles, sound, palettes, the Shockwave Support Folder, and what to do if your browser does not have the Shockwave plug-in installed.

General Authoring Tips

This section contains miscellaneous tips for Shockwave authors:

- Use the Cast Member Properties dialog box to see the size of your cast members in kilobytes. Find out the total size of several cast members by selecting them all in the Cast Window and selecting Modify, Cast Member/Properties from the menu. You can also access the cast properties by pressing the Control key on Macintosh or the right mouse button on Windows and clicking on a sprite on the Stage.

- Use small-sized cast members and then use the Sprite Properties dialog box to resize the sprite on the stage. Access the Sprite Properties dialog box by selecting Sprite/ Properties from the Modify menu or by pressing the control key on the Macintosh or the right mouse button on Windows and clicking on a sprite on the Stage. You can also use this dialog box to set key frame properties for animating sprites over time.

- Avoid long repeat loops that tie up the processor. Instead, loop on a frame. Transitions, such as Dissolve, ink effects, and animating sprite sizes, can be processor-intensive too, slowing down screen redraw, and tying up the user's machine.

- To set the background color of your Shockwave movie so that it matches the background color of your HTML document, choose Movie/Properties from the Modify menu and select a color for the background on the dialog box.

- Sprite locations are given relative to the stage. The Lingo commands stageRight, stageLeft, and so forth are given in absolute coordinates, relative to the monitor.

- Use the Lingo halt command to stop your movie when it is finished playing. This ensures that your movie won't eat up processor cycles after it has finished playing.

- Putting Shockwave movies inside table cels, especially nested table cels, tends to crash browsers.

- To test your Shockwave movie on a Macintosh, drag and drop the DCR file on the Netscape browser window.

Lingo Network Extensions in Shockwave

Shockwave comes with extensions to the Lingo scripting language that enable you to make asynchronous network calls. Your Shockwave movie can use the new network extensions to Lingo to branch to another Shockwave movie anywhere on the Web or to load another Web page.

You can also use Lingo network extensions to retrieve text-based data on the Internet or create richly interactive control bars or navigational panels that load HTML documents into separate frames. Figure 7.10 illustrates a 17 KB Shockwave movie that uses Lingo network extensions to collect data on the Internet and present it in a graphical display. With this Shockwave movie (less than 17 KB in size), wind surfers can find out about current weather conditions in the San Francisco Bay.

> **Warning**
>
> The network extensions are specific to Shockwave and only work within Shockwave. They do not work within the Director authoring environment.

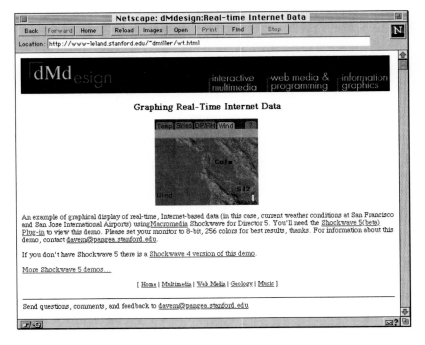

Figure 7.10

Graphical display of real-time Internet-based data using Shockwave.

One of the most annoying things about creating Shockwave animations that use the Lingo network extensions is that Lingo will give script errors for network commands whenever you run your movie in the Director authoring environment (see earlier warning). On the CD, you will find an external cast containing dummy handlers that will trap network Lingo calls so that you don't get compiler errors.

By uncommenting different lines within each handler, you can have the dummy handlers do nothing, put a message in the Message Windows, display an alert, or return data. You can link this cast to your Director movie during development. When you are ready to create your Shockwave movie, you can unlink the cast by doing the following:

1. Choose the Movie/Cast command under the Modify menu.

2. Select the cast name in the list box.

3. Click on Unlink.

Currently, you can only open four asynchronous network processes using the network extensions to Lingo. After the process is done or has returned the data you requested, use the NetDone() command to free up the process.

Disabled Director Features

Some Director features are disabled in Shockwave. These disabled features are listed at the end of this section. Most of the Lingo commands that provide access to the client hard disk, file system, or operating system have been disabled. This has been done for security purposes, so that downloaded applications do not have access to the local file system.

Here's a list of some of the Director features that are disabled Shockwave:

- You can't use Director's Movie-in-a-Window feature.

- Most of the Lingo commands that provide access to the client hard disk, file system, or operating system have been disabled. The disabled commands include the following:

```
openResFile
closeResFile
```

```
open window
close window

pasteFromClipboard member x of castLib y,
importFileInto member x of castLib y

saveMovie
printFrom
open, openDA, closeDA
quit, restart, and shutdown

fileName of cast
fileName of window
getNthFileNameInFolder
moviePath
pathName
searchCurrentFolder
searchPaths
set the filename of castlib
```

- mci (media control interface) Lingo commands in Director for Windows are disabled.

- FileIO, SerialIO, OrthPlay XObjects/Xtras are disabled.

- XObjects, XCMDs, XFCNs cannot be embedded as resources in a movie, but can be used in the Shockwave support folder (see section on the support folder later in this chapter).

- You can't use "Wait for" options in the tempo channel, but you can use Lingo to duplicate this feature.

The following Lingo commands and features have restricted usage under Shockwave. You can use these commands to access external files in the special Shockwave disk cache or support folder. See the later section on the Shockwave support folder for details.

```
openXLib
```

```
closeXLib
```

```
open castlib x
```

Text

Animated text is an easy way to draw attention to logos, bullet points, and other information. People who use presentation software are used to highlighting their text by using various forms of animation, such as sliding bullet points, and so forth.

In Director 5, there are two kinds of text-based cast members, as follows:

- Rich text or simply "text"
- Fields

Rich text contains many of the same formatting options you have in a word processing program. In addition, rich text can be anti-aliased against its background, so it looks good on-screen. (Anti-aliasing uses different techniques to blend or blur the jagged edges in computer images so that computer-generated imagery looks like a continuous tone photograph.) Rich text has access to fonts on the authoring machine. It is fully editable in the authoring environment, but cannot be edited in a projector or Shockwave movie.

To create rich text, use the Text tool or the Text Window. Figure 7.11 shows a rich text editor.

Figure 7.11

The rich text editor.

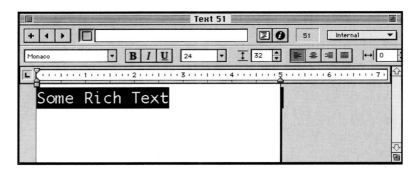

Field text has more limited formatting options compared to Rich text. Field text, moreover, is not anti-aliased. It can be edited in the authoring environment, but unlike rich text, it can also be edited by users in a projector or Shockwave movie. You make field text editable by selecting the editable check box in the Score, selecting the editable check box in the Cast Member property dialog box, or with the Lingo `editable of sprite` command.

Field text uses much less disk space than rich text or other bitmapped text; thus, it's especially useful for Shockwave movies. Because field text uses the fonts available on the playback machine, it's probably safest to stick with the standard fonts that come with most Windows and Macintosh systems, such as Times, Helvetica, Geneva, and Courier on

Macintosh, or Arial, Courier New, and Times New Roman on Windows.

To create Field text, use the Field tool on the Tools Palette or choose Field from the Control submenu on the Insert menu. Figure 7.12 shows a field text editor.

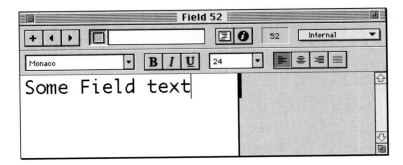

Figure 7.12

The field text editor.

You can also create bitmaps of text in the Director Paint window or import bitmaps of text from programs such as Photoshop.

1-Bit Graphics

One way to keep your file size small is to use bitmap graphics that have 1-bit color depth. To convert graphics to 1-bit in Director, do the following:

1. Select the cast member in the Cast Window.
2. Choose Transform Bitmap from the Modify menu.
3. Choose 1-bit from the Color Depth pop-up menu.

You can use an image processing program such as Debabelizer or Photoshop to convert graphics to 1-bit.

In Director, 1-bit graphics consist of two colors: foreground color and background color. You can change the forecolor and backcolor of sprites on the stage by doing the following:

1. Select the sprite.
2. Click on the color chips in the Tools Palette. This brings up a 256-color pop-up palette from which you can choose another color for the foreground or background.

Note

The contents of Fields can be changed while a Shockwave movie is running. Fields are a good way to provide status and help bars for users. Field text can be used for animated text effects. Many Field text properties, such as size and color, can be set by Lingo. For example, the following changes the point size of the text in the myFieldText cast member named to 18:

`set the fontSize of member "myFieldText" = 18`

Note

Dithering is a process used by many image processing programs when you reduce the bit depth of a graphic. Dithering uses patterns of pixels to approximate the colors and values of the original graphic. Dithering to 1-bit can produce some interesting effects.

Figure 7.13 illustrates choosing a foreground color from the pop-up palette.

Figure 7.13

Setting the foreground color of a 1-bit graphic.

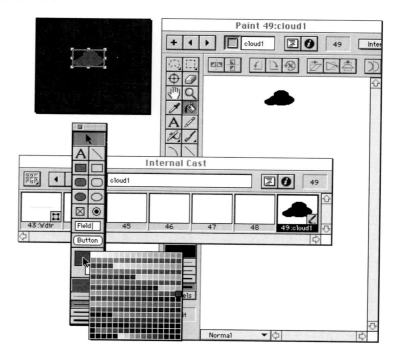

You can change the foreground color and background color of graphics using the Lingo commands `forecolor of sprite` and `backcolor of sprite`. On 8-bit systems, the 256 possible colors are referenced by a number between 0 and 255. For example, the following command sets the forecolor of the sprite in channel 12 to a random color between 1 and 255 in the currently active palette:

```
set the forecolor of sprite 10 to random(255)
```

To change the foreground color and background color of Field text, use the Lingo commands `forecolor of member` and `backcolor of member`.

The Trails Effect

The *Trails effect* leaves a copy of a graphic behind as it moves across the stage, as if the graphic were a paintbrush. Activate the Trails effect by selecting the Trails check box in the Score.

Trails can be an easy way to add multiple copies of a graphic
to the Stage, or to paint large areas of color. A drawback of
trails, however, is that trails will not be repainted if the user
covers and then uncovers the Shockwave movie with another
window.

Vector-Based Graphics

Vector-based graphics are different from bitmap graphics
because the computer stores vector-based graphics as a mathematical formulae rather than as a collection of pixels. Thus,
vector-based graphics are small and very useful for creating
Web-based animations.

Director 5 comes with a limited set of vector-based graphics
tools. In Director 5, vector-based graphics are called *shapes*.
Shapes include lines, ovals, rectangles, and rounded rectangles.
You access shapes from the Tools Palette, which also can be
used to change the type, line size, fill pattern, and color of
shapes. Figure 7.14 illustrates using the Tools Palette to create
shapes.

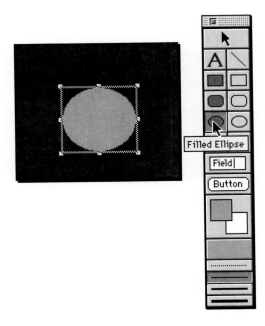

Figure 7.14

*Vector-based graphics
in Director.*

Note

New Lingo commands enable you to change the type of shape, fill, patterns, and line size of shape cast members from Lingo. For example, the following sets the line size of the shape sprite to four pixels:

```
set the lineSize of sprite
"myLine" = 4
```

But these fill the shape Cast myCircle with a solid color pattern:

```
set the filled of member
"myCircle" = TRUE
```

```
set the pattern of member
"myCircle" = 1
```

Ink Effects

Ink effects are an easy way to create interesting visual effects with 1-bit graphics without creating extra cast members. Ink effects control the way pixels in a 1-bit graphic are composited with underlying pixels. Some ink effects are processor-intensive and can slow screen redraw; see the documentation for details. Generally, ink effects lower down in the Ink effects pop-up menu are more processor-intensive.

Access the Ink effects pop-up from the Score Window, the Paint Window, or press the Command key on Macintosh or Control key on Windows and select a sprite on the stage. Text cast members only support Copy, Background Transparent, and Blend inks.

Tiles

Tiling is an efficient way to build backgrounds and create patterns in Director movies.

Access the Tile Settings from the Pattern Fill button on the Tools Palette (beneath the color chips) or in the Paint Window. Define a Tile pattern by choosing a rectangular region of any bitmap cast member. Figure 7.15 illustrates creating a tile from a cast member bitmap. You can define multiple tiles from the same bitmap. Tiles can be any rectangular size.

Figure 7.15

Creating a tile from a bitmap.

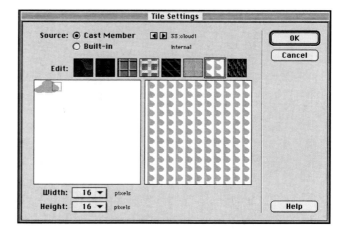

Once created, a tile can be used to fill a bitmap or vector-based shape. Figure 7.16 illustrates selecting Tile Settings to fill a graphic.

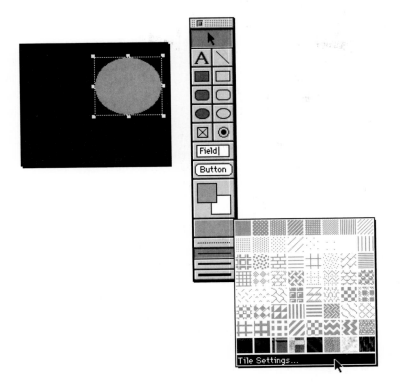

Figure 7.16

Using the Tile Settings to fill a graphic with a tile.

Sound

Sound is an important, though often neglected, element in multimedia. Shockwave movies are an easy way to add sound to a Web page. Unfortunately for Shockwave movies, the Afterburner compression utility doesn't compress sounds. Every kilobyte of digital audio you add to your movie will add a kilobyte to the size of the final Shockwave movie.

Play sounds in a Director movie by adding them to the sound channels in the Director Score, just like you add other cast members, or you can use the Lingo puppetsound command to play sound cast members.

Try to keep your sounds to 11 kHz (kilohertz) mono 8-bit or below. For sounds such as button clicks, you might get by with as little as 8 kHz. Test sounds with low sampling rate on different systems to see if the quality is acceptable. To loop sounds, set the Looped property in the sound cast properties dialog box.

> **Note**
>
> Endlessly looping sounds can be annoying, so provide a way for users to stop the sound—for example, the code stops the sound playing in sound channel 1 when the user clicks the mouse.
>
> ```
> on mouseDown
>   if soundBusy(1) then sound
>   stop 1
> end
> ```

Instead of using a sound editor to create fade ins and fade outs, use the Lingo commands sound `fadeIn` and sound `fadeOut`. Use the Lingo command `the volume of sound` to set the volume of a sound relative to the overall sound level of the user's machine.

You can use IMA (Interactive Multimedia Association)-compressed sounds in Shockwave, but, at this time, they can only be imported in the Macintosh authoring environment, although they will play back on Windows. To create an IMA-compressed sound on a Mac from a sound-only QuickTime movie in MoviePlayer, follow these steps:

1. Choose Export from the File menu.

2. Select Sound To AIFF.

3. Click Options.

4. Select IMA 4:1 for compressor.

5. Select a sampling rate of 11.025, and Mono.

Palettes

Your movie will probably play back on an 8-bit display. For playback on the Web, it's probably best to create 8-bit Shockwave movies. If you author in 16-bit or 24-bit, you can change the color depth of your Director movie by changing your monitor's color depth and then saving the movie.

The color in your 8-bit movie will be mapped to the currently active browser palette, unless you specify otherwise with the PALETTE parameter in the EMBED tag. This means that colors in your animation that aren't in the browser palette will be dithered to colors that are in the browser palette, which might make some of your graphics look speckled.

Note

Lynda Weinman, author of *Designing Web Graphics*, has placed the browser-safe palette on her Web site at the following:

`http://www.lynda.com/hex.html`

Netscape Navigator and Internet Explorer use a slightly different palette on Macintosh and Windows systems. These palettes share 216 colors. These 216 shared, non-dithered, cross-platform colors are the same colors as the middle 216 colors of the Macintosh system palette. If you use these colors, you can be assured that your graphics won't be dithered. A big drawback of this palette is its limited range of grays. If you aren't using custom palettes and want to provide the highest degree of cross-platform palette compatibility, you should probably stick to these colors.

You can embed a custom palette in your Shockwave movie and force the browser to use this palette using the PALETTE = FOREGROUND command. This command will probably shift all the colors in the rest of the display, which can be disorienting for some users. Also, if the user jumps to a new page, the palette might not get reset.

The Shockwave Support Folder

The Shockwave support folder is a new feature of Shockwave for Director 5. The *support folder* is a special folder or cache on the client hard disk that can be used for external files, such as linked QuickTime movies or digital audio, Xtras, XObjects, and external casts.

A drawback of the support folder is that users must download external files separately from the Shockwave movie, and also must make sure these external files are in the correct folder/directory on their hard drive (see following table). Possible uses of the support folder include support for online services or CD-ROM/Internet hybrids. An installer on the CD-ROM or online service software could automatically place external media, such as QuickTime movies, which would take a long time to download, in the Shockwave support folder. Then when the user accesses Shockwave movies on the Internet, the external files in the support folder are available to the Shockwave movie.

Platform	Support Folder	Location
68K Mac	NP-Mac68K-Dir-Shockwave folder	Plug-ins folder in the Netscape Navigator folder
PPC Mac	NP-MacPPC-Dir-Shockwave folder	Plug-ins folder in the Netscape Navigator folder
Win3.1	NP16DSW	C:\NETSCAPE\PLUGINS directory
Win95	NP32DSW	C:\Program Files\Netscape\Navigator \Program\Plugins directory

During authoring, place the external file in the same folder as the Director movie. When you call an external file from your

Shockwave movie, Shockwave searches the special support folder on the client hard disk.

Use the following Lingo commands to access files in the support folder:

```
openXLib
```

```
closeXLib
```

```
open castlib x
```

See the section. "Disabled Director Features," earlier in this chapter for a list of Lingo commands that will not work with external files under Shockwave at this time.

Use this code to open a Lingo Xtra or XObject in the startMovie handler:

```
on startMovie
    global gXtra

    if objectP(gXtra) then gXtra(mDispose)
    openXlib "NeatoXtra"
    set gXtra = NeatoXtra(mNew)

end startMovie
```

Close the Lingo Xtra or XObject when you are done using it. To be sure you don't forget and to free up memory, include the following code in the stopMovie handler:

```
on stopMovie
    global gXtra

    if objectP(gXtra) then gXtra(mDispose)
    closeXlib "NeatoXtra"

end stopMovie
```

During authoring, place the Xtra in the same folder/directory as your movie file. During playback, the Xtra must be in the appropriate Shockwave support folder on the client machine.

Lingo Network Extensions

Shockwave contains new network extensions to Lingo. These extensions enable you to start asynchronous network processes, go to other pages on the Web, and retrieve

Internet-based data, such as another Shockwave movie or a text file, all within your Shockwave movie. An asynchronous network process doesn't immediately return a result. The process runs in the background while your Shockwave movie continues to play. If you are interested in using the result returned from an asynchronous network call, such as the following:

```
GetNetText ("http://www.myserver.com/statuslog.txt")
```

then you will have to repeatedly make Lingo calls (for example, in an exitFrame handler) to query the process to see if it has returned a result. For example, first initiate an asynchronous network process by putting a call to GetNetText, such as the preceding listing, in an exitFrame handler. Then, in a subsequent frame, put the following handler in a frame script:

```
on exitFrame

    if netDone(getLatestNetID()) then
        put netTextResult() into field "Status Bar"
        go the frame +1
    else
        go the frame
    end if
end
```

This handler causes your Shockwave movie to loop continuously on a single frame, waiting for the result of your call to GetNetText. When it gets the result, it places the retrieved text in the field "Status Bar" and then jumps out of the loop to the next frame in the movie.

Currently, you can only open four asynchronous network processes at one time using the network extensions to Lingo. After the network process is done or has returned the data you requested, use the NetDone() command to free up the process.

Providing detailed tutorials on the powerful new network extensions to Lingo is beyond the scope of this chapter. The "No-Load Leader" example on the CD uses a single call to gotoNetMovie, if you'd like to see a simple implementation of an asynchronous network call.

For full documentation of the new network extensions to Lingo, go to the following:

```
http://www.macromedia.com/shockwave/director5/
create.html
```

Note

Frames are a Netscape extension to HTML that enable dynamic updating of regions of a Web page. *Target* is the HTML parameter used with the HREF tag that specifies the frame to be updated.

Targeting Frames

In Shockwave for Director 5, you can use the network extensions to Lingo to target frames in an HTML document. An example of this is a two-frame HTML document where one frame contains a Shockwave navigation bar or control panel and the second frame contains content that is accessed from the Shockwave control panel.

Shockwave for Director control panels can have features such as button and rollover feedback, and context-sensitive help. Figure 7.17 illustrates rich, responsive Shockwave control panels created using the interactivity features in Director.

Figure 7.17

Shockwave control panels illustrating rollover feedback and context-sensitive help.

The Net Lingo syntax for targeting frames follows:

```
gotoNetPage "chapter1.html","content"
```

The part chapter1.html is the HTML document that will be loaded into the frame named content. To integrate this into a navigation bar or control panel, you could place this command in the mouseUp handler of a button, for example.

Shockwave Unplugged

Chances are some browsers that hit your page will not have the Shockwave Plug-In installed. In Netscape Navigator 2.0 or compatible browsers, a broken icon appears if the Shockwave Plug-In is not present. At the very least, if you provide Shockwave content on your site, you should provide a link to the Macromedia Shockwave page so users can download the plug-in for their system at the following

```
http://www.macromedia.com/shockwave/
```

You can also use the PLUGINSPAGE parameter in the EM-BED tag to automatically point users' browsers to the Shockwave download page, as in the following example:

```
<EMBED SRC="myShockWave.dcr" WIDTH= 160 HEIGHT= 120
PLUGINSPAGE= "http://www.macromedia.com/shockwave/ ">
```

Using Shockwave and the <META> Tag

You can also use Shockwave and Lingo network extensions to detect the presence of the Shockwave Plug-In and automatically send the browser to a Shockwave-enabled page if the plug-in is present. This method was used by Macromedia on their home page. First, create a small Shockwave movie that contains the gotoNetPage command in a frame script, as in this example:

```
gotoNetPage "myShockwaveEnabledPage.html"
```

The page specified in the gotoNetPage command is your Shockwave-enabled page—in this case, myShockwaveEnabledPage.html. Embed this movie in an HTML document. Place the following HTML between the <HEAD></HEAD> tags of your HTML document:

```
<META HTTP-EQUIV=REFRESH CONTENT="20;
URL=myNonShockedPage.html">
```

When a user loads this HTML document, the little Shockwave movie loads and sends the browser to the Shockwave-enabled page if the user has Shockwave installed. If the user doesn't have Shockwave, then he will see the broken plug-in icon. If you use the PLUGINSPAGE parameter described earlier, the user will have the choice to go to a page to download the plug-in. The HTML in the <META> tag automatically sends the user to the non-Shockwave page after 20 seconds.

JavaScript Workaround for Netscape 2.0

The following JavaScript workaround is a variation on sample code from Macromedia's Shockwave Developer's Guide that is designed to provide a solution for the no-plug-in problem for the most number of browsers. Here's what it does. In Netscape 2.0-compatible browsers, the broken plug-in icon is displayed when there is no Shockwave Plug-In present and the PLUGINSPAGE parameter automatically points the user to a download site. In browsers that don't support Netscape-compatible plug-ins, it will usually display the HTML between the NOEMBED tags.

```
<script language="JavaScript">

    <!-- hide this script tag's contents from old
browsers

    document.write ( '<EMBED SRC="myShockWave.dcr"
WIDTH= 160 HEIGHT= 120  ' );
    document.write ( ' PLUGINSPAGE= "http://
www.macromedia.com/shockwave/ ">'  );

    <!—done hiding from old browsers -->

</script>

<NOEMBED>
    <IMG SRC="noPlugin.gif">
</NOEMBED>
```

JavaScript Workaround for Netscape 3.0

Another way to detect the presence of the Shockwave Plug-In requires Netscape 3.0 and uses a new feature of JavaScript. Following is HTML and JavaScript code that creates an HTML document on the fly based on whether the Shockwave Plug-In is installed on the user's machine. If JavaScript and HTML code makes your eyes freeze over, then skip this section. This code is different from the plug-in detection code published on Netscape's site, which didn't work properly as of this writing.

The function testForShockwave() within the HEAD tag returns true if there is a plug-in present that can handle the application/x-director MIME type. In addition, you could use this function to return the name of the Shockwave Plug-In installed—for example, "NP-PPC-Dir-Shockwave," which would tell you what type of machine the browser was on.

The JavaScript within the BODY tags first tests for the presence of the Shockwave Plug-In by calling the testForShockwave() function. Then, if the function returns true, the script uses document.write methods to generate a Shockwave version of the HTML document. If the function returns false, then the script writes out a non-Shocked version.

```
<HTML>
<HEAD>

<TITLE>ShockTest</TITLE>

<script language="JavaScript">

function testForShockwave()
{
numPlugs = navigator.plugins.length
for (p = 0; p < numPlugs; p++)
  {
    numMimes = navigator.plugins[p].length
   for (m= 0; m < numMimes; m++)
    {
      if (navigator.plugins[p][m].type == "application/
➥x-director")
          {
                 PlugInName = navigator.plugins[p].name;
                 return true;
             }
      }//end for loop
    }//end for loop

        return false;

} //end function

</script>

</HEAD>
<BODY>
<script language="JavaScript">
   <!— hide this script tag's contents from old
➥browsers


 if (testForShockwave())

   { // code to create a Shockwave-enabled HTML document

    document.write ( '<EMBED SRC="myShockWave.dcr"
```

```
➥WIDTH= 160 HEIGHT= 120  ' );
   document.write ( ' PLUGINSPAGE= "http://
➥www.macromedia.com">'  );
  }

else
  { // code to create a non-Shockwave HTML document

       document.write ( "<H3>Shock Not Here!</H3>"  );
  }

<!—done hiding from old browsers -->
</SCRIPT>
</BODY>
</HTML>
```

Procedure: No-Load Leader

When you begin downloading a large Shockwave movie, it doesn't display instantly. Instead, the Web page displays a white rectangle with a Macromedia logo in place of the Shockwave movie. This graphic is displayed until the movie has been completely downloaded to the user's disk cache. This tutorial uses a technique to replace this default graphic with a small movie that provides the user with feedback during the download time.

If you have a large movie with a long download time, first load a very small movie in its place—a *No-load Leader*. The movie should be small enough so that it loads in seconds—less than 10 KB, for example. The No-load Leader loads in a few seconds, then issues the gotoNetMovie Lingo command with the path name to your large Shockwave movie. When the No-load Leader issues the gotoNetMovie command, Lingo starts the download process of your large movie in the background, while still playing your small No-load Leader in the Web page.

When the larger movie has been completely downloaded to the client disk cache, it will appear in place of your No-load Leader movie. The No-load Leader movie should be the same dimensions as your large movie and should provide some low-bandwidth content to entertain your users during a long download. You can create your movie following these steps or use the movie "noldlder.dir" on the book's CD.

Follow these steps to create a No-load Leader:

1. Open Director with a new blank movie (see fig. 7.18).

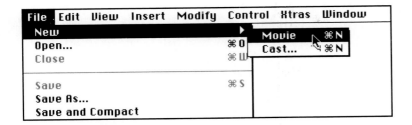

Figure 7.18

Creating a new Director movie.

2. Choose Movie/Properties under the Modify menu (see fig. 7.19).

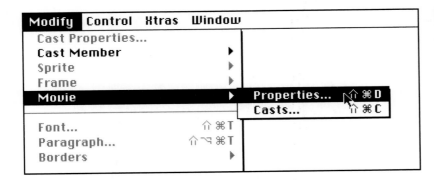

Figure 7.19

Choosing Movie/Properties.

3. Specify a stage size that matches your large Shockwave movie (see fig. 7.20).

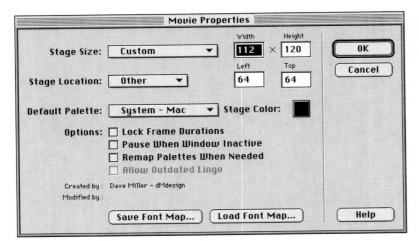

Figure 7.20

The Movie Properties dialog box.

4. Double-click in the Script channel in the first frame in the Score.

5. A Script Window should open with these lines (see fig. 7.21):

```
on exitFrame
  end
```

If you are using noldlder.dir, the script should be already there. Just uncomment the script.

Figure 7.21

The Script Window.

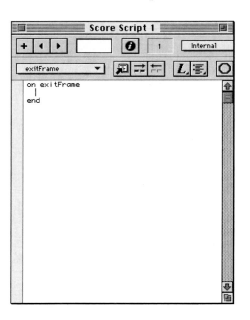

6. Between these two lines, type

```
gotoNetmovie "myBigShockwaveMovie.dcr"
```

where `myBigShockwaveMovie.dcr` is the name of your large Shockwave movie.

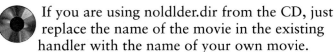 If you are using noldlder.dir from the CD, just replace the name of the movie in the existing handler with the name of your own movie.

7. The Script Window should look like this (see fig. 7.22):

```
on exitFrame
     gotoNetMovie "myBigShockwaveMovie.dcr"
end
```

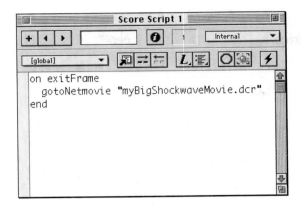

Figure 7.22

The Script Window with the gotoNetMovie handler.

8. Create a low-bandwidth animation or other indication for the user that downloading is in progress. The example on the CD uses Lingo animation to animate the hand of a clock.

9. Select the Afterburner Xtra from the Xtras menu.

10. Give your movie a name ending with the DCR extension.

Procedure: Score-Based Animation

This example uses Director to play back a sequence of animation frames created in another animation program. Director is used to add interactivity to the animation. You can use the animation frames and the movie "heart.dir" from the book's CD or use your own animation frames. To see the final version of the movie with all the interactivity, see the movie heartfnl.dir on the CD.

Use these steps:

1. First, create your animation frames in an animation program. The example on the CD used Extreme 3D, but you can use any animation program that outputs sequences of PICT files. The CD provides a series of graphics you can use for this exercise in the folder 6frames.

2. Process the graphics for the Web, as follows:

   ■ Reduce the size of the graphics to reduce the total file size and to fit the animation on a Web page. 160×120 pixels is a common size.

- Reduce the bit-depth of the graphics to 8-bit.

- Give the graphics a Web-compatible palette, such as the Macintosh system palette or the 216-color Netscape palette. Use any image processing program with batch capabilities, such as Equilibrium Debabelizer. The graphics on the CD were processed this way.

3. Put all the graphics in a single folder and make sure they have file names that are numbered sequentially.

4. Open Director with a new blank movie or use the movie "heart.dir" on the CD.

5. Choose Movie/Properties under the Modify menu.

6. Specify a stage size that matches the size of your animation (see fig. 7.23).

Figure 7.23

Specifying a stage size.

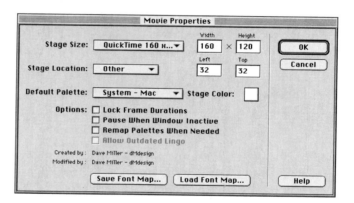

7. Open the Cast Window under the Windows menu.

8. Select an open cast slot. You want to have enough open cast slots in a row so that when you import your sequentially numbered PICT files, they all fit in a contiguous sequence in the Cast Window.

9. Choose Import from the File menu (see fig. 7.24).

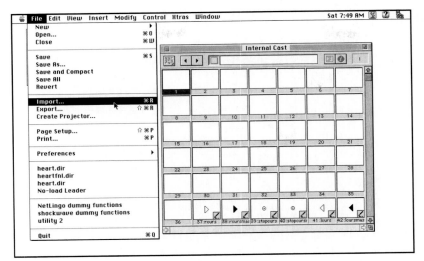

Figure 7.24

Choosing Import from the File menu.

10. Select the first graphic in your animation sequence. If the graphics are all in the same folder, select Import All. The CD provides a series of graphics you can use for this exercise in the folder 6frames (see fig. 7.25).

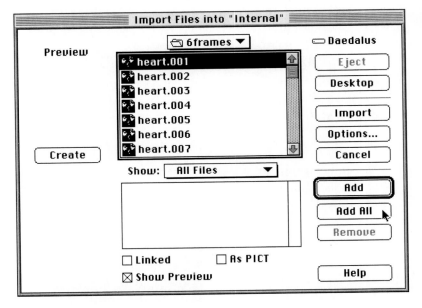

Figure 7.25

Importing animation frames into the Cast.

11. All the graphics will be placed in the Cast Window in sequence, based on file name (see fig. 7.26). That is why it is important to have sequentially numbered files.

Figure 7.26

Imported animation frames in the Cast Window.

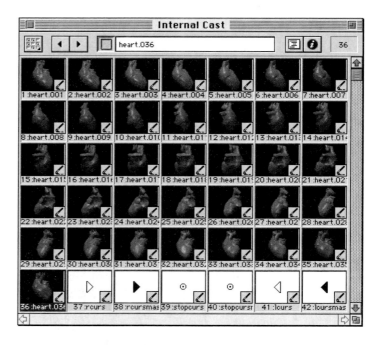

12. If you run out of memory during import, you can import files in smaller batches or quit Director and allocate more memory to the program.

13. In the Score, select frame 1, channel 1.

14. Click on the Cast Window to make it active. Select all the animation frames that you just imported into the Cast Window. Press the shift key to make a multiple, contiguous selection.

15. Choose Cast to Time from the Modify menu (see fig. 7.27).

Figure 7.27

Choosing Cast to Time.

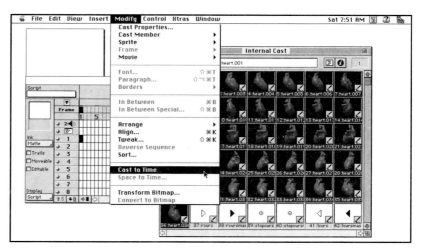

16. Selected cast members are placed sequentially into separate frames in the Score, beginning at frame 1, channel 1 (see fig. 7.28).

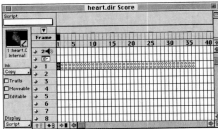

Figure 7.28

The Score Window after choosing Cast to Time.

Follow steps 17 and 18 if you are using the movie "heart.dir" from the CD.

17. Select frame 1 through 36 in the Script channel.

18. In the Script pop-up, select the score script named "interactivity" (see fig. 7.29).

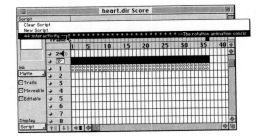

Figure 7.29

Selecting the "interactivity" script from the Script pop-up.

19. Select the Afterburner Xtra from the Xtras menu (see fig. 7.30).

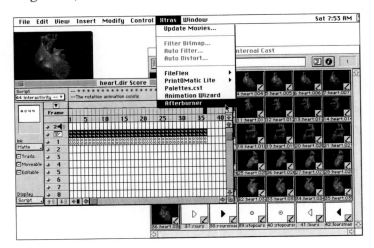

Figure 7.30

Choosing Afterburner from the Xtras menu.

20. Give your movie a name ending with the extension DCR.

Conclusion

This chapter only scratches the surface of things you can do with Shockwave and Director. Hopefully, it has provided you with a place to get started using Shockwave, or, if you already use Director, provided you with some tips for creating compact Shockwave movies.

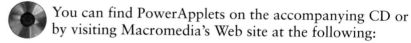 Director has a lot of competition these days in the Web animation arena. Several companies have released Netscape-compatible plug-ins and authoring tools for the creation of Web-based animations. Demos and beta versions of some of these products can be found on this book's CD. Competing products, such as WebPainter from TotallyHip, CelAnimator from FutureSplash, WebAnimator from DeltaPoint, Emblaze from the Interactive Media Group, and mBEDLets from mBED Software are generally cheaper than Director, provide very good animation tools, provide for interactivity (in some cases), and have been developed from the ground up for Web animation.

You can find PowerApplets on the accompanying CD or by visiting Macromedia's Web site at the following:

```
http://www.macromedia.com/
```

by William E. Weinman

Author Biography

William E. Weinman has earned his living as a technologist-for-hire for about 20 years. He has designed software for many large and small organizations, including IBM, Security Pacific Bank, KDD (the major long-distance company in Japan), and the Bank of New Zealand. Mr. Weinman has also designed and constructed electronic musical instruments for popular recording artists, fiber-optic systems for NASA and Bell Labs, and a broadcast ticker tape for a television station. He has been involved with online computing since he got his first acoustically coupled modem in 1978.

You can often find Mr. Weinman playing with Jezebel, his Gibson L6-S guitar, in blues bars around Texas; or studying Native-American shamanic medicine in Arizona; but it may be easier to send e-mail to wew@bearnet.com.

Server-Push Animation

Server-push is a clever technique that Netscape created that combines some features of the MIME[1] (Multipurpose Internet Mail Extensions) specification with features of the HTTP protocol to allow simple streaming animation. In a nutshell, this technique creates a multi-part "message" that the browser can display piece-by-piece as it is received.

In order to understand how these displays work, you first need to know a little about how data flows in an HTTP connection.

A Brief Introduction to HTTP

HTTP[2] (HyperText Transfer Protocol) is the protocol used by Web servers to negotiate the flow of data between the server and the client. The HTTP protocol defines a set of messages that fall into two categories, as follows:

- Request messages from the client (browser)
- Response messages from the server

Request messages are sent by the client to the server to request data. This is the basic format for an HTTP request message:

<method> URI *<HTTP-version>*

A typical request might look like this:

```
GET /cgibook/chap01/index.html HTTP/1.0
```

The server then sends a response to the client in the following form:

<response-header>

<data>

The first part of the response is the *response header*. It begins with a *status line* that contains the version of HTTP being used, a *status code,* and a *reason phrase*. The status line is followed by a series of MIME-formatted header lines that describe the details of the response.

The response header is always followed by a blank line to indicate that the header is finished. If there is a body of data associated with the response, it follows the blank line.

A response to the previous request might look like this:

```
HTTP/1.0 200 OK
Date: Mon, 22 Jan 1996 17:52:11 GMT
Server: Apache/0.6.4b
Content-type: text/html

<html>
<head>
<title>Chapter 1 &#183; "Hello, World!"</title>
</head>
<BODY bgcolor="#dddddd">

   . . . document body . . .

</body>
</html>
```

It is beyond the scope of this chapter to present all the definitions of all the possible fields in an HTTP transaction. This chapter provides what you need to know in order to successfully use the server-push technique. For all the gory details of

Warning

Newlines in HTTP Messages

When a computer is used to represent text or text-like information (like mail messages and message-oriented protocols such as HTTP), it must represent the end of a line with a code. That code is called a *newline.*

Newlines in HTTP messages are represented by both a carriage-return (0D*hex*) *and* a linefeed (0A*hex*). Some systems—including Unix systems and some software on Macs and PCs—do not normally use both characters in their line endings. Many servers and clients recognize line endings that are either a single carriage-return or a single linefeed; in fact, the current HTTP specification encourages them to do so. Some clients, though, don't recognize these line endings, and it's not required of them to do so.

Just make sure to end your lines with both characters, in the correct order, and your code will work with all clients without problem.

For more information about line endings, see Chapter 12 of *The CGI Book* (New Riders, ISBN: 1-56205-571-2), section 12.2.2.

HTTP, however, you can obtain a copy of the Internet Draft that describes it at `ftp://ftp.internic.net/internet-drafts/draft-ietf-http-v10-spec-04.txt`.

The important point here is that the server sends the client a stream of characters that represent the different elements of the response. If you know the format of the responses that an HTTP server sends, you can mimic its protocol and send customized responses to handle specific circumstances not otherwise supported by the server.

Normally, when you run a CGI program, the server intercepts the MIME-header and simply incorporates its elements into the overall header that it sends to the client. Because you need to generate your own HTTP responses for server-push, you need a way to prevent the server from changing your headers. The next section covers a technique for doing just that.

Technology Overview: Non-Parsed Header CGI

Most servers implement a special way of calling a CGI program that does not intercept the header—this is called Non-Parsed Header, or NPH-CGI. On most servers, the NPH method is invoked when the CGI program is in a file that starts with the letters, "nph-" (e.g., `nph-myprogram.cgi`). If this doesn't work on your server, talk to your system administrator or consult the server documentation to find out how to run NPH-CGI on your system.

Keep in mind that, unlike normal CGI, when you write an NPH-CGI program, you need to provide a valid HTTP response in your header. The following is a skeleton NPH-CGI program that does this in Perl. The technique should be obvious enough for you to see how to implement it in other languages.

```
#!/usr/bin/perl

# nph-skel.pl.cgi
#
# Hello World in NPH-CGI
#
# (c) 1996 William E. Weinman
```

> **Note**
>
> **For More Information**
>
> You may also want to see the following IETF RFCs (Internet Engineering Task Force Request for Comments) for more information on standard message formats for the Internet:
>
> *MIME (Multipurpose Internet Mail Extensions) Part One: Mechanisms for Specifying and Describing the Format of Internet Message Bodies.* N. Borenstein and N. Freed, RFC 1521, September 1983. `ftp://ftp.internic.net/rfc/rfc1521.txt`
>
> *Standard for the Format of ARPA Internet Text Messages.* D. H. Crocker. STD 11, RFC 822, August 1982. `ftp://ftp.internic.net/rfc/rfc822.txt`
>
> These documents are also included on the CD-ROM that accompanies this book.

```
$HttpHeader = "HTTP/1.0 200 OK";
$ContentType = "Content-type: text/html";

print "$HttpHeader\r\n";    # note the \r\n sequence!
print "$ContentType\r\n\r\n";

print "<http><head><title>NPH-CGI Hello World</title></
head>\n";
print "<body><h1>Hello, World!</h1></body></html>\n"
```

It really is that simple. Just make sure that you send the response header before anything else, that your newlines are carriage-return/linefeed pairs, and that the last line of the header is followed by two newlines.

The most common response status code that you will send is "200," which essentially means, "Okay, here's the data you requested." The other response codes defined in HTTP/1.0 are listed in table 8.1. For full definitions and usage guidelines, see the HTTP Internet Draft referenced previously.

Table 8.1

HTTP Response Status Codes

Status Code	Reason Phrase
Informational 1xx	
Undefined in HTTP/1.0	
Successful 2xx	
200	OK
201	Created
202	Accepted
204	No Content
Redirection 3xx	
300	Multiple Choices
301	Moved Permanently
302	Moved Temporarily
304	Not Modified
Client Error 4xx	
400	Bad Request
401	Unauthorized
403	Forbidden
404	Not Found

Status Code	Reason Phrase
Server Error 5xx	
500	Internal Server Error
501	Not Implemented
502	Bad Gateway
503	Service Unavailable

Now that you know how to do this, you're probably saying, "Well that's cool, but what do I do with it?"

I'm glad you asked.

How Server-Push Works

In a nutshell, server-push works by using an NPH-CGI program to push successive frames of an animation from the server to the client, one after the other, without waiting for subsequent requests from the client.

Server-push animation works with the special MIME-type, `multipart/x-mixed-replace`. The `multipart` content type is a method of encapsulating several entities (which the MIME specification calls "body parts") in the body of one message. The `x-mixed-replace` sub-type is an invention of Netscape (now also supported by a few other browsers) that enables each encapsulated entity to replace the previous one on a dynamic page.

The main part of the document is called a *container* because it is used to hold the contents of the subordinate entities. The container document uses boundary strings to delimit the individual entities so that they can be extracted by the client.

The correct syntax for the container's `Content-type:` declaration is as follows:

```
Content-type: multipart/x-mixed-
replace;boundary="random-string"
```

The boundary string is used with two leading dash characters (e.g., `--random-string`) to introduce the MIME-header of each subordinate entity; and with two leading *and* two trailing dashes to terminate the entire container (e.g., `--random-string--`). The following is an example of how a server-push stream should look:

```
HTTP/1.0 200 OK
Content-type: multipart/x-mixed-replace;boundary="foo"

--foo
Content-type: text/plain

Text string 1.

--foo

Content-type: text/plain

Text string 2.

--foo
Content-type: text/plain

Text string 3.

--foo
Content-type: text/plain

Text string 4.

--foo--
```

The boundary string, with its leading and trailing double-dashes, must be on a line by itself set off from the rest of the stream by carriage-return/linefeed pairs. The client software will expect this, and it is required by the RFC 1591 MIME specification. In other words, the preceding example would be coded with a string like this:

```
print "\r\n--foo\r\n"
```

and

```
print "\r\n--foo--\r\n"
```

The string used for the boundary needs to be one that is not likely to be found in the encapsulated entities, to avoid having the entities inadvertently split up. Such a problem is not likely with graphics files, of course, but you need to watch out for it—especially if your graphics files contain comment blocks.

Now, with all this background information, you're probably anxious to see it all come together. The next section presents a full working example of server-push.

Warning

Potential NCSA Bug?

According to Netscape's server-push document, there was a bug in an unspecified version of the NCSA httpd server that prevented the server from accepting a Content-type string with a space in it anywhere except directly after the colon. Obviously, this would be a potential problem if you wanted a space after the semicolon (";") and before the boundary declaration.

Netscape's statement appears dubious to me—after all, the server is not supposed to do anything with an NPH header anyway.

I have not been able to duplicate the anomalous behavior; in fact, my version of the NCSA server (version 1.5) works fine with a space after the semicolon. But just in case there was a bug in a previous version, I have left out the space in all the examples.

Procedure: A Complete Server-Push Example

First, you'll need a set of graphics to animate. I used Photoshop 3.0 to create a set of small pictures of Beethoven rolling inside a ball. Figure 8.1 shows all the frames of the animation.

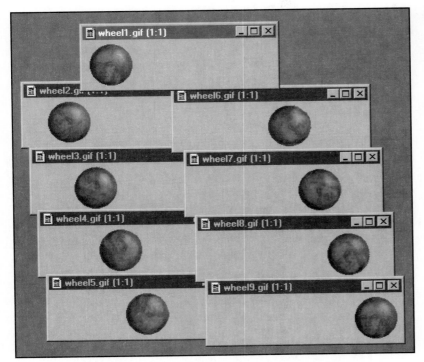

Figure 8.1

Individual files for animation frames.

It's very important to keep these images small. The larger they are, the more bandwidth they take, and the longer the user will have to wait for each frame of animation to display. The easiest way to keep your GIF files small is to use the smallest palette you can for the image. Sixteen-color GIF files are *much* smaller than their 256-color counterparts.

I saved each of these images as GIF files with transparent backgrounds so that they would appear to rotate when animated. Adobe's GIF89a plug-in for Photoshop works well for this.

Tools
Photoshop
GIF89a plug-in
NPH-CGI program (follows)

An NPH-CGI Program for Server-Push Animation

Now, you'll need an NPH-CGI program to send the individual GIF files to the client. This section presents a program that reads a list of GIF files and pushes them out to the client using server-push. First, though, you need to be forewarned of a danger.

It may be quite tempting to write your server-push program in one of the Unix shells. There are even some examples of shell scripts on the Net that implement server-push.

The problem is that most shells are not sophisticated enough to know when the client disconnects from the server and they may continue to run, needlessly wasting resources. This is especially serious when the animation is coded to run endlessly.

The Perl example presented here should serve well as a template for just about any animation you may need to do.

What follows is a skeleton NPH-CGI Perl program that reads a list of file names from a text file and sends them as parts in a multipart MIME stream, as documented earlier in this chapter.

```perl
#!/usr/bin/perl

# nph-push.pl.cgi
#
# (c) 1996 William E. Weinman
#
# Generic CGI Push Animation
#

# the list of files to animate
$listfile = "animate.lst";

# the delay time between each file (can be less than a
➥second)
```

```perl
$delaytime = .5;

# response header stuff
$httpokay = "HTTP/1.0 200 Okay";
$ct = "Content-type:";
$cl = "Content-length:";
$boundary = "foo";
$ctmixed = "$ct multipart/x-mixed-replace;
➥boundary=$boundary";
$ctgif = "$ct image/gif";

$| = 1; # force a flush after each print

# read the list
open(LISTFILE, "<$listfile");
@infiles = <LISTFILE>; # is perl suave, or what?
close(LISTFILE);

# send the main http response header
print "$httpokay\n";
print "$ctmixed\n\n";

# main loop
foreach $i (@infiles)
  {
  chop $i; # lose the trailing '\n'
  $clsz = (-s $i);  # the size of the gif file
  # inside boundaries have a leading '--'
  print "\n--$boundary\n";
  if ($sleepokay)
    {
    # this is perl's famous less-than-one-second sleep
    ➥trick! ;^)
    select(undef, undef, undef, $delaytime);
    }
  else
    { $sleepokay = 1;}
  # uncomment this to send the filename--useful for
  # debugging, harmless to the browser, and a bad
  # idea for production use, because it gives a poten
  ➥tial
  # intruder useful information.
  #
  # print "X-Filename $i\n";

  # the content-length header may be required by HTTP
  ➥1.1,
  # it's optional in HTTP 1.0, but some browsers will
  # use it to display progress to the user if you send
  ➥it.
  print "$cl $clsz\n";
  print "$ctgif\n\n";
```

```
# now send the GIF, keeping it open for a minimum
# amount of time.
open (INFILE, "<$i");
sysread(INFILE, $buffer, $clsz);
close(INFILE);
syswrite(STDOUT, $buffer, $clsz);
}

# the trailing boundary with both '--' indicators
print "\n--$boundary--\n";
```

A couple of things in the Perl source for this example are worth noting. One is the assignment, $¦ = 1;, near the top of the program. This is the Perlism for flushing an output stream buffer after each write to it.

It is necessary to flush the output stream buffers because most operating systems buffer their output most of the time. That means that the system may decide that it's more efficient to hold on to part of the output for a second or two, waiting for a more convenient time to send it. If it decides to wait in the middle of one of your graphic files, it will create a jumpy or wavy effect on the screen. The solution to this problem is to always flush the buffers after each write operation. In Perl, you do that by setting the special variable "$|" to a value other than zero.

Also notice the line select(undef, undef, undef, $delaytime);. This a neat Perl trick for getting a sub-one-second sleep. It's ugly, but it works well, and there's nothing like it in C or *sh*. sleep usually works only on one-second boundaries, so a command like sleep 1 will sleep for an unpredictable amount of time between zero and one second.

You can see the animation in action at http://www.weinman.com/wew/webanim/push-beethoven.html.

In light of the recent support for animated GIFs in Netscape 2.0 and later, server-push is not commonly used anymore for simple animations like the one in the previous example. Server-push is not dead yet, however—it is still useful for anything that must change continuously, based on external events.

One example of animating dynamic content is a clock. Server-push is ideal for this; in fact, this is an application that cannot be done with plain text and HTML.

Procedure: A Web-Based Digital Clock

The Web-based digital clock is built in two parts. One part is a program called *giftxt*, which is written in C. *giftxt* takes a string of text and builds a GIF on-the-fly out of corresponding characters. It uses the *gd*[3] library to manipulate the GIF file.

The other part of the program is written in Perl. It gets the current time from the system and calls *giftxt* with the appropriate string. By separating the program into two logical divisions, you end up with tools that you can reuse later for other purposes.

Tools

gd library (`http://www.boutell.com/gd/`)

ANSI C Compiler (e.g. gcc, `ftp://prep.ai.mit.edu/pub/gnu/gcc-2.7.2.tar.gz`)

giftxt program (follows)

GIFs (for numbers)

nph-clock.pl.cgi program (also follows)

The Text-to-GIF Converter

The *giftxt* program was written as a reusable tool. It takes a string of text, and creates a GIF by concatenating individual GIFs that are identified by each letter in the string. The source code in C for the *giftxt* program follows:

```
/*
 * giftxt.c
 *
 * (c) 1996 William E. Weinman
 *
 * create a gif of a text string.
 * for each character in the input string,
 * find a file named <character>.gif and
 * concatenate it to the output gif.
 *
 * uses Tom Boutell's gd library for handling the gifs.
 *
 * usage: giftxt <string> <outfile>
 *    omit <outfile> to use stdout
 *
```

```
 * compile:
 *   gcc -o giftxt giftxt.c -lgd -lm
 *
 * 1.1 -- wew - rewritten to dynamically allocate size
➥of gif and
 *              to maintain transparency
 * 1.0 -- wew - release for The CGI Book
 */

#include <gd/gd.h>
#include <stdio.h>

#define max(a,b) ((a > b) ? (a) : (b))

char infile[] = "X.gif";

void writegif(char * outfile, gdImagePtr img);
void makexcolor(gdImagePtr img);

int main(int argc, char ** argv)
{
static gdImagePtr imgout, imgin, imghold;
FILE * fpin;
int i;
int lastwidth;
char * instr;
char * outfile = NULL;

int curwidth = 0;
int curheight = 0;

if (argv[1]) instr = argv[1];
else exit(0); /* no input? bail. */

if (argv[2]) outfile = argv[2];

for (i = 0; instr[i]; i++)
  {
  *infile = instr[i];
  fpin = fopen(infile, "rb");
  if (fpin)
    {
    imgin = gdImageCreateFromGif(fpin);
    fclose(fpin);

    /* figure the new size */
    lastwidth = curwidth;
    curwidth += imgin->sx;
    curheight = max(curheight, imgin->sy);

    /* build the holding tank */
    if(imgout)
      {
      /* destroy and recreate in new size */
```

```
            gdImageDestroy(imghold);
            imghold = gdImageCreate(curwidth, curheight);
            makexcolor(imghold);
            gdImageCopy(imghold, imgout, 0, 0, 0, 0, imgout-
            ➡>sx,
                imgout->sy);
            gdImageCopy(imghold, imgin, imgout->sx, 0, 0, 0,
                imgin->sx, imgin->sy);
          }
        else
          {
          imghold = gdImageCreate(imgin->sx, imgin->sy);
          makexcolor(imghold);
          gdImageCopy(imghold, imgin, 0, 0, 0, 0, imgin-
          ➡>sx,
            imgin->sy);
          }

      /* create a new output image */
      if (imgout) gdImageDestroy(imgout);
      imgout = gdImageCreate(curwidth, curheight);
      makexcolor(imgout);
      gdImageCopy(imgout, imghold, 0, 0, 0, 0, imghold-
      ➡>sx,
        imghold->sy);

      /* clean up */
      gdImageDestroy(imgin);

      }
    }
writegif(outfile, imgout);
gdImageDestroy(imgout);

}

void makexcolor(gdImagePtr img)
{
int xcolor;

xcolor = gdImageColorAllocate(img, 0, 0, 0);
gdImageColorTransparent(img, xcolor);
}

void writegif(char * outfile, gdImagePtr img)
{
FILE * fpout;

fpout = outfile ? fopen(outfile, "wb") : stdout;
gdImageGif(img, fpout);
if (fpout == stdout) fflush(stdout);
else fclose(fpout);
}
```

The *giftxt* program was written with special attention to its flexibility in a variety of environments. *giftxt* can be used as a simple command-line tool for making GIFs of text strings; or it can be used as a "filter," taking a string in its input stream, and sending the GIF in its output stream. This flexibility is accomplished in the *writegif()* routine at the end of the source file. It checks to see if the output stream is *stdout*, in which case the program assumes it is being used as a filter; otherwise, it is probably writing to a file.

giftxt is also careful to preserve the transparency of the original GIF files. You will find this important when you use patterned backgrounds on your Web pages. The transparency bit in a GIF file's palette allows the patterned background to show through selected parts of the image.

For the clock, I created a series of GIFs of each of the numbers and the colon. Figure 8.2 shows these GIFs individually.

Figure 8.2

The individual numbers for the clock.

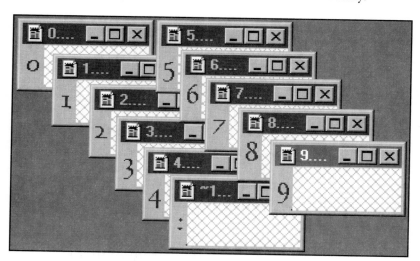

The Perl Part of the Clock

Once you have the text-to-GIF converter and the individual numbers in hand, the rest of the clock is implemented with server-push techniques learned earlier in this chapter. The Perl code for the clock follows:

```
#!/usr/bin/perl

# nph-clock.pl.cgi
#
```

```
# (c) 1996 William E. Weinman
#
# a server-push clock
#
# version 1.0 -- first release
#

# response header stuff
$httpokay = "HTTP/1.0 200 Okay";
$boundary = "foo";
$ct = "Content-type:";
$ctmixed = "$ct multipart/x-mixed-replace;
➥boundary=$boundary";

select STDOUT; $¦ = 1; # force a flush after each print

# send the main http response header
print "$httpokay\r\n";
print "$ctmixed\r\n\r\n";

# main loop
while (1) {
  # inside boundaries have a leading '--'
  print "\r\n--$boundary\r\n";
  if ($sleepokay) { sleep 1; }
  else { $sleepokay = 1;}

  print "content-type: image/gif\r\n\r\n";

  # now call giftxt with the time string
  system("giftxt `date +%H:%M:%S`");

  # for folks who forget they're connected . . .
  ($count++ == 60) && last;
}

# the trailing boundary with both '--' indicators
print "\r\n--$boundary--\r\n";
```

This Perl code works essentially like the generic server-push in the skeleton NPH-CGI program presented earlier in this chapter. The differences are in the *sleep* statement, which counts out one-second intervals, and the *system()* call, which calls the *giftxt* program presented earlier.

You can see the Web Clock in action at http://www.weinman.com/wew/webanim/push-clock.html.

Tip

Notice the line that says, ($count++ == 60) && last;. This code will cut off the clock after one minute. It's important to realize that a user may bring this page up and then go on a cruise to Alaska, forgetting that they have an open connection to your server. Whenever you create a server-push that loops indefinitely, remember to make an escape-hatch like this.

Conclusion

Server-push can be a useful tool for real-time dynamically updated animations. The techniques described in this chapter will enable you to create animated displays that contain any sort of information that you can generate as a graphic.

In this chapter, you have learned how to create server-push animations using NPH-CGI. You have also learned the necessary parts of the HTTP protocol, the required MIME extensions, and specific techniques for creating server-push code in Perl.

In addition, you have seen a real-world example of creating dynamic content on the fly with the Web Clock. This includes a useful tool in the *giftxt* program for creating GIF files in real time.

Recently, browser manufacturers discovered an alternative to server-push in the GIF89a specification. Although animated GIF files are not new—they've been around since 1989—they are new to the World Wide Web. The next chapter deals with techniques for creating them, and the unique options that they open for the Web designer.

For more details on CGI programming, see the author's book, *The CGI Book* (New Riders, ISBN: 1-56205-571-2).

---

[1] MIME is a method of defining and extending message types. It was originally created for use with internet mail, but has since been adapted to many other uses, including the World Wide Web.

---

[2] HTTP is currently under a massive revision process. The version of HTTP discussed here is HTTP/1.0, the latest version as of the time this was written.

---

[3] *gd* is a library of routines for manipulating GIF files. It was written by Tom Boutell, and is distributed free at `http://www.boutell.com/gd/`.

by Peter Chen

Author Biography

Peter Chen received his B.A. in Biochemistry and B.M. in Music Education from Oberlin College in 1995. Currently, he works conjunctively for the Stanford University Libraries and the Department of Biological Sciences as a consultant and developer of technological applications for the academic environment, including Web-based education.

On a Macintosh clone, Peter uses BBEdit for HTML authoring, Photoshop and FreeHand for graphical editing, and Opcode's Studio Vision for all his sound applications. On the receiving end, he uses the RealAudio Plug-In, LiveUpdate's Crescendo MIDI Plug-In, and Netscape Navigator 3.0 with its LiveAudio enhancement features.

A classically trained musician, Peter has been composing and working with computer-based music and MIDI over the past 10 years, and maintains a studio at home using equipment by Alesis, Emu, Korg, Lexicon, Opcode, Roland, Tascam, Yamaha, and Zeta.

Adding Sound and Special Effects to Animated Pages

Adding excellent sound effects to Web pages is what separates the presentation posterboards from the true multimedia experiences on the Web. Whether it's elevator music backgrounds or robot gurgles and explosions, having good sounds will capture your audiences' attention. Consider how the best computer games use sound effects and background music to enhance the experience. Without great sounds, most audiences quickly lose interest or their eyes just bug out from having nothing to do other than stare at the screen.

Creating good music and sound effects can be a daunting task, depending on how much effort you are willing to put into it. Given the effort that you have put into your animation, you should consider the visual experience as only half of it. Animation has a long history of incorporating all kinds of zany sounds and background music. (Remember the Road Runner cartoons? No speech, just lots of sound effects and music.)

Advertisers routinely pays thousands of dollars in licensing fees for songs or sound clips that people learn to associate with a particular product (like the Pentium ad). Suppose all your animation pages loaded up with a short five- or six-note jingle? Pretty soon your audience would learn to associate that sound with your work.

In this chapter, you will explore how audio has been developed for use on the Internet, how to create and edit sound files, and how to best use them to enhance your Web animation.

Computer Audio Basics: Digital Audio and MIDI

Audio designers are faced with two basic options when it comes to delivering sounds via the Web—digital audio or MIDI. *Digital audio* is the more familiar medium by which sound waves are recorded or *sampled* into a digital format and recorded on media like a disk. Digital compact discs, or "CDs," are a popular representative of a format for playing back recorded digital audio. Digital audio tape, or DAT, is another format for digital audio recording that enables audio-philes and home studio engineers the benefits of high-quality digital recording that, until recently, has been considerably expensive and out of reach. Instead of DAT, it is likely much more convenient for you to record directly to hard disk, which is the topic of this chapter.

In recent years, digital audio recording and home computing have undergone a renaissance that has benefited by some of the same innovations in technology. Since 1990, most home computers purchased have included sound boards or digital signal processing (DSP) chips that enable users to record digital audio directly to their hard or media drives. Putting such sophisticated sound cards and processors into computers has helped to fuel the boom in multimedia games and entertainment. Digital recording is simple because it is almost exactly the same as making tape recordings.

MIDI (Musical Instrument Digital Interface) is actually a language that has been developed and used by electronic musicians since the early 1980s. Originally designed to allow digital instruments and components (such as synthesizers, sequencers, and drum machines) produced by different manufacturers to "talk" to each other, today's computers now come with inexpensive DSP synthesizer chips that respond and communicate in the MIDI language. Despite the fact that many computers speak MIDI and come with synthesizer chips, they are more frequently used for storing and editing MIDI files composed on electronic musical instruments. Electronic musicians playing synthesizers or drum machines can record or "sequence" MIDI data on the computer via a MIDI interface, which is a box or card that connects serially to the computer on one end, and provides ports to connect a five-pin MIDI cable to the instrument.

By now you may be wondering, "What exactly are DSP chips and what do they do?" Or, "What is sampling, and does this MIDI thing mean that now I've got to learn another computer language?" Rest assured that these concepts will be explained thoroughly in the sections that follow. The important thing to recognize is that digital audio and MIDI represent two distinctly different types of sound mediums. This distinction is similar to the difference between digital video and animation.

Advantages and Disadvantages of Digital Audio and MIDI

The digital audio and MIDI means of delivering audio each have their advantages and disadvantages. One of the benefits of digital audio is that you can have absolute control of the sounds that your audience will hear. That is to say, "what you hear is what they'll get." This is not the case with MIDI, however. Because different manufacturers put different DSP synthesizer chips in their computers or cards, you might get a rich piano sound on one computer while another plays out the sounds like a dinky piano. (And remember that MIDI sounds are synthesized, meaning that they are generated from raw data. You won't be able to do voice-overs. Synthesis will be examined in more depth later in this chapter.)

Digital audio is also a simpler concept to handle for most users because all you have to do is press record, play, and stop. MIDI, on the other hand, requires you to compose your own MIDI files from raw sounds—which is easy enough if you just want to throw in special effects—but the language was designed to enable musicians to work easily with rich, complex compositions.

On the downside for digital audio, files can be very large and take a long time to download. This makes them hard to play in real time along with your animation. On the other hand, there is also a new type of technology called *streaming* (discussed at

Note

New technology for the Web develops fast. At the time of this writing, Netscape is releasing beta test versions of their 3.0 Navigator software with an enhancement feature called LiveAudio, which should be able to play streamed audio of higher sound quality. This streamed audio is embedded directly into the Web page.

greater length later in this chapter) that allows large sound files to be delivered in smaller packets that are somewhat seamlessly reassembled by a plug-in application and played with a slight delay. Currently, however, the audio quality of streaming sounds more like an AM radio (in other words, it can be fuzzy and lacking in stereo quality) and is prone to disruption on computers that have slower processors or are running through modems slower than 28.8 Kbps. Another current obstacle is that you also need to have a server that has software that delivers streaming. You'll have to see your system administrator about that.

MIDI files are compact and the sound resolution is generally quite good. Live Updates' plug-in helper application called Crescendo enables you to embed MIDI files in your Web pages and play the sounds back without delay. Crescendo will be discussed at greater length later in this chapter.

Table 9.1 compares selected features of digital audio and MIDI.

Table 9.1

Features of Digital Audio Recording vs. MIDI

Feature	Digital Audio	MIDI
Reproduction	"What you hear is what they'll get"	Dependent on DSP chip on computer
Resolution	Prone to compromises, especially if streamed	Very crisp and clear
Ease of use	Just click and record	Need some basic knowledge of synthesis
Memory requirements	Can be very large	Low memory usage
Server requirements	Requires server software	None
Coordinates with animation?	Only if streamed (and with slight delays)	Easy to time and synchronize

Digital Audio Recording

Digital audio is a technological medium that has grown mainly out of the demands of the music and recording entertainment industry. Although digital CDs have been available for over 10 years now, high-quality digital audio recording for home users has faced limitations until recently. The issue has largely been about the expense of disk space; only lately has the cost of read/write magnetic disk space come down, fueling a boom in disk-intensive multimedia production.

Read/write optical disks, like CDs, until very recently were relatively expensive for most users. A CD holds about 650 MB of data, which translates to approximately 70 minutes of stereo recording at 44.1 kHz. Over-the-counter music CDs that have already been "burned" with information are pretty cheap for the number of megabytes of information that they carry; however, unless you are churning them out in mass quantity, the money that you invest in the equipment to burn your own recordings is a waste, particularly for the purposes of adding sound to your animations.

Sampling

Digital audio recording is interchangeably referred to as "sampling." Modern rap music is notorious for its use of digital samples. Though sampling and playback are usually done with professional audio equipment, a couple important concepts from sampling carry over into computer-based digital audio recording. These include the following:

- Sample depth
- Sample rates
- Disk space considerations

> **Note**
>
> Digital audio recording is also sometimes also called "tapeless recording" because of its roots in the digital music realm, where musicians made short digital recordings of sounds like screams, belches, or bird chirps, and played them back in their compositions.

The sample depth refers to the number of separate dynamic levels at which the audio sample is recorded. Essentially, *sample depth* is how many different degrees of separation exist between the loudest and quietest sounds sampled. Audiophiles typically measure these dynamic differences in terms of decibel (dB) range. An 8-bit sample translates into 256 steps or a 48 dB range difference, whereas a 16-bit sample represents 65,536 steps or a 96 dB range. (Note that a larger decibel range does not mean that the sample is louder.) A 16-bit sample depth has about the same quality as CD recordings.

The *sample rate* is a measure of the frequency or rate at which music is recorded and played back. Without going into an intricate discussion on acoustical physics, the important thing to know is that the human ear can discern sounds between 20 Hz and 22 kHz. A Hertz (Hz) is a unit of measurement meaning "cycles per second." A kilohertz (kHz) is equal to 1,000 Hz.

Although the highest note on the piano has a frequency of 4.186 kHz, simultaneously heard sounds (known as overtones) in the higher frequency range color and flavor the sound. For a sound to be recorded, the sample rate has to be at least twice the rate of the highest frequency that you want to record, so a high-quality recording usually has a sample rate of 44.1 kHz. As mentioned earlier, this is the typical rate at which CDs are recorded.

So a top-quality recording has a sample depth of 16-bits and a sample rate of 44.1 kHz, but how much disk space does that take? In raw terms, a 16-bit sample taken 44,100 times per second in stereo (two channels) equals approximately 10.6 megabytes per minute. Even a five-second sound clip comes close to taking up 1 megabyte. Because it helps to make considerations about disk space and download time for your audio samples, it is important to understand the concepts of sample rate and sample depth in order to optimize your samples.

If you feel that your sample does not need so wide a dynamic range, you could reduce your sample depth to 8 bits. The drawback is that it may sound "tinnier," like an AM radio. If your sample doesn't have a lot of complex sounds, you could reduce the sample rate to 22, 11, or even 7 kHz. The downside to recording at lower frequencies is that your sample could end up sounding flat or "woofier" because the sparkle of overtones are diminished. You could probably get away with a lower sample rate if you were recording a simple bass line.

Another consideration concerning sound quality is whether you want to record in mono or in stereo. Higher-quality recordings done in stereo have two separate channels for left and right speakers, giving a more dimensional effect to samples. Recording in mono sometimes sounds fine, however, and it cuts disk space in half. Table 9.2 shows how all these factors affect storage space.

Table 9.2

Storage Requirements for Uncompressed Digital Audio Files

Sample Rate (kHz)	Sample Depth (bits)	Channels	Bytes per minute of recorded sound
44.1	16	stereo	10,584,000
44.1	16	mono	5,292,000
44.1	8	stereo	5,292,000
44.1	8	mono	2,646,000
22.05	16	stereo	5,292,000
22.05	16	mono	2,646,000
22.05	8	stereo	2,646,000
22.05	8	mono	1,323,000
11.025	16	stereo	2,646,000
11.025	16	mono	1,323,000
11.025	8	stereo	1,323,000
11.025	8	mono	661,500
7.418*	16	stereo	1,780,320
7.418	16	mono	890,182
7.418	8	stereo	890,182
7.418	8	mono	445,091

*Sample rates below 11 kHz are generally not recommended for musical sounds. However, spoken words are not rich with harmonic overtones the way musical sounds or singing voices are. Therefore, it is not recommended that anything other than speech be recorded below 11 kHz.

Sound Editing Software

There are a number of software packages for the Mac and PC that will be discussed later. At the very low end are packages like Sound Recorder (comes with Windows), which will record a snippet through a microphone.

A better basic package simply enables you to record and play back one or two tracks (stereo) and possibly vary the sample rate and depth. Even if you are planning on getting into mixing flashy or high-quality sound files, you can get a good multitrack program for a fairly inexpensive price. Using a sound editor to edit sounds is analogous to using an image editor like Photoshop to edit image files. In the more sophisticated programs, you get a graphic representation of the sound waves that you can cut, paste, and modify with effects. Recording in multitrack enables you to record and isolate separate sounds (much like the way you can work with layers in Photoshop) for modification and mix them to a balance that satisfies your tastes.

The graphical representation of sound is always presented as amplitude (waveform signal strength) versus time (see fig. 9.1). Because a high-resolution sample can oscillate up to 22.05 times per second, high-end editors enable you to zoom in closely for editing. Effects that can be added range from dynamic effects like sound amplification, audible compression and expansion, and equalization, to delay-based effects like reverberation, echo, pitch bending, flanging, and even inversions. You can also *interpolate*, or change the pitch of a sample without changing the speed, or change the speed without changing the pitch.

Figure 9.1

The typical graphical representation of a single sample waveform— a spoken voice.

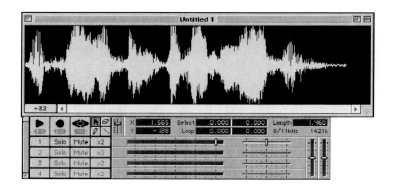

Sound File Formats

No doubt you already have some experience in dealing with different file formats in other mediums like word processing, graphics, or VRML. Sound files also deal with a multitude of formats or MIME (Multipurpose Internet Mail Extension) coding that have been developed by the hardware and software manufacturers. Although at least 20 different audio encoding formats for digital audio exist today, only a few of the more commonly used formats on the Web will be discussed in this chapter.

Audio Interchange File Format (AIFF)

Extension codes: audio/x-aiff .aif .aiff .aifc

This format was originally developed by Apple engineers and is now primarily used on Macs and Silicon Graphics workstations. The Mac operating system readily supports the playing of AIFF files, which is the preferred format for many Mac users. AIFF is very flexible in supporting mono and multiple channel recording, as well as different sample rates and depths.

Another nice feature for Mac users is that AIFF files can easily be compressed and played back directly in a format known as AIFF-C or AIFC using MACE (Macintosh Audio Compression and Expansion) at a ratio of 3:1 or 6:1. Compression playing will lose some resolution, but it is a convenient option for the space-savvy.

Windows WAVE Format

Extension codes: audio/x-wav .wav

This is Microsoft Windows and IBM's answer to Apple's AIFF format introduced with Windows 3.1. WAVE was originally developed for use with the Sound Recorder package included with the 3.1 OS applications. Using Microsoft's Sound Recorder is a simple way to record digital audio; however, you don't have much control of sample rate, depth, or many editing features. .WAV files are very common to find over the Internet and they also come in a variety of compression formats.

Sun Audio (AU) AKA NeXT Audio File Format

Extension codes: audio/basic .au

Also known as µ-law or a-law, this format has been primarily used by Unix users on Sun or NeXT workstations. It differs from the other formats by encoding the data logarithmically, as opposed to linearly. The advantage of this is that it spaces the sample depth levels further apart, allowing an 8-bit sample to have greater dynamic range. The downside of logarithmic data encoding is that recordings are prone to sounding noisy, meaning they frequently pick up external sounds.

System 7 or SND Files

Extension codes: audio/x-snd .snd

This is another Mac sound file format that is divided into two types—type 1 and type 2. Type 1 files are typically the system beep and short alert sounds that the Mac produces. Type 2 files were originally designed for use with Hypercard, but they have been carried over to being used on the Net on some occasions.

Sound Blaster VOC

Extension codes: audio/x-voc .voc

Because of the great popularity of Sound Blaster media cards being used in PCs, it is not at all uncommon to find files over the Internet that have the .voc extension. It is generally used best by Sound Blaster-compatible hardware; however, some software packages exist that can decode and play .voc files.

RealAudio RA Files

Extension codes: audio/x-pn-realaudio-plugin .ram .ra .pnre .pnra

Digital audio streaming, discussed in greater detail later in this chapter, is one of the more exciting new technologies available on the Web these days. Streaming enables developers to provide large sound files that can be heard in almost real time along with animation. Live radio broadcasts already are being streamed across the Net, as well as interactive demonstrations enhanced by streamed audio. Lo-fi quality sounds and the fact that it is processor-intensive are a couple drawbacks to streaming. When done in conjunction with animation, streamed audio competes for processor time, and things are bound to sound and look herky-jerky.

> **Note**
>
> It is not necessary to go into other existing formats too far because these are perhaps the most commonly used today. But if you are interested, Norman Franke, the creator of a wonderful little Mac sound application called SoundApp (included on the CD-ROM) has a resource page at the following:
>
> `http://www.bitnova.com/franke/`
> `SoundApp/formats.html`

Digital Audio for PCs

Historically, PCs possess that cumbersome characteristic of not all having the same features. This spawned a huge industry of third-party developers for all sorts of peripherals, such as sound cards. These packages, such as Creative Labs' Wave Studio, come bundled with software for sound recording and editing (some are pretty good).

Because there are so many different media/sound packages available to PC users, no single all-encompassing sound editing software application is recommended here. The bundled editor that you get is probably the best to use with that package. Most of them conform to enable you 16-bit sampling depth and sample rates up to 44.1 kHz. At the very least, Windows 3.1 and Windows 95 both come with Sound Recorder, which makes uneditable .wav files.

Although new PCs come bundled with multimedia packages with sound cards and software, owners of older PCs have many options when it comes to adding a sound card. As mentioned previously, the sound cards that you buy today will nearly always support CD-quality audio. Many sound cards also advertise the fact that they support "wavetable synthesis" or are "MIDI-compatible." Some cards are also sold as MIDI interface cards that enable you to communicate between your computer and a MIDI instrument, like a synthesizer, via a 5-pin MIDI cable. Connecting a synthesizer keyboard to your computer enables you to play and sequence sounds that come from the wavetable synthesis DSP chip. We'll explore these features when we discuss synthesis and MIDI.

If you don't have a good sound editor or you are not happy with the one that came with your PC sound card, there are a number of archives available on the Web full of Windows 3.1 and Windows 95 freeware or shareware. One such repository is the Shareware Music Machine (http://hitsquad.thehub.com.au/smm/edit/welcome.html). A good shareware editor for Windows 95 users is Sound Gadget Pro—a 32-bit editor that supports Win95 features and gives you a number of audio effects that can be applied separately to each of the stereo channels. Sound Gadget Pro can also be found at the following:

`http://www.cs.man.ac.uk/~magnayn/SGPro.html`

Digital Audio for Macs

Most Macs, like Power PCs and recent Performas and Powerbooks, as well as older AV-Quadras, support 16-bit digital sound. Also, virtually all Macs built since 1991 have ports for microphones, which allow for direct audio input, depending on what sort of drivers and software are used. It is also possible to upgrade some older Macs by adding a third-party digitizing board that will give you 16-bit sampling

Note

Many PCs bought in recent years come with sound cards that also support 16-bit audio. For PCs without 16-bit capabilities, a number of inexpensive multimedia packages, such as Sound Blaster, have 16-bit sound cards that provide PC users with high-quality audio. The Sound Blaster package is a popular option for many PC users who enjoy high-performance game playing.

Tip

Sound Gadget Pro for Windows works great for files in the .au format. It is shareware and available from the following:

`ftp://ftp.winsite.com/pub/pc/win95/desktop/sgpro101.zip`

quality. Macintosh has a long tradition of providing good built-in support for new users of sound software. The Sound Manager Extension is a utility that helps manage 16-to-8-bit file conversions and codec (compression/decompression) support, and enhances QuickTime's capabilities. Sound Manager is not actually a piece of software that you can manipulate; as an extension, it drives the audio software that you are running.

Apple's QuickTime 2.0 software is also designed to handle sound files in conjunction with the Sound Manager. QuickTime is Apple's multimedia driving software—what enables a Mac to display digital movies, animation, and sound. Running QuickTime movies and sounds as well as animation is still plenty heavy on processor use, so don't expect digital MTV videos on your computer screen yet. Still, Apple is firmly committed to develop, support, and improve the QuickTime platform for animation, video, and sound.

Say your Mac didn't come with a microphone input (that is, you have something before the Mac IIsi) or you have a Mac that only has 8-bit sound capabilities, and you'd like to do better. (A quick way to find out your computer's sound capabilities is to go to the Sound control panel [System 7.x] and to the "Sound Out" section. The maximum sample rates and depths allowed will be 22 kHz and 8-bits respectively.) Third-party NuBus cards that can bring your Mac up to specs are available. Some of these can be quite expensive—especially the models that are integrated video and audio capture cards. NuMedia makes an inexpensive card called the NuMedia 2 that can bring your older Mac up to par with an AV Mac. In fact, the synthesis DSP chip is the same as the one provided on AV models.

DA Software for the Mac

A good number of recording and editing software programs are freely available on the Net for Mac users. You can get pretty good results with freeware; however, once you've learned the tricks and played with more sophisticated studio recording software, you might not want to go back. As mentioned earlier, it is probably a good idea to familiarize yourself with programs like Sound Sculptor II 2.0 or Sound Effects 0.9.4, which give you a graphical representation of your sound file.

Some high-end sound editors popular with studio sound pros and hobbyists are Macromedia's SoundEdit 16 (part of the Macromedia Director Studio suite, but also sold separately for $399) and Opcode's Audioshop. Alaska software puts out DigiTrax, a PowerMac native editor that sells for about $150. Two other commercial editors available are Digidesign's Sound Designer II and OSC Media Products' Deck II.

A demo version of Sound Sculptor II 2.0 and Sound Effects 0.9.4 is included on the CD-ROM that accompanies this book. These two packages are fairly good sound editors that you can use almost right away. (The demo version of Sound Sculptor does not enable you to save files; however, by paying the $30 registration fee, you get full usage of a program that rivals high-end editors for nearly a steal.)

Sound Sculptor II 2.0 (demo)

Sound Sculptor II 2.0 is a fairly good four-track sound editor that comes with an array of really cool effects. Despite it being a demo kit, you can sample and play around with the effects, but you will not be able to save what you have done. The operations and controls may look a bit confusing if you have never operated a multitrack recorder—you will see two windows: one shows the waveforms and the other is a control panel. Having four tracks enables you to record four separate samples, edit and add effects to each one separately, and mix them down to a stereo or mono track. This also enables you to do a neat mixing trick called "Ping-Ponging," or adding more tracks on the empty tracks after mixing down, and then mixing them in. Theoretically, you could then infinitely layer your sounds.

The default sample rate is 44.1 kHz; however, you may sample as low as 5.563 kHz and as high as 48 kHz. You are also given options to sample in 16-bit or 8-bit, as well as in stereo or in mono. The Effects menu gives you 17 different ways to modify your sound, from fades and inversions to flanges and echoes.

The control panel enables you to select the tracks that you want to work with, adjust the volume or panning of individual tracks, or adjust the master volume. These types of features are a must-have for anyone who has been frustrated by a mix that had too much bass. The panel also gives you a level indicator to let you know if your signals are too weak or too strong. For in-depth information on using the controls, see the Read Me file on the CD.

Files can be saved in multitrack, stereo, or mono. You can also save them in AIFF, SND, Sound Designer II, or Sound Edit formats.

SoundEffects 0.9.4

SoundEffects is another recording program that is fully functional and available for use. (The author recommends that you do register all shareware. Paying the small shareware fee keeps you up to date with upgrades, bugs, and whatnot.) One cool feature of SoundEffects is that you can open as many channels as you need. (With these programs, channels and tracks mean the same thing.) You are only limited by the amount of memory that you can allocate to the program. In addition, there is also a catalog of more than 30 different effects to play with. The neat thing about this program is that the effects are actually plug-ins developed by other users of the program. If you ever tire of the effects that came with SoundEffects, check the archive at the following:

```
gopher://gopher.archive.umich.edu:7055/00/mac/sound/
soundutil/
```

Sample rates provided with SoundEffects are 44.1, 22.05, and 11.025 kHz and sample depth options are 16-bit and 6-bit. The one downside to SoundEffects is that it lacks mixing features. The author, however, has promised to make these features, as well as a spectrum analyzer, available in future releases.

Opening SoundEffects gives you the graphical main window (see fig. 9.2). The main editor window for SoundEffects enables you to manipulate your samples with more than 30 different plug-in effects. Clicking on the record button will open the recording panel, as shown in figure 9.3. Go through your settings and check to see that your microphone is connected. A nice feature of this program is the black strip that you see—this is a moving oscillograph. If the microphone is connected, tapping it should show some fuzzy green lines moving across the strip. When you click the record button, the lines turn red, indicating that the sound is being recorded. When the sound has been completely recorded, click on the stop button, and press play to see if you are satisfied with your sounds. Clicking record again will record over your sample.

When you are satisfied, click on Save. You will see a graphical representation of your sample in the main window. From there you can do whatever editing or effects processing that you need to do.

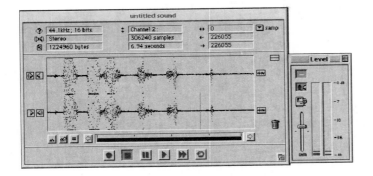

Figure 9.2

The main editor window for SoundEffects.

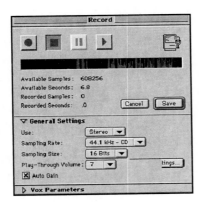

Figure 9.3

The Record window for SoundEffects.

Recording Directly from a CD on Your Mac

Inputting all your sounds via a microphone can be a pain, especially if you're sampling pre-recorded music. Anyone who has duplicated tapes knows that it is better to have a direct line input/output than to go via a microphone. You can also record sounds directly from your Mac CD-ROM drive from audio CDs. To do so, you have to change the input source from the microphone to the internal CD player via the Sound Manager. This can be done one of two ways. One way is to go into the Sound control panel and change the menu box to "Sound In." Clicking on the Options button reveals a window that enables you to switch to the internal CD as the sound source (see fig. 9.4). The second way to switch is from within the Sound Editor. Go under the Preferences menu (it might be a submenu under "File") and you will find an item labeled "Sound In" or "Recording Input." Again, there will be an Options button that will take you to the sound source window.

Figure 9.4

The sound source selection panel.

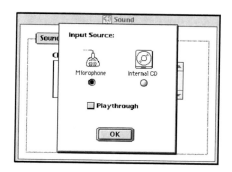

It should be noted that the practice of sampling directly from commercial recordings without proper authorization is a violation of copyright law and, although we know that the practice is fairly rampant, we cannot advocate such use. If you get a "cease and desist" letter from a lawyer representing ASCAP or some big record company, consider yourself previously warned. For years, musicians who sample short bits of other musicians' recordings for their own music have come under fire for violating copyright laws despite claims that they make about creative license. On the other hand, there are a number of commercially available CDs that are sold with the intention that you may sample and use their sounds. (They are actually made for sampling synthesizers to use, but the same technology carries over.) Many of these "sample CDs" jam-packed with sound effects can be found advertised in the backs of music magazines like *Electronic Musician* or *Keyboard*. They also can be purchased from music shops that sell electronic synthesizers and samplers.

More DA Sound Software for Macs

In addition to sound editing tools, it is also handy to have applications that are able to play and convert sound file formats. Because most Macintosh sound applications save to AIFF format, you may find it necessary to provide .wav and µ-law versions of your audio samples. SoundApp, which is included on the CD-ROM, is a handy application developed by Norman Franke that enables you to convert between the most common file formats.

Sound Machine by Rod Kennedy is another popular sound-playing application that also enables you to convert basic recordings and files. It gives you a handy control panel that looks like a cassette deck, as well as separate windows with sound file information. Older versions of Sound Machine also included a panel that enabled you to record samples via the

Note

Sound Machine can be found at the following Web site:

`http://online.anu.edu.au/rsise/teleng/Software/welcome.html`

microphone or CD drive. This microphone recording is gone
in version 2.6.2, though you can still import CD audio to AIFF
files.

Publishing Your Sound Files with Your Web Pages

Once you have your sound file and have uploaded it to your
Web server, referencing it in your Web page is essentially the
same as any hyperlink using the <A HREF></A> tag. An
audience user will have to download your sound and play it
with a helper application, so make considerations about the
size of your sound files.

The harsh reality of multimedia on the Web is that it is sort of
like buying a shiny new model Ferrari that has a real cool
picture on the box, and then finding that more than just a little
assembly is required. It is not as simple to deliver simulcast or
synchronized audio and visual media on the Web as it is to
make Macromedia Director movies. We'll get there eventually,
but for now there are cutting-edge tools that can help bring us
closer.

Streaming with RealAudio

The problem with publishing sound files on the Web in .aiff,
.wav, .au, or some other format is that these files have to be
downloaded and opened with some helper application like
Sound Machine. This shift in time makes it impractical to try
to play alongside a streamed animation embedded in your Web
page. The solution is to use an application to stream the audio
so that it plays nearly in real time with your animation. In
mid-1995, Progressive Networks released its first version of
RealAudio for both PCs and Macs. Since then, it released a
version 2.0 that has been accompanied by a number of developers releasing "Web broadcasts" via the RealAudio server
software. Streamed sounds aren't terrific. At 28.8 cubs, it
sounds a bit like AM radio. It is also prone to bumping, and
"fuzzes out" if you open some other processor-heavy task to
run simultaneously. Figure 9.5 provides a basic overview of
how streaming works.

Figure 9.5

Activating a RealAudio metafile.

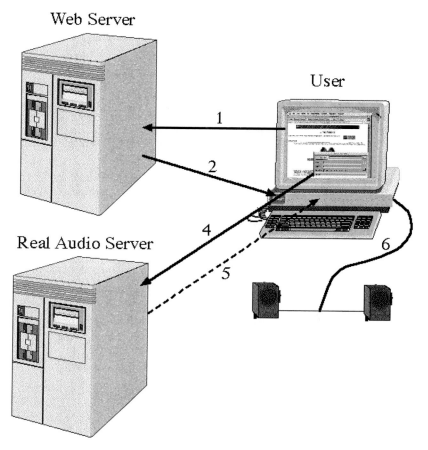

Here is what is happening in the figure:

1. The user clicks on a hyperlink that the Web server will access as a metafile.

2. The metafile sends back to the user's computer an URL address that identifies the location of the audio file on the RealAudio server.

3. The RealAudio Player is launched.

4. The RealAudio Player requests the audio file from the RealAudio Server.

5. The server delivers the audio file to the user's computer by stream.

6. The file is played over the speakers on the user's computer.

To get an idea of how well RealAudio works and whether streaming is a viable option, several radio stations and programs stream to you a virtual real-time broadcast or archives. The way streaming works is that sound data of any length is sent in small packets that are buffered (thus producing slight delays), seamed together, and dumped in a continuous stream. It is a lot like reading ticker tape.

Three key pieces of software make RealAudio streaming work:

- The RealAudio Player
- The RealAudio Encoder
- The RealAudio Server

The RealAudio Player is a freely distributed program that enables users to listen to streamed sound files or broadcasts. You open streamed files or broadcasts either by entering the URL (which begins with the protocol "pmn://") or by opening a metafile that identifies the URL (see fig. 9.6).

The RealAudio Encoder is another freely distributed program that enables you to convert your .aiff, .wav, or .au sound files to .ra streamed files. Finally, the RealAudio server is an application that allows your server to stream the sound file. RealAudio comes with a browser plug-in application that enables you to open links to streaming sites. A RealAudio metafile, (coded with extension .ra or .ram), which can be both anchored in your Web page or downloaded to the user's computer, sends a command to find the URL that sends the streamed audio file.

> **Note**
>
> RealAudio products are easily obtained by download from their home page at the following:
>
> `http://www.realaudio.com`

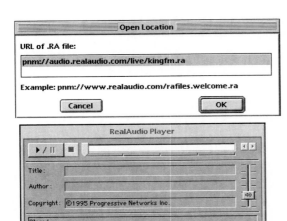

Figure 9.6

The RealAudio Player interface and a window indicating a RealAudio streaming URL.

Converting Sound Files to RealAudio Streams

Once you have your sound file in .aiff, .wav, or .au format, it is a simple task to convert it into a RealAudio stream by using the RealAudio Encoder (see fig. 9.7). The Encoder interface provides you with simple options to identify your stream file with a title, author, and copyright information. Depending on the platform that you are working on, the Encoder may also be able to convert files of different formats as well. The encoded file is compressed and ready to be delivered once it is uploaded to the server and referenced.

Figure 9.7

The RealAudio Encoder interface.

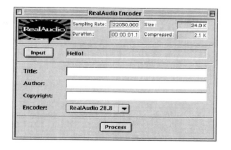

Referencing RealAudio streams is done with a metafile link put in your Web page. The contents of a metafile are simply a text reference that contains the address of the stream, such as the following:

```
pnm://yourserver.xxx/youraccount/
➥yourstream.ra
```

i.e., this is the only line you need to write in the file:

```
http://yourserver.xxx/youraccount/
➥metafile.ram
```

The metafile itself will be accessed by a hypertext reference in the Web page, such as the following:

```
<A HREF "http://yourserver.xxx/
➥youraccount/metafile.ram"> Stream

</H>
```

That is basically all you need to do to stream your audio. Once streamable, a user who has the RealAudio Player and browser plug-in loaded can go to your Web page, click on the metafile reference, and hear the streamed sounds while your Web animation is playing.

RealAudio Servers

The problem that presents itself now for most users is whether you have a server that runs the RealAudio server application. Progressive Networks is distributing two categories of server software. Because RealAudio has many commercial applications, the regular RealAudio Server program is sold by license mainly to businesses of various sizes. These packages enable you to deliver from five to 100 simultaneous streams. The Personal Server category enables individuals who are running their own servers to deliver one local and two Internet streams simultaneously. At the time of this writing, RealAudio has been distributing free beta test versions of the Personal Server software with the promise that the first 10,000 will be entitled to a free copy of the final release. Progressive Networks has also indicated that its suggested retail price for the released Personal Server will be $99.

> **Note**
>
> Information about the Personal Server can be obtained at the following:
>
> `http://www.realaudio.com/persserv/`

The Cutting Edge—Streaming via Netscape

At the time of this writing, Netscape is releasing beta versions of its 3.0 Navigator for testing. The new version of Netscape features enhancements for 3D VRML, video, and audio through packages called Live3D, LiveVideo, and LiveAudio, respectively. The idea is to enable Web authors to embed VRML, video, and audio files directly into their Web pages. Embedding is also a lot smoother than running a simultaneous RealAudio stream, so the audio quality is supposed to be much better. LiveAudio is also designed to stream .aiff, .wav, .au, as well as .mid (that's the MIDI extension) files so you don't have to convert files or modify servers.

One of the best features of the new Navigator with enhancements is that it saves the general public from the arduous task of searching for plug-ins and helper applications before they can view really cool multimedia pages. What makes this possible is the <EMBED> tag, which is an HTML 3.0 code that Netscape 3.0 supports (but Microsoft Internet Explorer doesn't... yet).

Figure 9.8

*Netscape's LiveAudio
information page features
some embedded sounds.*

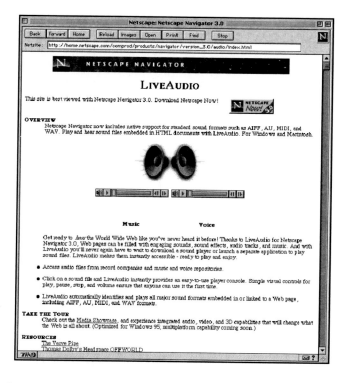

Note

Netscape's LiveAudio info page,
as shown in figure 9.8, can be
found at the following:

`http://home.netscape.com/
comprod/products/navigator/
version_3.0/audio/`

To refer to your audio file as an embedded sound, use the
following syntax:

```
<EMBED SRC="/mysoundfiles/mysound.xxx" AUTOSTART =
A VOLUME = V

WIDTH = 144 HEIGHT = 60 CONTROLS =
Console>
```

There is no closing tag (</EMBED>). The attributes can be
described as follows:

- AUTOSTART—(True/False). Setting AUTOSTART to
  "True" will automatically begin streaming your file as
  soon as the page begins loading. If set on "False," you
  must be sure to provide a "console" under the CON-
  TROLS attribute to enable your viewers to start the
  sound file.

- VOLUME—(0-100). Sets an author-defined volume level
  from a scale of 0-100.

- WIDTH—This is set by default to "144" to provide a
  space for the console graphic that Netscape Navigator 3.0
  automatically inserts.

- HEIGHT—Also set by default to "60" for the console graphic.

- CONTROLS—You should indicate "console" that will present a small console in the Web page where you embedded the sound. This enables the user to start and stop the audio stream, and adjust the volume.

Synthesis and MIDI Basics

Digital sound synthesis experienced a huge boom in the 1980s with the mass production of affordable keyboard synthesizers. Microprocessor technology, which fueled the growth of the computer industry, has often spilled over into the electronic music industry. In fact, electronic synthesizers and samplers really are just specialized computers that are dedicated to the task of producing sound. Owners of sophisticated instruments known as workstations often bemoan the lack of disk space, the need for more on-board RAM, and the need for SCSI CD-ROM drives the same way computer owners do. Some instruments also upgrade their RAM with the same sort of SIMMs computers use.

The basic principle behind synthesis is about how one generates a sound wave and then modifies it. Synthesized sound waves are generated by one or a series of digital oscillators and can take the shape of a repetitive sine curve, sawtooth, square, triangle, or other shape. Different wave shapes place different levels of emphasis on the harmonic overtones, which then give the sound a basic timbre. The basic signal is then passed through filters that can emphasize or de-emphasize specific frequencies, thereby continuing to color the sound. Envelope filters are then used to specify dynamic type characteristics, such as attack, peak, decay, sustain, and release, over time.

All this may sound quite simple, but, over the years, developers have created a number of different ways to apply and modify the arrangements of filters and insert all sorts of other bells and whistles into the process, thereby giving their instruments interesting characteristic sounds. FM (frequency modulation) synthesis, introduced by Yamaha, produced very popular sounds for a number of years until Roland introduced Linear/Arithmetic (L/A) synthesis. Meanwhile, other methods like

Phase Distortion Synthesis (PDS), Pulse Code Modulation (PCM), and vector synthesis have been incorporated. Advanced Integrated (AI) synthesis is a popular technique that was introduced by Korg, only to soon be followed by Kurzweil's Variable Architecture Synthesis Technology (VAST).

Samplers, on the other hand, do not generate their own waveforms. Sometimes referred to as "sampling synthesizers," they actually represent a different type of technology. Earlier in this chapter, we discussed how digital audio recording has its roots in sampling. Whereas synthesizers use oscillators to generate waveforms of regular shapes, samplers start with irregularly shaped waveforms from externally produced sounds that have been recorded in their memory banks. Samplers also come with a variety of modifying envelopes and on-board effects that shape the sounds. Some of the more recently produced electronic instruments hybridize synthesizers and samplers to form a more complex sound. Two of the more recent synthesis techniques, AI and VAST synthesis, use sampled waves as a basis for synthesizing sounds.

In 1982, electronic music instrument developers came together to discuss the advantages of microprocessor capabilities and develop a standard to allow their independently produced instruments to communicate with each other. The product of the talks was the MIDI specification that enables musicians to "network" their components produced by different manufacturers. The basic idea of MIDI connectivity was to give musicians playing one instrument, known as a controller, the ability to produce sounds from another instrument, known as a slave.

Though electronic keyboards have generally come to symbolize the basic MIDI controller, there are also drum controllers, guitar controllers, wind controllers, violin controllers, and even some experimental controllers like the MIDI glove. A controller doesn't actually produce sound. When a musician plays the controller, it produces digital information that specifies parameters for each note like "Note On/Note Off," "MIDI Volume," "MIDI Velocity," "MIDI Aftertouch," and "MIDI Channel." These concepts are not vital to learn; however, it is important to recognize that the information produced by a controller comes out as a digital code that is in the MIDI language. A slave is usually a synthesizer sound module—a box that contains all the chips with digital oscillators, filters, and envelopes. When the slave receives MIDI information from the controller, it processes it and generates sound. The benefits of the MIDI language really shined when developers came out with *sequencers*—machines (now often sold as software) that record and play back MIDI information coming from a controller. Sequencers enable musicians to compose, edit, and play numerous tracks of sound to create more complex and detailed work. Sequencers work like multitrack recorders that assign each track a specific MIDI channel (often up to 16, but sometimes 32, 64, and even as many as 128 or 512!), which is assigned on the synthesizer, a specific patch, or sound. A sequencer becomes a controller when it is playing back a sequence through a (slave) sound module. As we shall soon see, sequencers also are a way to transport and deliver music because of their relatively small demands on disk space.

Because most synthesizer keyboards integrate both controllers and sound modules, you often don't need to string together a whole network in order to get a sound. Many manufacturers today also include sequencers and on-board effects, making a package referred to as a workstation. Still, like computers, there is so much more to take advantage of if you have the means to be networked.

Early sequencers were small boxes that could save your tracks onto a magnetic disk, not unlike 3.5" floppies. In fact, the problem was that some manufacturers used 3.5" floppies while others used 2.75" floppies and so on. There was a miniature sequencer box war as manufacturers vied to create the standard. Eventually, someone figured out that many musicians owned computers and that it would be much easier to write software and standardize the platform there. Thus, the MIDI interface box, which went between the 5-pin MIDI cable and the computer's serial connection, was developed. A computer released by Atari once had MIDI In, Out, and Thru ports; however, today you still need a MIDI interface or interface card to connect your controllers and/or sound modules to your computer, Mac, or PC.

A *MIDI interface* is a device that converts MIDI data from a MIDI component to data that the computer can interpret, and vice versa. Software sequencers can then record compositions, and Editor/Librarian software can be used to manipulate and catalog sounds on different instruments. The basic MIDI interface has one IN and three OUTs, and allows basic back-and-forth traffic on 16 channels between the computer and instrument. More sophisticated interfaces for PCs also have synthesizer DSPs as part of a sound card package. Other interfaces for both Macs and PCs come with multiple in/outs, support 32 channels or more, and are also designed to synchronize information with MIDI Time Code (MTC) or SMPTE Time Code.

Instrument manufacturers have come to realize the somewhat "symbiotic" relationship that they have with the computer industry, and over the years they have made addendums to the MIDI specification. In the late 1980s, two major improvements were made to the MIDI specification. The first was the development of the Standard MIDI File (SMF) format and the second was the General MIDI or GMIDI specification.

Because of the multitude of sequencer programs and computer platforms (at this time, Atari and Amiga were still important players to the MIDI world), no portable standard for sequence files had been implemented. SMF was introduced as a standardized language compatible across all computer and software platforms, thereby enabling one to run a sequence made with PC software over to the Mac. This also spawned a whole cottage industry of homegrown MIDI clips that can be bought from stores or found on newsgroups like alt.binaries.sounds. midi. (Read the FAQ at http://incolor.inetnebr.com/williss/ absmfaq.shtml.)

GMIDI was created soon thereafter as a standard list and order of sounds that would be defined for every MIDI device. No matter if Korg's grand piano did not sound as grand as Kurzweil's—it would be assigned patch no. 1 on all sound modules that followed GMIDI specification. Before GMIDI, a sequence created for the sound banks of a Roland MT-32 would play very different-sounding instruments when played on an E-mu Proteus. GMIDI assigns specific types of sounds to the first 128 patches of a synthesizer or sound module (see table 9.3). Because of this generic standard, computer users now benefit because manufacturers of PC sound cards and Mac computers build in DSP chips with GMIDI sounds on them.

Table 9.3

The General MIDI Patch List

1.	Acoustic Grand Piano	33.	Acoustic Bass
2.	Bright Acoustic Piano	34.	Fingered Bass
3.	Electric Piano 1	35.	Picked Bass
4.	Honky-Tonk Piano	36.	Fretless Bass
5.	Electric Piano 2	37.	Slap Bass 1
6.	Electric Piano 3	38.	Slap Bass 2
7.	Harpsichord	39.	Synth Bass 1
8.	Clavichord	40.	Synth Bass 2
9.	Celesta	41.	Violin
10.	Glockenspiel	42.	Viola
11.	Music Box	43.	Cello
12.	Vibraphone	44.	Bass Violin
13.	Marimba	45.	Tremolo Strings
14.	Xylophone	46.	Pizzicato Strings
15.	Tubular Bells	47.	Harp
16.	Dulcimer	48.	Timpani
17.	Organ 1	49.	String Orch 1
18.	Organ 2	50.	String Orch 2
19.	Hammond Organ	51.	Synth Strings 1
20.	Church Organ	52.	Synth Strings 2
21.	Reed Organ	53.	Choir Aahs
22.	Accordion	54.	Voice Oohs
23.	Harmonica	55.	Vox Synth
24.	Bandeon	56.	Orchestra Hit
25.	Nylon String Guitar	57.	Trumpet
26.	Steel String Guitar	58.	Trombone
27.	Jazz Guitar	59.	Tuba
28.	Clean Electric Guitar	60.	Muted Trumpet
29.	Muted Electric Guitar	61.	French Horn
30.	Overdriven Guitar	62.	Brass Section
31.	Distorted Guitar	63.	Synth Brass 1
32.	Guitar Harmonics	64.	Synth Brass 2

continues

Table 9.3, continued

The General MIDI Patch List

65.	Soprano Sax	97.	Ice Rain
66.	Alto Sax	98.	Soundtrack
67.	Tenor Sax	99.	Crystal
68.	Bari Sax	100.	Atmosphere
69.	Oboe	101.	Brightness
70.	English Horn	102.	Goblins
71.	Bassoon	103.	Echo Drops
72.	Clarinet	104.	Sci-fi
73.	Piccolo	105.	Sitar
74.	Flute	106.	Banjo
75.	Recorder	107.	Shamisen
76.	Pan Flute	108.	Koto
77.	Bottle Blow	109.	Kalimba
78.	Shakuhachi	110.	Bag Pipe
79.	Whistle	111.	Fiddle
80.	Ocarina	112.	Shanai
81.	Square Wave	113.	Tinkle Bell
82.	Sawtooth Wave	114.	Agogo
83.	Calliope	115.	Steel Drums
84.	Chiffer Lead	116.	Woodblock
85.	Charang	117.	Taiko Drums
86.	Vox32	118.	Melodic Toms
87.	Samtooth Wave in 5ths	119.	Synth Drums
88.	Bass & Lead	120.	Reverse Cymbal
89.	Fantasia	121.	Guitar Frets
90.	Warm Pad	122.	Breath Noise
91.	PolySynth	123.	Seashore
92.	Synth Choir	124.	Birds
93.	Bowed Glass	125.	Telephone Ring
94.	Metal Pad	126.	Helicopter
95.	Halo Pad	127.	Applause
96.	Sweep Pad	128.	Gun Shot

Where to Start if You've Never Used MIDI Before

The truth is, getting into making MIDI music can be a bit of an investment. You will probably need to get a keyboard, an interface, and sequencing software. You might also need speakers, cables, and more. Though your computer or sound card might have perfectly good synthesizer sounds, they are generally there as slaves, and you don't yet have the means to trigger them and write MIDI files. Some programs do give you a software interface to play the sounds on a virtual keyboard, but they are mostly designed as educational aids and tools.

Your best bet is to look for a secondhand keyboard that supports GMIDI. The format has been out long enough that there are now plenty of good GMIDI keyboards in the used market for as low as a few hundred dollars. Look for a keyboard from a reputable manufacturer—reading through back copies of *Keyboard* and *Electronic Musician* is a good way to familiarize yourself with some of the better manufacturers out there.

Once equipped with all the essentials, take some time to familiarize yourself with the sounds and experiment with sequencing multiple tracks. If you buy a workstation, you may find the on-board sequencer a good introduction to writing multiple tracks. Although it helps to have some music background, many of these keyboards already sound so good, you can have a great time making atmospheric sounds with an Atmosphere patch on one channel over Ice Rain on another channel.

PCs and MIDI

Although Macs originally had the leg up on the MIDI world, PCs have made great inroads in this market as well. The large number of options for third-party sound cards has spawned a number of amateur electronic musicians who had never hummed an original tune until their PCs got them into it. Again, like sound cards, PC users have many options for integrated packages that PC users have.

Opcode has recently started making interfaces for PCs, working under the name Music Quest. The Pro model interface is called the 8Port/SE and, like the Studio 4, is rack mountable, drives 128 MIDI channels, and syncs with SMPTE and MTC. Music Quest also makes a lower-end interface, called the MIDI Engine, in four different configurations. If you already have a MIDI-compatible sound card that does not provide 5-pin MIDI IN or OUT ports, low-cost MIDI adapters that connect to the card via the 15-pin port can be used. At the very least, you can buy a PC MIDI card for under $100. Look for MPU-401 compatibility when shopping for these. MPU-401 is the code name for a Roland sound chip that was put on many early sound cards.

MIDI Software for PCs

The most complete sequencing package for Windows PCs is Twelve Tone System's Cakewalk Pro. The high-end package is Cakewalk Pro Audio, which integrates digital audio recording with MIDI sequencing. Opcode has recently released a version of Vision for PCs, and Passport Designs has put out a PC version of Master Tracks Pro 6. For entry-level sequencers, Voyetra makes MIDI Orchestrator Plus and PG Music puts out Power Track Pro.

Macs and MIDI

For Mac musicians and users who want to use their Macintoshes for sequencing and other MIDI applications, a set of software called the MIDI Manager consists of an INIT, a driver, and a PatchBay program. Like AppleTalk, the MIDI Manager enables you to make changes with your serial ports to enable routing of MIDI information through your modem or printer serial port by using the PatchBay to make virtual connections. The MIDI Manager software package often comes with MIDI software like sequencers for the Mac.

For all Mac users, QuickTime 2.0 comes with a set of GMIDI sounds licensed from Roland. These are enabled by the QuickTime Musical Instruments extension. Any file with MIDI information can play and trigger the instrument sounds in your Mac—not great sounds, but entertaining. If you have a MIDI sound module, like the Roland Sound Canvas, and interface it with your Mac, you can assign the PatchBay to trigger the sound module instead and get better sounds.

Opcode makes a number of MIDI interfaces for the Mac. On the Pro end are the Studio 5 and Studio 4 interfaces that are rack mountable and allow up to 512 and 128 separate MIDI channels respectively. At the other end are the MIDI Translator II and the MIDI Translator Pro, both well under $100. Mark of the Unicorn puts out another Pro interface called the MIDI Time Piece II for either the Mac or PCs.

MIDI Software for Macs

Macs have been well-supported with a number of high-end sequencers. One package considered the industry standard is Opcode's Vision 3.0 sequencing package. It is a huge program designed to operate best with the Opcode Studio 5 MIDI interface. Vision (and Studio Vision Pro, which allows sophisticated digital audio recording and mixing, and can convert digital audio files to MIDI) comes bundled with the Galaxy patch Librarian that organizes sound patches. Opcode's scaled-down version, EZVision is a good, inexpensive, entry-level sequencer that will get you rolling. Some other good sequencers available for the Mac include Passport Design's Master Track's Pro 6 and Mark of the Unicorn's Performer. Trax is another inexpensive entry-level sequencer, which really is Passport's Pro 5 "lite."

The Crescendo Plug-In for PCs and Macs

Once you have created your MIDI sequence, it is a simple step to embed it into your Web page. Earlier in this chapter, you were introduced to the <EMBED> tag, part of the new HTML language that Netscape has begun incorporating into newer versions of Navigator. A MIDI file that has been uploaded to your server can be immediately referenced by using the <EMBED> tag. For Microsoft's Internet Explorer browser, however, a different tagging scheme, <BGSOUND>, is used. Note that Navigator does not recognize <BGSOUND> and Internet Explorer does not recognize <EMBED>. Therefore, it is a good idea to include both references in your Web page, as follows:

```
<EMBED SRC="/mysoundfiles/myseq.mid"
WIDTH=0 HEIGHT=2>

<BGSOUND SRC="/mysoundfiles/
myseq.mid">
```

As you can see, the <BGSOUND> tag functions much like other background tags. According to Netscape, the 3.0 release of Navigator includes a feature called LiveAudio, which is supposed to read embedded MIDI files. At the time of this writing, for Internet Explorer users, MIDI background music is enabled by a plug-in, Crescendo, by Live Update. Having Crescendo will enable the Web browser to download the MIDI sound file and trigger the computer's on-board MIDI sounds as soon as you reach a page with the <EMBED> or <BGSOUND> reference. The MIDI file is looped so that as long as your browser points to the Web page, the music continues playing in the background. Live Update claims that the attributes "WIDTH=0 HEIGHT=2" are "magic" specifications that tell Navigator to make the plug-in "invisible" and operate in the background on current 2.x browsers. To get the Crescendo Plug-In and see some example sites that embed MIDI sound files, go to http://www.liveupdate.com/crescendo.html.

Conclusion

In this chapter, we explored the technology, background, and future of sound on the Web. Hopefully, this overview of audio on the Web is a good basis for rounding out your multimedia Web production.

Whether you experiment with digital audio or plunge into MIDI, both should continue to be supported well into the future. While the impending release of Navigator featuring LiveAudio may make streaming digital audio as seamless and integral as playing MIDI files in the background, it is important to consider that digital audio files still take up a great deal of disk space. With other similar developing technologies that enable voice-overs and speech simulation, the Web promises that the future will not be a quiet one.

What's On the CD

This appendix provides you with information about the Netscape-compatible animation plug-ins, HTML and Java editors, and other utilities on the *Designing Web Animation* CD-ROM. The plug-ins presented here work with one or more of the following platforms:

- MacPPC

- Mac68k

- Win31

- Win95

At the time of this compilation, none of the Netscape Plug-Ins support the Unix platform.

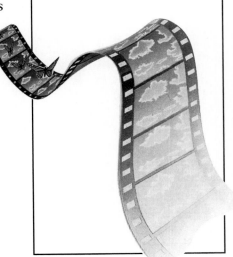

Product: Animated Widgets

Company: InternetConsult

Address: P.O. Box 1934
          Merrimack, NH 03054-1934

Telephone: 603-424-1621

Fax: 603-424-1621

E-mail: brad@InternetConsult.com

Web site: For more information, visit http://www.InternetConsult.com/

Platform: Win95

Notes: Compressed file format.

Product: Debabelizer

Company: Equilibrium Technologies

Address: 3 Harbor Drive, Suite 111
          Sausalito, CA 95052

Web site: For more information and updates, visit http://www.equil.com

Product: Emblaze

Company: Interactive Media Group

E-mail: info@geo.co.il

Telephone: 972-3-5733288

Fax: 972-3-5733290

Web site: For more information and updates, visit http://
Geo.inter.net/Geo/technology/emblaze/downloads.html

Platforms: MacPPC, Mac68k, Win95, Win31

Description: Animation plug-in player and authoring tool.

Notes: Streaming animation; Emblaze Creator authoring tool
for Mac is also available.

Product: FutureSplash

Company: FutureWave Software, Inc.

Address: 8305 Huennekens Street, #210
        San Diego, CA 92121-2929

Telephone: 619-552-7680 or 1-800-619-6193

Fax: 619-552-7689

E-mail: info@futurewave.com

Web site: For more information and updates, visit http://
www.futurewave.com

Platforms: MacPPC, Mac68k, Win95, Win31

Description: Animation plug-in player and authoring tool.

Notes: Streaming, scaleable, interactive, vector-based anima-
tions; inexpensive CelAnimator authoring tool (Mac and
Win95) for creating Web animations; supports Netscape's
LiveConnect.

Product: GraphicConverter

Web sites: For more information and updates, visit http//
hyperarchive.lcs.mit.edu/HyperArchive/Archive/gst/grf/graphic-
converter-24.hqx

or

http://members.aol.com/lemkesoft

Description: Graphic Converter can convert approximately 80
graphic file formats. It also includes many useful features like
slide show and batch conversion.

Product: mBED

Company: mBED Software Inc.

Telephone: 415-778-0930

Fax: 415-778-0933

Web site: For more information and updates, visit http://
www.mbed.com/

Platforms: MacPPC, Mac68k, Win95, Win31

Description: An object-oriented multimedia description language for creating animated, interactive Web pages. This plug-
in allows playing of Mbedlets, or multimedia applets defined
by Mbd files.

Notes: Easy-to-use for non-programmers; includes mBEDlet
Designer authoring tools; supports multiple media types;
supports Netscape's LiveConnect.

Product: MooVer

Company: esp Software

Address: 1112 Oceanic Drive
        Encinitas, CA 92024-4007

Web site: For more information and updates, visit http://hyperarchive.lcs.mit.edu/HyperArchive/Archive/gst/mov/moover-12.hqx

Platforms: 68K- and PowerMac-compatible

Description: MooVer is Macintosh utility software that creates a QuickTime movie from a sequence of Macintosh Pict files or System 7 sound files dripped on it.

Notes: MooVer is used for creating computer animations, slide shows, or batch converting images or sounds to the QuickTime movie format. Subtitles can be optionally added under each image frame, using either the name of each Pict file or the lines of a special "subtitle" text file. It is a System 7-only fat application (68K- and PowerMac-compatible). It requires at least System 7 and QuickTime versions 1.6 or newer.

Product: Movie Cleaner Lite 1.1

Company: Terran Interactive

Address: 2 North First Street, Suite 215
        San Jose, CA 95113

Web site: For more information and updates, visit http://www.terran-int.com/

Description: Movie Cleaner Lite is a MacOS shareware program for QuickTime video compression.

Notes: This shareware version includes an expert system to help beginners configure their parameters properly. Software includes an electronic user's manual and a README file.

Also included on the CD from Terran Interactive are movies compressed with various parameters to illustrate aspects of low data-rate movies. For more online examples, visit http://www.terran-int.com.

Product: NET TOOB Multimedia Player v.2.51

Company: Duplexx Software

Address: 35 Congress Street
Salem, MA 01970

Fax: 508-741-2543

Web site: http://www.duplexx.com

Platforms: Windows 3.x, Win95, Win NT

Description: NET TOOB Multimedia Player is a single, cost-effective tool for viewing any video format that is encountered on the Web.

Notes: NET TOOB plays *all* of the digital video formats found on the Internet (MPEG-1, AVI, MOV, and FLC/FLI), with synchronized sound, as well as real-time audio *and* video. NET TOOB is a "software-only" solution, meaning that no add-on hardware is required to play digital video. It is extremely easy to use and has a VCR-like interface. Installation of the software is simple and automatic, taking less than three minutes. Playing a video requires no more knowledge than an understanding of the play, stop, and pause buttons of a standard VCR. NET TOOB includes mouse-operated VCR-like controls and adds screen size adjustment features, enabling users to play MPEG, AVI, and MOV video at 1/8, 1/4, and full-screen sizes. It also incorporates a frame rate control for MPEG, AVI, and MOV so that users can adjust playback from 1 to 30 frames per second. NET TOOB automatically installs and integrates itself as the Web browser video helper app for Netscape and many other browsers. Users can also save their favorite video clips and run them as screen savers. Complete product support is provided.

NET TOOB has been rated the Number 1 Multimedia Player on the Internet by Stroud's Consummate Winsock App List and The Windows Utility Report, and as a "Must Have" by The Ultimate Collection of Windows Software (TUCOWS). It was recently ranked by Wired Magazine as the second most popular Winsock Application after Netscape Navigator.

In addition, NET TOOB is posted on *all* the most visited MPEG Archives; is the "Recommended Viewer" on America Online; has been the "Site Of The Day" on The Microsoft Network; is in PC Magazine's "Internet Tool Kit;" is an AT&T Business Solution; and is a featured selection by ZD Net and CNet.

Product: PointPlus

Company: Net-Scene

Address: Merkazim Building
         32 Maskit St.
         P. O. Box 12394
         Herzliya, Israel 46733

Telephone: +972-9-558260

Fax: +972-9-558262

E-mail: info@net-scene.co.il

Web site: For more information and updates, visit http://www.net-scene.com/

Platforms: Win95, Win31

Description: Net-Scene's PointPlus enables users to immediately experience true online presentations by easily publishing colorful, dynamic, and compelling Microsoft PowerPoint presentations on the Net.

Notes: Using special compression methods and streaming technology, PointPlus eliminates download waiting time. Use it to repurpose PowerPoint files; supports Netscape's LiveConnect.

Product: PowerMedia

Company: Rad Media

Address: 745 Emerson Street
          Palo Alto, CA 94301

Web site: For more information and updates, visit http://www.radmedia.com/

Platform: Win95

Description: Viewer for applications created with Rad Media's authoring tool.

Notes: PowerMedia is the first multimedia presentation software designed for business communications using the World Wide Web to deliver exciting interactive sales, training, marketing, and advertising applications on corporate intranets, CD-ROM, and the global Internet.

Product: Premiere

Company: Adobe

Address: 1585 Charleston Road
          Mountain View, CA 94039

Web site: For more information and updates, visit http://www.adobe.com

---

Product: Macromedia Shockwave/Director

Web site: For more information, visit http://www.macromedia.com/Tools/Shockwave/index.html

Platforms: MacPPC, Mac68k, Win95, Win31

Notes: Includes Director-based PowerApplet animation templates; repurpose Director files; cross-platform; no streaming animation; requires Director for authoring.

Product: Macromedia Shockwave/Authorware

Web site: For more information and updates, visit http://www.macromedia.com/Tools/Shockwave/index.html

Platforms: MacPPC, Mac68k, Win95, Win31

Notes: Repurpose Authorware files; cross-platform; streaming playback; requires Authorware for authoring.

Sausage Software Products

Company: Sausage Software

Address: Suite 1, 660 Doncaster Road
Doncaster, VIC 3108 Australia

Products:

HotDog (Demo)	HTML Editor
HotDog Prox	HTML Editor
BookWorm	Java Editor (Lists)
Clikette	Java Editor (Buttons)
CrossEye	Image map Editor
Dummies	HTML Editor
Egor	Java Editor (Animations)
Flash	Java Editor (Status Bar Messages)
FrameGang	Frame Editor
Swami	Java Editor

Web site: For more information and updates, visit http://
sausage.com/

Product: Sizzler

Company: Totally Hip Software Inc.

Address: 301-1224 Hamilton Street
         Vancouver, BC V6B 2S8

Telephone: 604-685-6525

Fax: 604-685-4057

Web site: For more information, visit
http:/www.totallyhip.com/

Platforms: MacPPC, Mac68k, Win95, Win31

Description: Sizzler Viewer and conversion tool.

Notes: Sizzler Plug-in for Netscape Navigator is a multimedia software program that enables Web users to play live, real-time interactive animation and multimedia on the Web. The Sizzler converter enables creative Web page designers to convert their Web site. Free download is available from www.totallyhip.com.

Sizzler is an easy-to-use conversion playback technology. The Sizzler viewer for Macintosh is available for Cyberdog, Netscape Navigator, and Microsoft's Internet Explorer. Windows versions are available for Netscape Navigator and Microsoft's Internet Explorer. The Sizzler converter enables users to convert PICS files, QuickTime movies for Macintosh, or AVI or DIB list file formats for Windows to the Sizzler file format. Because it utilizes stream-based technology, the Sizzler viewer and converter significantly improves network performance for latency-critical applications such as animation and multimedia delivery. This streaming technology also enables users and developers to move beyond the present "store, forward before you can play" technologies for multimedia and animation delivery on the Internet.

Sizzler enables you to see moving pictures (animation) on the Web instead of the typical static images you currently see, making the Web come alive! You'll be able to see a plane flying by with a logo swaying behind versus the static "letterhead" logo you may currently see. The WebPainter animation authoring tool (Mac) is also available.

Product: SoundApp 2.0.3

Web site: For more information and updates, visit http://www-cs-students.stanford.edu/~franke/SoundApp/

Notes: SoundApp will play or convert sound files dripped onto it. Currently, it supports the following sound formats: SoundCap, SoundEdit, AIFF, AIFF-C, System 7 sound, QuickTime Moov, Sun Audio AU and NeXT.snd, Windows WAVE, Sound Blaster VOC, many varieties of MODs, Amiga IFF/8SVX, Sound Designer II, PSION sound files, DVI ADPCM, Studio Session Instruments, and any "snd" resource file. SoundApp can convert all of these formats to System 7 sound, sound suitecase, AIFF, WAVE, and NeXT formats. Using QuickTime 1.6 or later, SoundApp can also convert audio CD tracks. MOD playback is PowerPC-accelerated on Power Macintoshes.

Product: SoundEffects

Web site: For updates, visit ftp://ftp.alpcom.it/software/mac/Ricci/

Description: SoundEffects is a powerful sound editor for the Mac.

Notes: SoundEffects' strength resides in the capability of applying many digital effects to record sounds, and because the effects are plug-in modules, you can enhance the program at any time by just adding any new modules as they become available. Not only can SoundEffects change sounds in many ways through its variety of effects, but it can also handle multi-channel sounds, sampled at any rate up to 64 kHz and with any sample size between 1 and 32 bits. Recording rate and sample size are only limited by your Mac and your sound input device.

Product: Sculptor II 2.1

Web site: For more information and updates, visit http://members/aol.com/sculptorii/

Product: Wavelet

Company: Summus, Ltd.

Address: 950 Lake Murray Blvd.
Irmo, SC 29063

Telephone: 803-781-5674

Fax: 803-781-5679

E-mail: wavelet@summus.com

Web site: For more information and updates, visit http://www.summus.com/

Platforms: MacPPC*, Mac68k*, Win95, Win31

Description: Summus' Wavelet Image is a compressed image format that compresses and decompresses super-fast while maintaining excellent image quality, even at high compression ratios.

Product: WI Netscape Plug-In

Company: Summus, Ltd.

Address: 950 Lake Murray Blvd.
Irmo, SC 29063

Telephone: 803-781-5674

Fax: 803-781-5679

E-mail: wavelet@summus.com

Platforms: Win31, Win95, WinNT, Mac

Description: Summus' WI Netscape Plug-In is a Wavelet Image Viewer for displaying wavelet images over the World Wide Web via Netscape Navigator. Both the Windows and Macintosh versions feature progressive decompression with the capability to enable Web page designers to control how the image will be displayed by setting increments between intermediate image displays.

Summus' WI Netscape Plug-In for MS Windows has an image map feature that enables Web page designers to use WI images for graphical hypertext links. This feature is as easy to use as GIF and JPEG image maps. The Windows version of the WI Plug-In also contains an image-sharpening switch that brings fuzzy images into clearer focus. These features are currently being incorporated into the Macintosh WI Plug-In.

Product: WI Viewer

Company: Summus, Ltd.

Address: 950 Lake Murray Blvd.
          Irmo, SC 29063

Telephone: 803-781-5674

Fax: 803-781-5679

E-mail: wavelet@summus.com

Platforms: Win31, Win95, WinNT

Description: Summus' Wavelet Image Viewer for MS Windows is a stand-alone desktop WI viewer. It features a slide-show capability, smoothing, sharpening, fast decompression, progressive decompression, and viewed images that can be saved in bmp, tif, tga, pgm, and ppm image file formats.

Product: WebMotion Plug-In

Company: Terran Interactive

Address: 2 North First Street, Suite 215
          San Jose, CA 95113

Web site: For more information and updates, visit http://www.terran-int.com/

Product: WebPainter

Company: Totally Hip Software Inc.

Address: 301-1224 Hamilton Street
Vancouver, BC V6B 2S8

Telephone: 604-685-6525

Fax: 604-685-4057

Web site: For more information, visit http://www.totallyhip.com/

Description: WebPainter is a seamlessly integrated, easy-to-use cel animation package that combines a set of comprehensive painting tools with extensive importing and exporting capabilities.

Notes: With WebPainter, users can create attention-grabbing, dynamic Web pages that will capture the interest of Web surfers. WebPainter enables Web page designers to easily create bitmap animations, banners, and static images for their Web pages. Complete with all the essential elements of a 2D color bitmapped painting application, WebPainter also has unique animation tools like onion-skinning, multiple cel editing, and foreground/background layering. The product also includes a library of pre-designed animation, making it easy for novice users to incorporate animation to their Web site.

Product: VDOLive

Company: VDOnet

Address: 4009 Miranda Avenue, Suite 250
Palo Alto, CA 94304

Web site: For more information and updates, visit http://www.vdolive.com/

Platforms: MacPPC, Mac68k, Win95, Win31

B

Additional Netscape-Compatible Animation Plug-Ins

This appendix provides you with information about additional Netscape-compatible animation plug-ins. These plug-ins work with the following platforms:

- MacPPC
- Mac68k
- Win31
- Win95

At the time of this compilation, none of the Netscape Plug-Ins support the Unix platform.

Product: Action

Company: Open2U

Address: 5256 Countryside Lane
　　　　　San Jose, CA 95136

Web site: http://www.open2u.com/action/action.html

Platforms: Win95, Win31*

Description: MPEG player.

Notes: Synchronized audio.

Product: Astound Web Player

Company: Gold Disk Inc.

Web site: http://www.golddisk.com/awp.html

Platform: MacPPC*, Mac68k*, Win95, Win31

Description: Plays Astound multimedia files.

Notes: Easy to repurpose Astound presentations for the Web; requires Astound for authoring.

Product: CoolFusion

Company: Iterated Systems, Inc.

Address: 3525 Piedmont Road
Seven Piedmont Center, Suite 600
Atlanta, GA 30305-1530 USA

Fax: +1-404-264-8300

Web site: http://webber.iterated.com/coolfusn/download/cf-loadp.htm

Platforms: MacPPC*, Mac68k*, Win95

Description: AVI player.

Notes: Streaming AVI; limitations of AVI format; no Win3.1 support.

Product: InterVU

Company: InterVU Inc

Web site: http://www.intervu.com/prevu.html

Platforms: MacPPC, Mac68k, Win95

Description: Streaming video; proprietary format.

Product: KM's Multimedia Plug

Developer: Kevin McMurtrie

Web site: ftp://ftp.wco.com/users/mcmurtri/MySoftware/

Platforms: MacPPC, Mac68k

Description: Player for multiple multimedia formats, including QuickTime and AIFF sound files.

Product: MacZilla

Company: MacZilla

Web site: http://MacZilla.com/

Platforms: MacPPC, Mac68k, Win95*, Win31*

Description: Player for QuickTime; AVI, MPEG movies; au, wav, midi, aiff, mp2 audio.

Notes: Handles many multimedia formats; can add new modules, including games, and update itself over the Net.

Product: Media Splash

Company: PowerSoft

Web site: http://www.powersoft.com/media.splash/product/index.html

Platforms: Win95, Win31*

Description: Interactive animation player.

Notes: Easy-to-use authoring.

Product: MovieStar

Company: Intelligence at Large

Address: 3508 Market Street
        Philadelphia, PA 19104-3316

Telephone: 215-387-6002

Fax: 215-387-9215

E-mail: info@beingthere.com

Web site: http://www.beingthere.com/

Platforms: MacPPC, Mac68k, Win95, Win31

Description: Streaming QuickTime; MovieStar Maker authoring tool (Mac) also available.

Notes: Supports multiple platforms; streaming and Fast-Start playback; inexpensive authoring tool.

Product: Neuron

Company: Asymetrix Corporation

Web site: http://www.asymetrix..com

Platforms: Win95, Win31

Description: Player for Asymetrix ToolBook 4.0.

Notes: Repurpose Toolbook files; need Toolbook for authoring.

Product: SCREAM

Company: Saved by Technology

Web site: http://www.savedbytech.com/sbt/Plug_In.html

Platforms: MacPPC*, Mac68k*, Win95, Win31

Notes: Animation and sound; streaming.

Product: TEC Player

Company: TEC Solutions, Inc.

Web site: http://www.tecs.com/TECPlayer_docs

Platforms: MacPPC, Mac68k, Win95*, Win31*

Description: QuickTime player.

Product: WebActive

Company: Plastic Thought, Inc.

Address: 10260 - 112 Street
         Edmonton, Canada AB T5K 1MK

Voice mail: 403-429-5051 or 1-800-635-5715

Fax: 403-426-0632

Web site: http://www.3d-active.com/

Platforms: MacPPC, Mac68k*

Description: 3D-Model viewer.

Notes: Includes authoring tool.

Product: WebAnimator

Company: Deltapoint Inc.

Address: 22 Lower Ragsdale Drive
         Monterey, CA 93940

Main telephone number: 408-648-4000
                       M-F 8 a.m. to 5 p.m. PST

Main fax: 408-648-4020

E-mail: sales_support@deltapoint.com

Web site: http://www.deltapoint.com/

Platforms: MacPPC, Mac68k, Win95*, Win31*

Description: Inexpensive authoring tool.

Index